W9-CCK-983

Ethnic Entrepreneurs

SAGE SERIES ON
RACE AND ETHNIC RELATIONS

Series Editor:
JOHN H. STANFIELD II
College of William and Mary

This series is designed for scholars working in creative theoretical areas related to race and ethnic relations. The series will publish books and collections of original articles that critically assess and expand upon race and ethnic relations issues from American and comparative points of view.

Ethnic Entrepreneurs

Immigrant Business in Industrial Societies

Roger Waldinger
Howard Aldrich
Robin Ward

with the Collaboration of

Jochen Blaschke
William Bradford
Hanneke Grotenbreg
Hermann Korte
David McEvoy
Annie Phizacklea
Pnina Werbner

Jeremy Boissevain
Gavin Chen
Isaac Joseph
Ivan Light
Mirjana Morokvasic
Marlene Sway
Peter Wilson

**Sage Series on Race
and Ethnic Relations**

v o l u m e   1

SAGE PUBLICATIONS
The International Professional Publishers
Newbury Park   London   New Delhi

For our parents

For information address:

SAGE Publications, Inc.
2111 West Hillcrest Drive
Newbury Park, California 91320

SAGE Publications Ltd.
28 Banner Street
London EC1Y 8QE
England

SAGE Publications India Pvt. Ltd.
M-32 Market
Greater Kailash I
New Delhi 110 048 India

Printed in the United States of America

Library of Congress Cataloging-in-Publication Data

Waldinger, Roger David.
   Ethnic entrepreneurs : immigrant business in industrial societies
/ by Roger Waldinger, Howard Aldrich, and Robin Ward with the
collaboration of Jochen Blaschke . . . [et al.].
      p.   cm. — (Sage series on race and ethnic relations ; 1)
   Includes bibliographical references.
   ISBN 0-8039-3710-5. — ISBN 0-8039-3711-3 (pbk.)
   1. Minority business enterprises — United States.   2. Minority
business enterprises — Europe.   I. Aldrich, Howard.   II. Ward,
Robin, 1937-   .   III. Title.   IV. Series.
HD2341.W325   1990
338.6′422′094 — dc20   89-24247
                                                                           CIP

FIRST PRINTING, 1990

Contents

Foreword

Race and ethnic relations have taken on critical dimensions as the twentieth century draws to a close. Everywhere we turn in the United States and abroad, race and ethnicity are central structuring and reality interpretation factors in politics, popular culture, nation-building (and decline), education, labor market transformations, social movements, and technological development. The international centrality of race and ethnicity in what is becoming the twentieth-century world demands an expansion of, if not revision of, conventional wisdom in academic race and ethnic relations literature. This is the purpose of the Sage Race and Ethnic Relations Series.

One of the ways in which this series will attempt to contribute significantly to the race and ethnic relations field is by publishing monographs and anthologies written by social scientists utilizing historical and comparative theories and research methodologies. We plan to publish such works to enrich the conventional race and ethnic literature, which at most only superficially utilizes historical logics of inquiry and tends to focus attention on one society or one population. Thus we are proud to publish as the first volume of this series *Ethnic Entrepreneurs: Immigrant Business in Industrial Societies* by Roger Waldinger, Howard Aldrich, Robin Ward, and associates as a stimulating illustration of the importance of comparative analysis in a fragmented research area in ethnic and immigrant studies. *Ethnic Entrepreneurs* promises to provoke much-needed discussion about how similar and different cultural, political, and economic characteristics of immigrants and of the industrial societies in which they settle influence the development and transformation of immigrant small businesses.

John H. Stanfield II
Series Editor

Preface

This is neither an edited book nor a single-authored book. Instead, it is a team book. At various stages in its preparation, as many as 16 people have been involved. For some chapters, a team leader assembled material submitted by team members, and for other chapters, one person took responsibility for most of the material in the first draft. Almost all the ideas in this book were generated by collective discussions at two conferences. The final draft of the book was put together by Roger Waldinger, Howard Aldrich, and Robin Ward, as will be discussed more fully below.

The idea for this book grew out of a proposal, submitted by Howard Aldrich and Robin Ward in October 1984 to the Council for European Studies, that asked for funds to hold a research planning meeting on "minority business development in industrial society." The idea was to bring researchers together from the disciplines of sociology, economics, geography, political science, anthropology, and business management to compare and contrast approaches to explaining the growth of ethnic businesses. We observed that there had been an expansion of ethnic businesses in continental Europe, the United Kingdom, and North America. For the conference, we sought researchers who were actively pursuing empirical research on this topic. The proposal was funded and resulted in two conferences.

The first conference was organized by Robin Ward and held in Birmingham, England, at the University of Aston, in June 1985. Over a period of two and a half days, we debated various approaches to explaining ethnic businesses. We began the conference with each investigator talking briefly about his or her research interests and key findings. We had precirculated copies of investigators' major publications, so people came to the conference prepared to discuss points that had arisen in their reading of other investigators' work. Various subgroups were formed to pursue particular issues more fully, and plans were made for people within each subgroup to draft a report for a follow-up conference.

In the fall of 1985, the various subgroups circulated working drafts among their members. In the early spring of 1986, drafts from the various subgroups were circulated to the entire planning group.

A second conference was organized by Roger Waldinger and held in April 1986, in New York City, at the City University of New York Graduate Center. During two and a half days, the various subgroups presented their preliminary papers, and plans were drawn up for a book.

Over the next three years, the book slowly took shape. Roger Waldinger took responsibility for Chapter 2, on trends in ethnic business in the United States, and Jochen Blaschke took responsibility for Chapter 3, on trends in European businesses. Working with notes prepared by David McEvoy, Roger Waldinger also took responsibility for preparing Chapter 4, on dimensions of opportunity structures.

Jeremy Boissevain led a team of six people preparing Chapter 5, on ethnic resources and strategies. Initially this chapter was thought to have a strong methodological component, being based on observational studies carried out by the members of the team. However, the theme of ethnic strategies also turned out to be a core component of the overall model eventually developed for Chapter 1. Chapter 6, on the garment industry in three cities, was drafted by Mirjana Morokvasic and then reworked by Roger Waldinger, with contributions from Annie Phizack-lea. Finally, William Bradford headed a team of six people drafting a statement on public policies toward ethnic businesses. The various members of the team put together material on their own countries, and Bradford wrote an initial draft, bringing the material together. Roger Waldinger then substantially revised and expanded the statement so that it fit into the concluding chapter.

Once the draft chapters were completed, Howard Aldrich took responsibility for coordinating the rewriting of the chapters to make sure that they were integrated into a theme that runs throughout the book. Chapters were rewritten to ensure consistency in the use of terms, redundancies were eliminated, common themes were linked across chapters, and references and statistics were brought up to date. Howard Aldrich and Roger Waldinger went through many drafts of each chapter, striving to bring out the common threads that linked material from the various investigators and countries.

This book would not have been possible without the very generous support of the Council for European Studies and its executive director, Dr. Ioannis Sinanoglou. The CES provided the majority of the funding for the two conference meetings in Birmingham and New York, and Sinanoglou also provided additional funding, making it possible for the principal authors to meet on several occasions. Arthur Young, PLC, also provided funding for the 1985 meeting in Birmingham, and the 1986 meeting in New York was underwritten by additional funds from the Morton Globus Lecture Fund of the City College, CUNY, and the Minority Business Development Administration. We would like to thank Arline McCord, formerly dean, Division of Social Sciences, City College, and Gavin Chen, MBDA, for arranging funding from their respective institutions. Alan Gartner and *Social Policy* magazine graciously assisted with funding for the New York meeting. Roger Waldinger gratefully acknowledges support from the Robert F. Wagner, Sr., Institute on Urban Public Policy, City University of New York, which supported his work on this book during 1988-1989.

A number of people participated in one of the conferences but for various reasons did not take part in drafting chapters. We wish to acknowledge the contributions that Thomas Bailey, Richard Randall, Risa Palm, Timothy Mescon, and Hedwig Rudolf made in our conference sessions.

Pyong Gap Min and Ivan Light read through all seven chapters and made very helpful comments; Marlene Sway reviewed and made useful suggestions for Chapter 5; Alejandro Portes and Silvia Pedraza-Bailey read and commented on Chapter 2. The series editor, John Stanfield, pushed us to make certain that the final draft of the book represented an integrated, coherent statement rather than a series of discrete chapters. We thank him for his enthusiastic backing of the project, and we also thank Mitch Allen, our editor at Sage, for keeping everything on schedule. Steven and Daniel Aldrich provided the computer expertise for constructing Figure 1.1. Two people deserve special mention: Greg Floyd helped us with the references, and Sharon Byrd was the ultimate link between our drafts and the printed copy and computer disks we turned over to Sage.

Roger Waldinger
Howard Aldrich
Robin Ward

1

Opportunities, Group Characteristics, and Strategies

Roger Waldinger
Howard Aldrich
Robin Ward

With the recent growth of new ethnic populations in Europe as well as the United States, ethnic business is no longer a matter of strictly historical interest; neither is it a parochial American concern. Because the new ethnic populations have grown at a time when Western economies are in a phase of slow growth and massive technological change, ethnic adaptation and mobility are central issues in ethnic research. Large numbers of immigrants are caught in the conjuncture of changing economic conditions — international competition, a new international division of labor, and changing comparative advantages. They find themselves in marginal economic positions, disproportionately affected by changes in their host societies.

Some ethnic groups have responded by entering business ownership, and indeed some observers have seen ethnic entrepreneurship as a possible avenue out of disadvantage. But not all groups have entered equally into self-employment, and not all have been equally successful.

How are we to explain both immigrant groups' entry into business and their different fates? In this chapter, we propose a model based on immigrant groups' access to opportunities, group characteristics, and the embeddedness of opportunities and resources within a specific set of historical conditions encountered by emigrating groups. Understand-

13

ing the forces stimulating entry into business (and possible success therein) may help policymakers formulate policies to improve the lot of ethnic communities.

THE PURPOSE OF THIS BOOK

There is growing evidence of the spread of ethnic enterprise on both sides of the Atlantic, but existing scholarly work has generated little consensus on its determinants and implications. For example, some researchers argue that small business can play an important role in promoting upward mobility, whereas others see immigrant enterprise as confined to peripheral positions offering only low returns and little potential for growth.

Regardless of theoretical approach, much of the work on ethnic business remains exploratory. Until recently, many studies were designed to generate, not test, hypotheses. Indeed, some of the case studies were accidental by-products of labor market studies, in which immigrant enterprise became an object of attention only once it appeared that competition between native and immigrant workers was mediated by competition between native and immigrant firms.

In the remainder of Chapter 1, we present a model of immigrant enterprise that will serve as a context for the chapters that follow. The model emphasizes the changing opportunity structure confronting immigrants in Western capitalist societies as well as the distribution of resources and the terms on which they are available to ethnic minorities. We emphasize that immigrant economic activity is an interactive consequence of the pursuit of opportunities through the mobilization of resources through ethnic networks within unique historical conditions.

The remaining chapters of this book fall into three main parts. Chapters 2 and 3 use the model developed in Chapter 1 to analyze the trajectory of ethnic business in the United States and Europe, drawing upon publicly available data and fieldwork by the contributors to this volume. Chapter 2 focuses on the United States, first reviewing general small and ethnic business trends, and then comparing the experiences of four ethnic groups—Afro-Americans, Chinese, Koreans, and Cubans. Chapter 3 examines four European countries—England, France, West Germany, and the Netherlands—showing how the model elaborated in Chapter 1 can account for interethnic differences as well as variations in the timing of ethnic business development.

The next three chapters elaborate on the model set forth in Chapter 1, first examining different components of the model, and then bringing together the two sides of the model within the context of a single case study. Chapter 4, which treats the influence of spatial arrangements on ethnic business, takes group characteristics for granted and examines how variations in opportunity structures affect the level and pattern of business development. Chapter 5, which looks at the strategies pursued by ethnic entrepreneurs, assumes that opportunities arise under the conditions reviewed in previous chapters and asks how ethnic entrepreneurs mobilize resources to exploit the niches they encounter. Chapter 6 then brings the two sides of the model back together, by looking at the interaction of opportunity structures and group characteristics in the same industry in three societies — the garment business in the United States, England, and France.

The third part of the book, Chapter 7, summarizes and concludes the volume, and reviews and assesses the policies that national, regional, and local governments have adopted toward ethnic minorities in business.

Scope of the Book

Ethnic entrepreneurship is important because it is one way immigrants and ethnic minorities can respond to the current restructuring of Western industrial economies. This concern defines the scope of our book. Temporally, we focus on the post-World War II period, although historical material from the late nineteenth and early twentieth centuries is often introduced for comparative purposes. Geographically, we examine Western industrial societies. Though we deal mainly with five countries — France, Germany, the Netherlands, the United Kingdom, and the United States — this treatment primarily reflects the development of research on ethnic business and not the actual presence or significance of ethnic business in specific Western societies.

Finally, the groups we consider all share a migrant experience. Most of the groups are immigrants; Afro-Americans, a group discussed in Chapters 2, 4, and 7, are the major exception. Nonetheless, their inclusion in this book is relevant on at least two counts. First, Afro-American migration to cities in the northern United States in the twentieth century provided the crucible out of which black businesses were formed, as we show in Chapters 2 and 4. Second, as we argue in Chapters 2 and 7, it is precisely the situational difference between Afro-Americans and contemporary immigrants that helps us understand the difference in business activity between blacks and other American ethnic groups.

BACKGROUND

Since World War II, the recruitment of immigrant labor to the industrial societies of the West has been linked to the emergence of labor shortages at the bottom of the job hierarchy. Initially, the orientations of the immigrants and the characteristics of the jobs appeared congruent, because the immigrants first came as temporary migrants and the jobs were so simple that they were easily filled by a succession of often unskilled sojourners. Over time, however, the immigrant population settled down and the liabilities of the initial entry-level positions became more severe. These positions were often detached from the main lines of structured mobility within the primary sector of the labor market. Moreover, poor language facility and inappropriate or inadequate skills often barred immigrants from entry into positions that were rationed on the basis of approved apprenticeship training or exams.

The likelihood of successful economic adaptation for many of these new immigrant groups seems further clouded by recent economic trends. The new ethnic populations are heavily overrepresented in precisely those industries most affected by economic stagnation, declining product demand, lost jobs following technological innovation, and intensified world competition. With growth concentrated in the advanced services and new technologies that demand technical proficiency and emphasize interpersonal communication, the mismatch between job requirements and immigrants' skills has steadily widened. Moreover, in a climate of decreasing public expenditure and low economic growth, political support for radical governmental interventions has contracted sharply.

Ethnic small business, in this context of changing economic conditions, has been viewed by both policymakers and academics as an alternative and possibly more viable route to upward economic mobility for immigrant groups. This view is rooted in historical experience, the changing economics of small business, and new evidence on the growth of ethnic entrepreneurship.

Historical Evidence

Small business played an important role in the economic progress of several earlier immigrant groups in the United States: Jews, Chinese, Italians, Greeks, and others (see Light 1972; Bonacich and Modell 1980; Baron et al. 1975, for case studies). Their proportionately higher involvement in entrepreneurial activities continues to differentiate these groups from much of the native population (Goldscheider and Kobrin 1980; Light 1979, 1980; Ritterband and Cohen 1984). Given Europe's more stable and ethnically homogeneous population, the precedents for mobility through business in western European economies are not so striking. Still, the experiences of British and French Jews (Pollins 1984; Green 1986) and, to a lesser extent, Italians and Cypriots in Britain (see the essays in Ward and Jenkins 1984) point to a pattern that the more recent arrivals might emulate.

Changing Economics of Small Business

We are aware that many definitions suggest a distinction between entrepreneur and manager on the basis of the former's unique innovative functions. But neither economists (Baumol 1968: 66) nor social scientists (Kilby 1971: 27-29; Wilken 1979: 60) seem able to implement this distinction to permit the unequivocal exclusion of any owner/manager from the class of entrepreneurs. We, therefore, operationally define "entrepreneurs" as owners/operators of business enterprises (Greenfield et al. 1979).

The future of the small business sector looks much brighter today than it did two decades ago. Far from being marginal, it is now apparent that business activity engages substantial proportions of the working-age populations in all of the countries with which we are concerned. In the European Community as of 1982, 11.9% of the nonagricultural labor force were employers, self-employed, or family workers. In the United States, 13.5% of all employed persons were business owners in 1983 (Haber et al. 1987). A substantial portion of the labor force now works in relatively small concerns. The OECD (1986b) estimates that each self-employed person employs two other people, on average. In the United States, according to Granovetter (1984), four out of every ten workers work in establishments of fewer than 100; and in Britain, according to Curran and Burrows (1986), small firms employ one-third of the private labor force. A new source of data from the United States,

Table 1.1 Self-Employment Rates in Major U.S. Metropolitan Areas

	Men		Women	
	All Persons %	New Immigrants %	All Persons %	New Immigrants %
Chicago	9.0	6.4	3.6	2.4
Los Angeles-Long Beach	12.4	9.1	4.1	3.1
Miami	15.2	13.8	3.9	3.1
New York-New Jersey	10.6	9.3	2.6	2.3
San Francisco-Oakland	12.7	10.6	4.9	3.8

SOURCE: 1980 Census of Population, 5% Public Use Microdata Sample.
NOTE: "New Immigrants" include all immigrants who arrived in the United States between 1965 and 1980.

indicating that 26.4% of nonagricultural workers hold jobs in sole proprietorships, further underlines the employment implications of the small firm sector (Haber et al. 1987).

Business ownership is significant in quantitative terms, and it is also on the upswing, largely because the current economic situation is damaging to large industry while increasingly supportive of small firms. In the United States, the decline in the number of persons working on their own account outside of agriculture finally bottomed out in the mid-1970s, and the number has continued to grow ever since (Fain 1980; Becker 1984; see also Chapter 2). Small firms accounted for the bulk of new jobs generated during the 1970s and 1980s (Birch 1987); and even in manufacturing, in the past decade, small firms have succeeded in maintaining a stable share of employment (Granovetter 1984).

In western Europe, the picture is more mixed. As Table 1.2 shows, between 1969 and 1984, England experienced a very substantial increase in the proportion of the labor force that was self-employed: The data suggest that the profound economic restructuring of the early 1980s produced an environment that was significantly more conducive to small firms than previous conditions. By contrast, self-employment rates fluctuated around a stable midpoint in Germany and the Netherlands and slightly diminished in France.

Sectoral factors were also important in the European countries. Between 1970 and 1982, the proportion of employers, self-employed, and family workers in manufacturing was either up or stable in the four countries treated in this book. Some of this increase may reflect the types of situations described in Chapter 6, in which immigrant piece-rate workers or homeworkers are formally engaged as "independent contractors" (OECD 1986a). In contrast to the situation in manufacturing, only the United Kingdom and the Netherlands appear to have experienced growing self-employment rates in the services (Bechhofer and Elliot 1985). Data on small businesses' role in job creation are not as readily available in Europe as in the United States, but an OECD review concluded that all studies in England, France, and Germany show that employment grew only in start-ups while declining in older firms. Among new establishments/enterprises, employment growth was concentrated in small rather than in large firms (OECD 1985).

Growth of Ethnic Entrepreneurship

The revival of small business has been widely accompanied by the infusion of new ethnic owners into the ranks of petty proprietorship. By 1980, self-employment already accounted for a substantial share of employment among those newcomers who had moved to the United States in the years since the renewal of large-scale immigration in 1965. In four of the five principal immigrant-receiving metropolitan areas — New York, Los Angeles, Miami, and San Francisco — immigrant self-employment rates among males were close to or above the 10% mark, as can be seen in Table 1.1. The immigrant imprint is most dramatic in Miami, where a 30-year influx of Cuban refugees has transformed a decaying, stagnant city into a booming economy that some analysts have called the "capital of Latin America" (Rieff 1987; Levine 1985). Elsewhere, it has been more a matter of immigrants finding niches where small businesses could thrive. In industries like garments, restaurants, petty retailing, taxis, and so on, newcomers have found a supportive environment in which entrepreneurial activity has flourished — as will be seen in the chapters that follow.

In Britain, the percentage of Indian males in self-employment increased from 6% in 1971 to about 18% in 1982, with the equivalent figures for Caribbean males at 2% and 7% (Ward and Jenkins 1984; Department of Employment 1988). Cypriots and Asians revived London's dying East End clothing trade (Saifullah Khan 1979) and created a new one in the West Midlands (Ward et al. 1986). Chinese and Cypriot immigrants have come to dominate the traditional fish and chips trade. Indian and Pakistani entrepreneurs are now prominent in several other areas of retailing (chemist's shops, small grocery stores, discount air-

Table 1.2 Self-Employment Trends, 1969-1984, in Four European Countries (employed persons in nonincorporated business as percentage of civilian, nonagricultural employment)

	1969 %	1973 %	1979 %	1981 %	1984 %
France	N.A.	9.7	8.7	8.7	9.1
Germany	7.6	7.6	7.7	7.6	8.2
Netherlands	N.A.	3.7	4.1	5.6	4.9
United Kingdom	7.3	7.3	6.6	7.9	9.6

SOURCE: OECD (1986: 45).

line tickets), even in areas such as Glasgow, where South Asian settlement has been on a relatively small scale (Krcmar 1984).

In France, immigrants still lag far behind the French national population in their rate of self-employment: In 1984, only 6% of the immigrant population was self-employed, in contrast to 17% for the total population (see Chapter 3). But the overall trend is toward a narrowing of the gap: While small business is losing its attractiveness for the native French population, the proportion of immigrants working on their own account is steadily increasing. As in other countries, the immigrant effect is more visible in those localities with immigrant concentrations than elsewhere. In Paris, for example, one out of every ten store owners is foreign-born (Ma Mung and Guillon 1986).

Elsewhere on the Continent, the expansion of ethnic business has been held back by restrictive "immigrant policies" that constrain movement out of wage and salary employment. In many areas, the terms of entry for migrant workers do not allow self-employment, and the legal/institutional arrangements for small business constitute a further barrier. Despite this, there is evidence of a growing ethnic small business sector, as we discuss in Chapter 3. In the Netherlands, the overall rate of self-employment is considerably lower than in France, but substantial business activity has sprung up among Chinese immigrants, and Hindustani and Turkish entrepreneurs have reintroduced garment manufacture to Amsterdam. In Germany, where there has been no national census since the 1970s, reliable national estimates of immigrant business rates do not exist. Nonetheless, the case study literature points to a growth of immigrant entrepreneurship, as economic restructuring has spurred immigrants to seek out alternatives to wage and salary work in the traditional immigrant-employing industries (Blaschke and Ersoz 1986; Morokvasic 1986).

Our interactive model of ethnic business development is built on two dimensions: opportunity structures and characteristics of the ethnic groups. As shown in Figure 1.1, opportunity structures consist of market conditions that may favor products or services oriented toward co-ethnics and situations in which a wider, nonethnic market might be served. Opportunity structures also include the routes through which access to business is obtained. Group characteristics include premigration circumstances, a group's reaction to conditions in the host society, and resource mobilization through various features of the ethnic community. Ethnic strategies emerge from the interaction of all these factors, as ethnic entrepreneurs adapt to the resources made available in opportunity structures and attempt to carve out their own niches.

THE OPPORTUNITY STRUCTURE

We begin with the characteristics of opportunity structures to emphasize the role played by historically contingent circumstances in shaping the prospects open to potential ethnic business owners. Groups can work only with the resources made available to them by their environments, and the structure of opportunities is constantly changing in modern industrial societies. Market conditions may favor only businesses serving an ethnic community's needs, in which case entrepreneurial opportunities are limited. Or market conditions may favor smaller enterprises serving nonethnic populations, in which case opportunities are much greater. Even if market conditions are favorable, immigrant minorities must gain access to businesses, and nonethnic group members often control such access.

Market Conditions

For a business to arise, there must be some demand for the services it offers. The initial market for immigrant entrepreneurs typically arises within the immigrant community itself — the immigrant community has a special set of needs and preferences that are best served, and sometimes can only be served, by those who share those needs and know them intimately, namely, the members of the immigrant community itself.

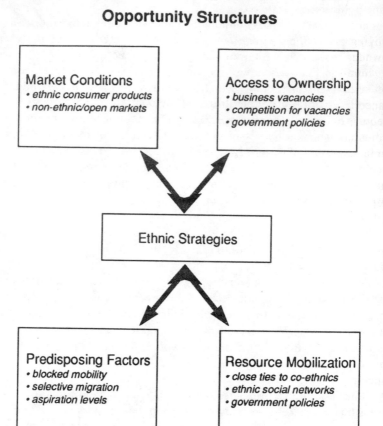

Figure 1.1. An Interactive Model of Ethnic Business Development

Ethnic Consumer Products

Generally, the businesses that develop first are purveyors of culinary products — tropical goods among Hispanics, for example, or Oriental specialties among Asians. Businesses that provide "cultural products" — newspapers, recordings, books, magazines, clothes, jewelry —

are also quick to find a niche in the immigrant community. The important point about both types of activity is that they involve a direct connection with the immigrants' homeland and knowledge of tastes and buying preferences — qualities unlikely to be shared by larger, native-owned competitors (Aldrich, Cater, et al. 1985).

Immigrants also have special problems that are caused by the strains of settlement and assimilation, which are aggravated by their distance from the institutionalized mechanisms of service delivery. Consequently, the business of specializing in the problems of immigrant adjustment is another early avenue of economic activity, and immigrant-owned travel agencies and law firms as well as realtors and accountants are common in most immigrant communities. Such businesses frequently perform myriad functions far beyond the simple provision of legal aid or travel information and reservations (Ladbury 1984).

To a large extent, these services to immigrants are unfamiliar and unintelligible to the newcomer unaccustomed to bureaucratic procedures. In some cases, they may impinge on the often dubious legal status of immigrants and their families. Trust is thus an important component of the service, and the need for trust pulls the newcomer toward a business owner of common ethnic background. In addition, in many of the societies from which the immigrants come, people prefer personalistic relationships over reliance on impersonal, formal procedures. Such predispositions further increase the clientele of those businesses that specialize in adjustment problems.

If immigrant business stays limited to the ethnic market, its potential for growth is sharply circumscribed, as shown in studies of white, black, and Puerto Rican businesses in the United States (Aldrich and Reiss 1976) and of Indian and white businesses in the United Kingdom (Aldrich et al. 1983). The obstacle to growth is the ethnic market itself, which can support only a restricted number of businesses because it is quantitatively small and because the ethnic population is too impoverished to provide sufficient buying power. Moreover, the environment confronting the ethnic entrepreneur is severe: Because exclusion from job opportunities leads many immigrants to seek out business opportunities, business conditions in the ethnic market tend toward a proliferation of small units, overcompetition, and a high failure rate, with the surviving businesses generating scanty returns for their owners.

These conclusions may be too pessimistic because the immigrant market may also serve as an export platform from which ethnic firms may expand. One case in point is the experience of Cuban refugees in Miami, Florida, discussed in Chapter 2. The early refugees converged on a depressed area in the central city, where housing costs were low and low-rent storefront vacant space was available. As the refugee population grew, and the customer base expanded, retail businesses proliferated (Mohl 1983). The availability of a nearby, low-cost labor force linked together through informal networks further enabled Cuban entrepreneurs to branch out in other industries, such as garments or construction, where a nonethnic clientele could be secured. Once in place, these "export industries" then served as a base for additional expansion of the ethnic economy: The export industries generated a surplus that trickled down to merchants serving the local, specialized needs of the Cuban communities. The export industries also enabled ethnic entrepreneurs to diversify, by moving backward or forward into related industries. As the vibrant Cuban ethnic economy has turned Miami into a center for investments from Latin America as well as an entrepôt for trade with that area, Cuban entrepreneurs have been able to move into more sophisticated and higher-profit fields (Levine 1985).

The same pattern of development can be detected among the Chinese refugees who have settled in Paris in growing numbers since 1975. A variety of factors have facilitated the development of a burgeoning Chinese business sector: population concentration, especially in the 13th arrondissement; specialized and distinctive consumption tastes; informal capital-raising networks; and linkages to sources of financing and cheap consumer goods in the Far East. Chinese entrepreneurs have quickly used their access to their ethnic market to develop ties to French customers and suppliers and reduce their dependence on Asian customers:

> Already, shops producing beancurd have been started in the Parisian region and in Paris itself. In the 13th arrondissement, the Sojato company, for example, produces several tons of beancurd each day, furnishing it at the same time to local merchants of the neighborhoods and to wholesalers at the Halles de Rungis. Other enterprises making fresh food are in the planning stage. . . . An opening is perceptible toward non-Asian suppliers and at the same time toward a more diversified clientele (the stores make an ever greater effort to translate the prices and labels into French). (Guillon and Taboada-Leonetti 1986: 117)

These examples notwithstanding, we note that the growth potential of immigrant business hinges on its access to customers beyond the ethnic community. The crucial question, then, concerns the types of economic environments that might support neophyte immigrant entrepreneurs.

Immigrant Business in the Open Market

The structure of industry is a powerful constraint on the creation of new business organizations. New firms are unlikely to arise in industries characterized by extensive scale economies and entry costs. However, most Western economies contain niches where techniques of mass production or mass distribution do not prevail. Under these circumstances, immigrant businesses can grow in the open market.

Underserved or abandoned markets. One such niche consists of markets that are underserved and often abandoned by the large mass-marketing organizations. The fact that immigrants are so heavily concentrated in the core of urban centers means that they live in areas that are at once ill-suited to the technological and organizational conditions of large enterprise and favorable to small enterprises. The agglomeration of urban populations allows immigrants to start businesses with virtually no capital at all, as demonstrated by the experience of Senegalese traders in Paris (Salem 1984) and the upsurge of street peddling among a variety of immigrant groups in the United States (Greenberg et al. 1980).

A more important influence is the cost structure of the food retailing industry: Overhead costs in central city locations keep store sizes down, thus diminishing the scale economies that give large chain operations an advantage over small independent grocery stores. In France, where food distribution is increasingly concentrated in large suburban supermarkets, or *hypermarchés,* immigrant retailers have found a niche as small neighborhood retailers (Simon and Ma Mung 1987). Retailing in the United Kingdom is experiencing a similar trend; for example, two firms account for more than half of all package grocery sales in London. But the inner urban areas of largely working-class populations are shunned by the large chains, and Asian shopkeepers now dominate these areas, whatever the ethnic origins of local residents (Ward 1986, 1987). Similarly, in New York City, large national chains play a very limited role in the food retailing industry; consequently, the industry has been entered easily by small immigrant concerns that do well in competing against local, nonimmigrant chains that lack the economies of scale to achieve significant market power (Waldinger 1986).

Within the central cities of the United States, black urban ghettos are particularly underserved by retail chains. For example, North Lawndale, a heavily black community in Chicago of over 60,000 persons, contains only one supermarket (Wacquant and Wilson 1988). In turn, black neighborhoods such as North Lawndale have seen an influx of Korean, Arab, and other immigrant merchants who thrive in the absence of competition from larger, native-owned and -operated organizations (see Chapter 2). In general, this pattern of immigrants selling to a nonimmigrant clientele can be characterized as a "middleman minority" situation, which is discussed in Chapter 4.

Low economies of scale. Markets where economies of scale are so low that immigrant entrepreneurs can achieve the highest levels of efficiency by engaging in self-exploitation are another fertile field for immigrant business. Given the competitive weakness of native-owned food stores, as noted above, self-exploitation is a strategy that small immigrant store owners can successfully pursue. As Ma Mung and Guillon (1986) observed, the immigrant-owned neighborhood shops of Paris offer the same products as their French counterparts, but provide different services: longer hours, year-round operation, easily available credit, and sales of very small quantities. Another case in point is the taxi industry in the United States, where immigrants have been able to move rapidly into ownership positions. What is distinctive about the taxi industry is that virtually no advantages accrue to the large firm. Because the owner-operator of a single cab operates at essentially the same costs as a fleet of 20 to 30 cabs, the key to cost reduction is keeping the vehicle on the road for the longest possible time. Thus if immigrants are amenable to self-exploitation or, better yet, can pool resources to buy a taxi and then split shifts so that the cab is in use 24 hours a day, they can effectively compete with native-owned firms (Russell 1985; Orlick 1987).

Instability and uncertainty. A niche for immigrant firms also arises in markets affected by instability or uncertainty. When demand falls into stable and unstable portions, and the two components can be separated from one another, industries may be segmented into noncompeting branches (Piore 1980): One branch is dominated by larger firms, handling staple products; a second, composed of small-scale firms, caters to the unpredictable and/or fluctuating portion of demand. Hence segmentation processes in industries like clothing or construction give rise to small-scale sectors specializing in products that larger firms cannot effectively supply. As we show in Chapter 6, the small-scale sector, with its low entry barriers and high labor-to-capital ratios, offers immigrant entrepreneurs an accessible route into the general market.

Ethnic goods. A final niche in the general market arises where the demand for exotic goods among the native population allows immigrants to convert both the contents and the symbols of ethnicity into profit-making commodities. Selling exotic goods and services offers a fruitful path of business expansion because immigrants have a special product that only they can supply or, at the very least, present in conditions that are seemingly authentic (Palmer 1984). Immigrants not only lack competitors in "exotic markets," they can also offer their products at relatively low prices and thereby capture a clientele priced out of the businesses run by native entrepreneurs (see Ma Mung and Guillon 1986). Indeed, the demand for exotic products such as Indian cuisine in the United Kingdom and Indonesian cuisine in the Netherlands may become so dominant as to force many native businesses offering traditional alternatives out of business.

In conclusion, what distinguishes the variety of processes giving rise to immigrant business is an environment supportive of neophyte capitalists and the small concerns that they establish. Ethnic consumer tastes provide a protected market position, in part because the members of the community may have a cultural preference for dealing with coethnics, and in part because the costs of learning the specific wants and tastes of the immigrant groups are such as to discourage native firms from doing so, especially at an early stage when the community is small and not readily visible to outsiders (Aldrich, Cater, et al. 1985).

If the ethnic market allows the immigrant to maintain a business at somewhat higher-than-average costs, the other processes outlined above reduce the cost difference between native and immigrant firms. Small capital-to-labor ratios keep entry barriers low, and consequently immigrant businesses should be most common in industries where this condition prevails. Where there are problems in substituting capital for labor because changes in demand might idle expensive machines, immigrant businesses with labor-intensive processes can operate close to the prevailing efficiencies. When small markets inhibit the realization of economies of scale, small firms can achieve efficiencies close to or better than their larger competitors and without the heavy overhead and administrative costs that the latter must shoulder.

A second characteristic of industries supportive of immigrant firms is that the technical barriers to entry are also low. The best example is taxis, in which the essential skill — driving — is one that almost everybody has. More commonly, the required skills do not involve high levels of specialization and can be learned through informal, on-the-job training and developed through work experience.

Consequently, the crucial factor is whether the would-be entrepreneur can pick up the needed business know-how while still an employee. One case in point is the rehabilitation-and-renovations sector in construction: Not only are jobs smaller in size, but fewer master construction skills are needed, making on-the-job training easier to obtain. A similar situation applies in another province of immigrant businesses — restaurants — where the hierarchy of skills ranges from dishwashers at the bottom to cooks at the top. Although one way of going to the top in this industry is going to a culinary school, a newcomer can also move up through observation and learning by doing: today, a dishwasher, tomorrow a sandwich man; eventually, a cook.

Access to Ownership

Given the existence of markets conducive to small business, the would-be immigrant entrepreneur still needs access to ownership opportunities. Immigrants' access to ownership positions largely depends on two factors: (1) the number of vacant business-ownership positions, and the extent to which natives are vying for those slots, and (2) government policies toward immigrants.

Business Vacancies

In the immigrant-receiving countries of the late nineteenth and early twentieth centuries, rapid economic growth created new industries, allowing immigrants to take up business activities without substantial competition from, or displacement of, natives. As we shall show in Chapter 6, the clothing industry offers the classic illustration of this process: Because the influx of Jewish immigrants to Paris, London, and New York coincided with a burgeoning demand for factory-made clothes from the 1880s on, immigrants could move into newly emerging small business positions. In the late twentieth century, however, economic growth is proceeding more slowly; there are relatively fewer opportunities for the self-employed, even though the ranks of those working on their own account have generally increased during the past

10 to 15 years. Under these conditions, ownership opportunities for immigrants are principally determined by the supply of native entrepreneurs. Should the supply of native owners for a small business industry dwindle, immigrants may take over as replacement owners.

At the neighborhood level, replacement opportunities for immigrant owners selling to their coethnic neighbors emerge as a result of ecological succession (Aldrich and Reiss 1976). As the native group in a residential area no longer replaces itself, native entrepreneurs seek out business opportunities outside the local area. Given a naturally high rate of failure among all small businesses, the absence of members from the older established group willing to open up new firms in "changed" neighborhoods creates vacancies for potential immigrant businesspeople (see Chapter 4).

In the general economy, the crucial factor is that the petite bourgeoisie often does not reproduce itself, but survives through the recruitment of owners from lower social classes (Bechhofer and Elliot 1981). To some extent, it is the very marginality of the small business position that discourages heirs from taking up their parents' modest enterprises. As Berteaux and Berteaux-Wiame (1981: 166) write about artisanal bakers in France:

> If the baker's trade was still a good trade, as it was for centuries, the sons of bakers would have chosen this profession and one of them would be ready to take over his parents' business. . . . But the baker's trade is not what it used to be. . . . So most bakers orient their sons away from the trade. . . . So when the time for retirement comes, they do not find any baker's child to take over the business; neither their own nor the children of their colleagues.

In the central cities of the United States, where small business has been concentrated among European immigrants and their descendants, the changing social structure of Italian, Jewish, and other European ancestry groups has further diminished the allure of petty enterprise. Assimilation, high levels of educational attainment, and the dwindling of corporate discrimination have lowered the barriers to desirable positions in large organizations. Among groups like Italians or Jews, self-employment tends to be higher among fathers than among sons, and higher among fathers of older cohorts than among their younger counterparts (Goldscheider and Kobrin 1980; Cohen 1983). Similar pro-

cesses have been observed among the long-established Jewish population in the United Kingdom (Pollins 1984).

A variety of studies note how the growth of replacement demand has
altered the ethnic complexion of the small business class. A large
proportion of Moroccan storekeepers in Paris have taken over small
neighborhood shops from older French owners in areas of relatively low
immigrant settlement. Ma Mung and Guillon (1986: 122-123) pointed
out that French owners who sold their businesses were "a relatively
aged commercial population which had not found a buyer among those
French to whom they would have . . . preferred to have sold rather than
to 'foreigners.'" Similarly, in New York, Korean grocery store owners
have taken over from Jewish or Italian proprietors who were just too
old, tired, and scared of crime to keep on minding their stores.

> Korean immigrants are able to buy shops from white minority shopkeep-
> ers, especially Jews, because the second- or third-generation children of
> these older immigrants have already entered the mainstream of the Amer-
> ican occupational structure, and so they are reluctant to take over their
> parents' businesses. In fact, experienced Korean shopkeepers have ad-
> vised less experienced Korean businessmen that "the prospect is very
> good if you buy a store in a good location from old Jewish people." (Kim,
> 1981: 111)

When native groups falter in their recruitment to small business, their
share of the small business sector inevitably declines, if for no other
reason than the high death rate to which all small businesses are prone.
Birch's (1987) studies, for example, have shown that 8% of all firms in
U.S. metropolitan areas are lost each year, which means that half of all
firms in any area must be replaced every five years for the area simply
to break even. For small firms and for new businesses, the failure rates
are higher still; indeed, the majority of new businesses do not last longer
than four years.

The burgeoning of immigrant business in New York's clothing industry shows how the diverging appeal of small business for immigrants
and natives creates a favorable environment for immigrant entrepreneurship by reducing the competition for business positions. Immigrant
clothing factories fail at a higher rate than their native-owned counterparts, but the crucial difference is that immigrants set up new businesses
at a very high rate. By contrast, there are virtually no natives replacing
other natives whose businesses fail. The remaining native proprietors

are the aging owners of long-established factories, with little hope for the industry (Waldinger 1986).

Government Policies

Access to ownership is also affected by government policies setting the terms on which immigrants enter and by policies affecting the ease with which businesses can be started. In most societies, new immigrants, because of their terms of entry, are free to settle wherever job opportunities are best. However, governments often attempt to influence where immigrants settle. In the United States, for example, the government tried to spread Cuban and Vietnamese refugees across the country. The policy failed for Cubans, as they recongregated back in the Miami area. In England, the government tried to direct the flow of Asian refugees from Uganda in the early 1970s, again with little long-term success. In Germany, the government initially treated Turkish workers as only temporary residents, making it difficult for them to bring their families with them. Nonetheless, families did reconstitute in German cities, creating markets for ethnic goods and services.

National and local governments vary in the extent to which they set restrictive conditions on which businesses can be started. In the Netherlands, for example, in some trades licenses are required and prospective entrepreneurs must show that there is a "need" for their business. In Germany, the legal right to open a business is contingent upon obtaining a residence permit, which is awarded after many years of labor migrant status. Formal requirements for starting craft and trade firms in various sectors were liberalized in the 1980s, making it easier for immigrants to open businesses.

GROUP CHARACTERISTICS

Thus far, we have discussed two opportunity-structure conditions for the development of immigrant business: a niche in which the small business can viably function and access to ownership positions. But if there is a demand for small business activities, why do immigrants tend to emerge as the replacement group? We hypothesize that some immigrants are predisposed toward business and that they can also draw on informal ethnic resources that give them a competitive edge. We emphasize the fit between immigrant firms and the environments in which they function, including not only economic and social conditions but also the unique historical conditions encountered at the time of immigration.

Predisposing Factors

The reasons that immigrants emerge as a replacement group rest on a complex of interacting economic, social, and psychological factors. Blocked mobility is a powerful spur to business activity. Immigrants suffer from a variety of impediments in the labor market: unfamiliarity with the language of the host country, inadequate or inappropriate skills, age, and discrimination. Lacking the same opportunities for stable career employment as natives, immigrants are more likely to strike out on their own and to experience less aversion to the substantial risks that this course entails.

Immigrants' limited range of job- and income-generating activities also spurs them to acquire business skills. Native workers will tend not to acquire particular skills if the returns to the needed investment in education and training are lower than those for comparable jobs. By contrast, the same skills might offer immigrants the best return, precisely because they lack access to better remunerated jobs (Bailey 1987). Immigrants' willingness to put in long hours — needed to generate working capital or to maintain economies of scale — is similarly conditioned. For those without access to jobs with high rates of hourly return, such activities as driving a cab or running a store from early morning to late night offer the best available rewards for their work effort.

There are also psychological components to the entry of immigrants into small business. Much of the sociological literature has characterized the small business owner as an anachronistic type impelled by a need for autonomy and independence (Mills 1958). Auster and Aldrich (1984) noted that this approach assumes that entrepreneurship reflects the decisions of isolated individuals and thus ignores the issue of why certain groups disproportionately channel new recruits into small business.

The traditional perspective also fails to account for the social pressures that condition groups and individuals for small business activity, including immigration itself. The process of leaving one's home to take up life in a new society is self-selective: The workers who enter the immigration stream tend to be more able, better prepared, and more inclined toward risk than those who stay home. These same characteristics also give immigrants an advantage in competition with native groups in the low-wage labor market, against whom they compare favorably in terms of motivation, risk propensity, and an ability to adjust to change (Chiswick 1978). Immigrants are also more satisfied than native-born workers with low profits from small business because of wage differences between their origin and destination countries (Light 1984).

Immigrants' social origins also alter the way they perceive the chances of getting ahead, because they have a more favorable view of low-level work than do natives. Immigrants perceive their jobs' status, as well as economic rewards, in terms of the much different job hierarchies of their home societies (Piore 1979). Quite the same disparity would give the immigrant a distinctive frame of reference from which to assess the attractiveness of small business opportunities that open up as previously incumbent groups move on to other pursuits. A young native aspiring to work as a manager behind the desk in a clean, air-conditioned bank might well look askance at the idea of taking over the neighborhood grocery store or small local factory that becomes vacant when an aging owner retires. By contrast, in a newcomer's eyes, taking over a petty proprietorship is likely to be a positive alternative to working for someone else, as well as the best chance of getting ahead. Immigrants in general and sojourners in particular are more concerned with economic mobility than with social status.

Resource Mobilization

Resource mobilization is intimately bound up with the dynamics of ethnic identity, and, therefore, we present our conceptualization of ethnicity before turning to the routes through which resources are acquired.

Conceptualization of Ethnicity

Ethnic is an adjective that refers to differences between categories of people (Petersen 1980). By contrast, when it is linked to the noun *group*, it implies that members have some awareness of group membership. In this book, we begin with the assumption that what is "ethnic" about "ethnic business" may be no more than a set of connections and regular patterns of interaction among people sharing common national background or migration experiences. Consequently, our concern here begins with the subcultural dimension of ethnicity — that is to say, the social structures through which members of an ethnic group are attached to one another and the ways in which those social structures are used. These social structures consist, broadly speaking, of two parts: (1) the networks of kinship and friendship around which ethnic communities are arranged (Zimmer and Aldrich 1987) and (2) the interlacing of these networks with positions in the economy (jobs), in space (housing), and in civil society (institutions).

From our perspective, ethnicity — that is, self-identification with a particular ethnic group — is neither primordial nor imported prior to contact with a host society. Rather, ethnicity is a *possible* outcome of the patterns by which intra- and intergroup interactions are structured. Our central contention is that ethnicity is acquired when the social connections among ethnic group members help establish distinct occupational, industrial, or spatial concentrations. Once established, these concentrations promote frequent and intensive face-to-face interactions that breed a sense of commonality and identification with members of the same ethnic group. Ethnic concentrations may also give rise to common ethnic interests, reinforcing a sense of identity. In addition, industrial or business concentrations foster competitive cross-ethnic contact, which in turn promotes ethnic consciousness and solidarity.

Our conceptualization implies that the emergence of ethnic communities and networks may generate the infrastructure and resources for ethnic small businesses *before* a sense of group awareness develops. Once in place, an ethnic business niche may give rise to, or strengthen, group consciousness. Ethnic entrepreneurs, as we note in Chapters 5, 6, and 7, may find themselves in conflict with other ethnic groups or with state officials. As a group's level of self-employment rises, the protection and growth of the ethnic business niche may come to define the group's interests and, therefore, the meaning of ethnicity.

Close Ties Between Coethnics

Information about the host society (accurate or misleading) is transmitted through communication or personal interaction between migrants and their home communities, and the picture portrayed by the migrant prompts other natives to take their chances abroad. A similar chain of events conditions the process of settlement: Once arrived in the new society, who does one turn to but those friends or relatives already situated with a home and a job? To be sure, home and job are not quite as glittering as the newcomers had imagined or the settler had promised. The new arrivals frequently secure jobs where many, or even most, of the workers are immigrants as well.

Because of a preference for familiarity, the efficiency of personal contacts, and social distance from the host society's institutions of assistance, immigrants rely on connections with settlers to find shelter and work and thus find themselves in the ethnic occupational-and-residential ghetto. Should this process repeat itself time and again, two consequences ensue. First, intense interaction within a common milieu intensifies the feeling of commonality and membership with the group. Second, there is the buildup of that critical mass needed for formal ethnic institutions — a church, a mutual aid society, perhaps a trade union, maybe a political club — which in turn serve to reinforce ethnic identity.

Thus far, this is a familiar, though greatly simplified, story; however, we will use it to extract several less familiar lessons. The first is that immigrants may be vulnerable and oppressed, but, because they can draw on connections of mutuality and support, they can also create resources that offset the harshness of the environment they encounter. The second is that the social structures of the immigrant community breed organizations, both informal and formal, in a context that might otherwise tend toward anomie. The third lesson, of particular importance to the discussion that follows, is that such informal organizational resources might give immigrants an advantage against natives should the institutionalized arrangements that normally connect individuals with organizations be undeveloped and/or malfunctioning.

Ethnic Social Networks

Because entrepreneurs need to mobilize scarce and, therefore, valued resources, activating strong ties to kin and coethnics is important in the formation and maintenance of immigrant firms, as we shall discuss at greater length in Chapter 5. Strong ties are likely to be particularly important to immigrant business owners, who start out with few resources and lack access to mainstream sources of credit or technical assistance. Such ties are embedded in the migration experience: The immigration process selects immigrants who are integrated into kinship networks, and the tendency of immigrants to move under the auspices of settlers and their subsequent interdependence for information and support fosters a reciprocal flow of exchanges. Of course, the characteristics of the migration process are likely to affect the closeness and density of ties within immigrant communities. Migration streams characterized by circular movements, frequent return migrations, or a preponderance of single individuals are less likely to support closely tied networks than those in which households move on a permanent basis. Closely tied networks are likely to unravel over time because settlement makes migrants less dependent on one another and may also give them the skills needed to enter mainstream institutions (Bailey 1987; Portes 1987).

The very process of entry into a new society, in which newcomers both occupy distinct positions and find themselves in conflict with natives, hastens ethnic group formation (Olzak 1983). Conditions that raise the salience of group boundaries and identity, leading persons to form new social ties and action-sets, increase the likelihood of entrepreneurial attempts and raise the probability of success (Aldrich and Zimmer 1986). The more deeply entrepreneurs are embedded within their networks of kin or coethnics, the more salient ethnic group boundaries will be. Therefore, it is more likely that immigrants will engage in the receipt and transmittal of business support and information with other coethnics. Moreover, the circumstances of migration spur the conscious widening of connections within the ethnic community. Even among communities made up of permanent immigrants, home-country familial networks are unlikely to be transplanted fully. Precisely because connections to kin are truncated, nonkin ties must be cultivated for social and economic support (Lessinger 1985).

Such closely tied social networks provide the confidentiality and social control required for the types of informal credit-raising mechanisms that Ivan Light and other subsequent analysts have identified for Japanese, West Indians, Jews, Koreans, Chinese, Tunisians, and others (Boubakri 1985; Guillon and Taboada-Leonetti 1986; Light 1972, 1980; Tenenbaum 1986). Other groups have managed to leap over capital barriers without access to rotating credit associations or their analogues. However, informal ties to other coethnics with capital have a strong impact on the ability to gain start-up capital, as Portes (1987) has shown for the Cubans.

In addition to capital, owners also need to rely on trusted acquaintances to obtain reliable information about permits, laws, available business sites, management practices, and reliable suppliers. Relatives or friends with business experience are likely to be a source of good and low-cost information. Where such ties do not flow from a home-society context, they can be created after migration, as in the case of Koreans in New York who attend churches because "they are looking for jobs or job information, want to obtain business information, make business contacts, conduct business negotiations, or seek private loans" (Kim 1987).

Partners are also to be secured through contacts with coethnics. Partnership is a crucial ingredient, allowing immigrant owners to pool capital, reduce the need for outside labor, and maintain outside wage-earning activities, thereby reducing risk. Informal networks within an ethnic community also enable entrepreneurs to connect with persons in higher positions. Immigrants excluded from the formal credit system may develop close ties to higher-status members of an ethnic community and thereby secure loans or money partners. Professionals within the ethnic community provide a wide variety of valued services (Ladbury 1984).

Labor recruitment. Small business industries such as clothing, restaurants, construction, or retail are the environments in which new immigrant businesses have sprung up. In these industries, size of establishments and competitive conditions constrain the development of internal labor markets. Firms turn to the external market to secure a labor force and, consequently, the factors that influence employment and training characteristics are generated outside the firm (Granovetter and Tilly 1988).

The central issue confronting small firms is how to increase the probability of hiring workers who are capable of learning required skills and who will remain with the firm and apply their skills there. "Hiring," as Spence (1974: 2-3) has put it, "is investing under uncertainty." Employers are uncertain about the productive capabilities of job applicants prior to hiring and even for some time after the hiring decision has been made. In many cases, native workers have dropped out of the labor supply in which immigrants are concentrated (see Waldinger and Lapp 1988 for an example). Native employers, therefore, have little choice but to recruit immigrants, and this dependence causes special problems in stabilizing the employment relationship.

Trust may be low due to stereotyping of immigrant labor; in addition, situational constraints may provide little room for trust to develop. For example, high turnover — which may arise because of seasonality, frequent travel to home societies, or return migration — will hinder the development of stable relationships on which trust might be based. A firm with high turnover is also apt to be caught in a vicious circle, because the costs of constantly hiring make it uneconomical to exercise much discretion over the recruitment process.

Whereas native employers confront a shortage of native workers, immigrant employers usually have no such problem. They recruit an attached labor force by mobilizing direct connections to the ethnic community from which they emigrated. One means of securing a labor force is to recruit family members. Because the characteristics of kin, unlike those of strangers, are known and familiar, their behavior is likely to be predictable, if not reliable. Furthermore, trust may already inhere in the family relationship.

Newcomers turn to settlers for help in job finding and may first seek out employment in an immigrant firm where they can work in a familiar environment with others who know their language. Newcomers' dependence on their bosses/patrons makes them likely to accept conditions that may fall below standard; it is also the case that owners will be more likely to place trust in workers who depend on them.

Native- and immigrant-owned firms further differ in their handling of internal strains. Where management and labor are ethnically distinct, social distance tends to preclude managerial acceptance of informal shop-floor norms. Repeated conflict over production quotas, behavioral rules, absenteeism, and instability tends to take on an explicitly racial character as management interprets workers' behavior in racially stereotyped ways. When immigrant or minority workers are employed by members of the majority group, the economic disparities between the two groups fuel discontent with wages, personnel policies, and general working conditions, making work just another instance of inequitable treatment (Waldinger 1986).

In immigrant firms, however, ethnicity provides a common ground on which the rules of the workplace are negotiated. The social structures around which the immigrant firm is organized help stabilize the employment relationship; they are also relationships of meaning suffused with expectations that actors have of one another. One consequence is that authority can be secured on the basis of personal loyalties and ethnic allegiance rather than on the basis of harsh discipline, driving, and direct-control techniques. Furthermore, ethnic commonality provides a repertoire of symbols and customs that can be invoked to underline cultural interests and similarities in the face of a potentially conflict-laden situation (Wong 1987).

If ethnic commonality is a device for securing the immigrant worker's loyalty, the expectations bound up in the ethnic employment exchange impinge on the owner's latitude as well. Immigrant workers can anticipate that the standards of conduct prevailing in the broader ethnic community will extend to the workplace as well (see, for example, Herman 1979). The immigrant firm is also likely to offer an environment where the worker is sheltered from some of the rules and regulations of the host society: a place where hours are not carefully watched, wages are paid in cash or under the table, and machinery is used for personal needs (Gold 1985). Similarly, the terms under which immigrant owners obtain kin or hometown friends as laborers may include an understanding that the employment relationship is meant to be reciprocal (Ladbury 1984). In return for the immigrant worker's effort and constancy, the immigrant owner may be expected to make a place for newly arrived relatives, to help out with financial problems, or even to provide a loan needed for starting up a new business. This issue is taken up again in Chapter 5.

Ascribed ties, such as ethnic commonality, may also make relations between businesses more effective. The cost of transactions between firms is likely to be lower when they have a basis for trusting each other and can thus work more effectively together. Owners in ethnic business communities may be involved in such regular cooperative activities with suppliers, subcontractors, and customers, thus justifying the label "custom of cooperation" (Dei Ottati 1986). These may be business/ residential communities that are ethnically very distinct, such as, for example, Pakistanis living in a particular urban district in Britain or village/small town communities in which the "industrial district" consists largely of families with recent background in agriculture. In each case, the "custom of cooperation" is underpinned by a range of sanctions, positive and negative, that structure village life, with the prospect that firms that betray trust lose further orders as word of their opportunistic behavior spreads.

Government Policies

Governments vary substantially in the level of economic assistance they provide to immigrants and ethnic minorities. In the United States, minority businesses were ignored by the federal government until the 1960s, when the civil rights movement, civil disorders, and other political conditions coalesced into support for "black capitalism." Minority set-aside provisions were introduced into government contracting procedures, and special minority enterprise investment programs were created. The amount of money allocated was never very large, but the effort was a politically significant symbol of minority business's importance in American society. The long-term economic significance of these programs was small, and little concrete evidence of their consequences could be found in the 1980s.

The British government's interest in minority business was also heightened by widespread civil unrest, which occurred in 1981. Subsequent investigations showed that few government measures had specifically targeted minority businesses, but since 1986, the central government has taken some steps to reach minorities in England's largest cities. Most programs directed to ethnic businesses, however, have been implemented by local authorities.

West Germany, the Netherlands, France, and most other European countries have no funding programs directed primarily at immigrant businesses. If ethnic minorities and immigrants do benefit, they do so as part of the small business constituency, not as members of an ethnic minority. We address these issues more fully in Chapter 7.

Differences Among Ethnic and Immigrant Groups

Why do some ethnic and immigrant groups do better in business than others? The historical record shows considerable disparities in self-employment among the various European immigrant and Afro-American populations in the United States (see Chapter 2) and the various immigrant groups in Europe (see Chapter 3). Jews, for example, were far more successful in business in the United States than were the Irish, and Italians achieved higher rates of self-employment than did the Poles. Similar differences hold for the newcomers who arrived in the United States between 1970 and 1980. According to the *Census of Population,* Koreans ranked first, with 11.5% self-employed; lagging far behind were the Mexicans, among whom less than 2% worked for themselves. In the United Kingdom, South Asians (Indians and Pakistanis) have recently achieved rates of self-employment much higher than the native population, whereas West Indians are underrepresented in self-employment (Ward 1987). In France, Moroccans, Tunisians, and Chinese have high levels of business activity, whereas immigrants from Spain and Portugal are rarely involved in business ventures (Ma Mung and Guillon 1986; Guillon and Taboada-Leonetti 1986).

Various explanations have been proposed for these differences. We believe the most useful approach is multivariate, which implies that the terms of the interaction among the various factors are indeterminate. What we can do at an analytic level is to specify the variables that affect self-employment outcomes; it remains for empirical work to determine their effects on a case-by-case basis, and we will report on some research findings in the following chapters.

We can separate the conditions that influence the self-employment process into three categories: (1) premigration characteristics, (2) the circumstances of migration and their evolution, and (3) postmigration characteristics. First, premigration attributes include skill, language, business experiences, kinship patterns, and exposure to conditions (such as a high level of urbanization and industrialization) that would foster entrepreneurial attitudes. Second, the circumstances of migration are the conditions under which the immigrants move, whether as temporary workers or as permanent settlers, as well as the factors influencing their settlement type. Third, characteristics such as economic and occupational position and discrimination (or the lack thereof) would fall under the postmigration rubric. Our discussion implies that no single characteristic — whether premigration or postmigration experience or circumstance of migration — will in and of itself determine the level of self-employment; rather, the critical factor will be how these various characteristics interact with one another and with the local opportunity structure.

Premigration Characteristics

The likelihood of succeeding in business is enhanced if immigrants come with skills that are useful to business success in both general and specific ways. A good historical illustration is the case of turn-of-the-century Russian Jews who, by virtue of prior experience in tailoring, a high level of literacy, and a historical orientation toward trading, moved rapidly into entrepreneurial positions in the garment industry in the United States. The educational level of recent immigrants to the United States today is much higher than was true for the earlier immigrant waves, and thus a considerable proportion arrive with general skills that are relevant for business success. But among U.S. immigrants there appears to be only a weak correlation between education and self-employment. It is not the immigrants with the highest or most developed general skills that flock to business; rather, it is those whose general skills are not quite appropriate to the new context.

Relatively fewer immigrants arrive with skills that are specific to the business fields they enter. For example, New York's fur industry contains a high proportion of Greeks, both as workers and as owners, almost all of whom have come from the province of Kastoria, where they were apprenticed as furriers at a relatively young age. Yet the bulk of Greeks in business are active in the restaurant industry, and cooking is not a skill that most Greek males appear to have brought with them, especially when one considers that Greek restaurants mainly specialize in "American food." Thus the crucial issue is how skills are acquired upon arrival in the host society. One answer, which follows from our discussion of ethnicity as organizational resource, is that groups with strong informal networks will do better in transmitting skills to newcomers. However, it is also true that these informal networks are important because of the conditions in small business industries; hence, for all groups, positional factors will be an important influence on self-employment rates.

Occupational training is not the only skill affecting immigrants' chances. Social and cultural differences also affect the job opportunities available, especially language skills. College-educated Koreans, for example, often confront a language barrier in the United States that hampers their chances of employment, especially in jobs requiring higher education and contact with the public (Min 1984).

Circumstances of Migration

Whether newcomers arrive as temporary migrants or as permanent settlers, migration scholars increasingly agree, is a crucial condition of mobility and integration into the host society. Piore (1979) argued that most labor migrations to industrial societies begin as movements of temporary workers. Because workers see themselves as temporary migrants, they constitute a satisfactory work force for dead-end jobs that native workers reject: As long as the migrants maintain the expectation of return to the home country, their concern is with the accumulation of capital to be brought home and invested in a business or farm, not with the attainment of social mobility in the societies to which they have migrated. Even though Piore focused mostly on access to structured job ladders of large organizations, rather than the attainment of business ownership, his argument suggests a framework for evaluating how the circumstances of migration will affect entrepreneurial success.

Whether conditions are perceived as opportunities or obstacles to mobility depends upon the eye of the beholder. The same factors that condition temporary migrants for work in low-level, dead-end jobs will also dampen the frustration that spurs other immigrants to start up in business on their own. As long as migrants anticipate returning home, as long as their stint in the host society is punctuated by periodic trips home, as long as they evaluate success in terms of their original standard of living, they will continue to furnish a supply of low-level labor. But those same low-level jobs will be unacceptable to permanent settlers whose ambitions extend to the positions occupied by natives as well as to the rewards generated by those positions. Consequently, blocked mobility will impinge more severely on settlers than on their counterparts among the birds of passage.

Permanence is also likely to add an edge to the settler's quest for opportunity: If one does not succeed, there is no going back. It is for these reasons that permanent immigrants have a reputation for being more self-assertive than temporary migrant groups. Thus the circumstances of migration breed an affinity with the requirements of entrepreneurial success: Only the driven immigrant will be foolish or desperate enough to start up a business when anyone can observe how many new concerns fall victim to a quick but painful death.

In addition to influencing aspirations, the circumstances of migration are also likely to affect immigrants' behavior in a way that will condition the likelihood of setting up on their own. One characteristic of temporary migrants is that their settlement and work patterns are too haphazard and variable to promote the acquisition of needed business skills and are also disruptive of the informal networks that play such an important role in organizing the immigrant firm and its labor force. By contrast, we can expect permanent immigrants to be more deliberate in their quest for economic progress. For example, P. Young (1983) described the foresight and planning with which Korean greengrocers in New York pursue their trade — they may spend months scouring the city for the best possible location, and often deliberately open stores next to supermarkets so as to capture part of the latter's walk-in trade.

The alternative to this argument is the possibility that immigrants who move as sojourners — with a clear intention of returning home — will opt for business over employment as the better way of rapidly accumulating portable investment capital (Bonacich 1973). There are two major problems with this hypothesis. One is that setting up a business is a more risky endeavor than working for someone else. If we assume that even the most entrepreneurial of sojourning immigrants begin as employees, it is likely that they will accumulate a nest egg that can be either safely banked for returning home or invested in a small business whose chance for success is always open to doubt. Faced with these options, the prudent sojourner is likely to keep on working for someone else, as Ward (1984) has shown in a study of East Asian immigrants in Britain.

Though Bonacich (1973) has argued that these East Asian immigrants illustrate the influence of sojourning on ethnic business activity, Ward's study shows that they are in fact more likely to prefer employment over business in areas where high wages are paid to those prepared to undertake hard and unpleasant work, resorting to business only in those cities where the available jobs are relatively poorly paid. Moreover, Aldrich (1977) found that a sojourning orientation made no difference in the business practices of Asians in London, as owners who intended to return to their native lands used the same competitive business practices as those who had no intention of returning. Aldrich, Cater, Jones, and McEvoy (1983) replicated this finding on another sample of Asian business owners in three English cities.

Another condition of immigrant business activity is settlement pattern. Permanent immigrants usually either come with family or import immediate relatives shortly after settling; temporary immigrants leave family members at home. The consequence for temporary immigrants is that they must continue to funnel remittances that are needed to support relatives still living in the home country rather than use those monies to start up a business. Kessner (1977: 167) pointed out in his comparison of Italian and Jewish immigrants at the turn of the century that "the large sums of money sent back over the ocean to Europe drained [the Italians of] risk capital [for] investment and enterprise." Also, if family members do not migrate with the sojourner, then they will not be available as a source of cheap labor for a small business.

Postmigration Characteristics

Another factor that will exercise a strong effect on self-employment outcomes is a group's position in the economy. This factor follows from the argument made about opportunity structures, namely, that certain environments are more supportive of small businesses than others. The likelihood that immigrants will take advantage of supportive conditions is greatest if immigrants are already concentrated in those industries where small business is the prevailing form.

First, the motivation to go into business presupposes other conditions; for example, having some information about business opportunities that in turn can be used to assess the likelihood that one's efforts will be rewarded. Second, neophyte capitalists will do better if they have some knowledge of the activities that the new role of ownership will entail. Such knowledge is usually better if it is obtained firsthand rather than through indirect methods. One characteristic of environments supportive of small business is precisely that the know-how needed to run a business can be acquired through on-the-job training. Thus immigrant groups concentrated in small business industries will have access to more and better information about small business opportunities and will also have more opportunities to acquire the relevant skills than those groups concentrated in industries where small businesses are not prevalent.

Emphasizing position, however, begs the question of why groups occupy one position and not another. To some extent, this is a matter of prior skill; to some extent, purely random factors come into play, such as arriving at a time or place where small business industries generate a demand for immigrant labor. One important influence is the degree of native-language facility, and looking at the effects of language provides a good illustration of how pre- and postmigration experiences interact to affect self-employment outcomes. Immigrants who arrive in the United States with English-language facility have a broader range of employment opportunities than do those newcomers whose English is virtually nonexistent or barely serviceable. Having a broader range of opportunities, immigrants facile in English are more likely to find employment in industries where the organizational form tends to be large.

Even within a small business industry, some occupations are more strategic than others in terms of providing an employee with exposure to the skills and contacts needed to start up a small business. In the garment industry, for example, the typical new manufacturing business is set up when a salesman and a textile cutter get together: The salesman has the necessary knowledge of the market, and the cutter knows the production side. In restaurants, waiting tables is the logical occupational bridge to becoming a restaurateur: The waiter learns how to size up the customer, direct him or her to the appropriate choice, and then hustle the customer off when a new patron is ready to take the table. In retailing, selling is also the point of departure for many employees who decide to start up on their own.

For prospective immigrant capitalists, the question is how to gain access to these strategic occupations. This problem is particularly serious because many of these occupations involve face-to-face interaction, in which case natives' desire to maximize social distance from immigrants will obstruct the latter's recruitment into these key positions. What is at work is an instance of the principle of cumulative social advantage: Immigrants belonging to a group whose characteristics favor business success will also be more likely to be hired by coethnics and thereby gain access to needed business skills. By contrast, those immigrants whose characteristics are less conducive to entrepreneurship will be more likely to work for natives, which in turn will reduce the likelihood of their gaining access to strategic occupations.

ETHNIC STRATEGIES

Ethnic strategies emerge from the adaptations ethnic entrepreneurs make to the resources available to them, building on the characteristics of their groups. As we explore at length in Chapter 5, ethnic business owners commonly confront seven problems in founding and operating their businesses: (1) acquiring the *information* needed for the establishment and survival of their firms; (2) obtaining the *capital* needed to establish or to expand their business; (3) acquiring the *training and skills* needed to run a small business; (4) recruiting and managing efficient, honest, and cheap *workers*; (5) managing relations with *customers* and *suppliers*; (6) surviving strenuous business *competition*; and (7) protecting themselves from *political attacks*.

Information is typically obtained through owners' personal networks and via various indirect ties that are specifically linked to their ethnic communities. The structures of such networks differ, depending upon the characteristics of the group. Some groups have very hierarchically organized families and a clear sense of family loyalty and obligation, whereas others have more diffusely organized families. Ritualized occasions and large-scale ceremonies also provide opportunities for acquiring information, and some groups have specialized associations and media that disseminate information.

Most entrepreneurs, immigrant or not, raise the bulk of their capital from personal savings. After this primary source, some arrange loans within their communities through institutions such as rotating credit associations. Norms about borrowing from family and friends differ widely across groups, as we show in Chapter 5.

Training and skills are typically acquired on the job, often while the potential owner is an employee in a coethnic or family member's business. Ties within the ethnic economy widen workers' contacts, increasing the probability of their moving up through a variety of jobs and firms in which skills are acquired.

Family and coethnic labor is critical to most ethnic small businesses. Such labor is largely unpaid, and kin and coethnics work long hours in the service of their employers. Ethnic entrepreneurs manipulate family perseverance and loyalty to their own advantage, but they also incur obligations in doing so.

Customers and clients play a central role in owners' strategies, as building a loyal following is a way of offsetting the high level of uncertainty facing ethnic small businesses. Some owners provide special services, extend credit, and go out of their way to deliver individual services to customers. Often, however, providing special services to coethnics causes trouble for owners, who then are faced with special pleading to take lower profits for their efforts.

The intense competition generated in the niches occupied by ethnic businesses is dealt with in at least four ways: through (1) self-exploitation, (2) expanding the business by moving forward or backward in the chain of production or by opening other shops, (3) founding and supporting ethnic trading associations, and (4) cementing alliances to other families through marriage. We discuss these more extensively in Chapter 5.

Finally, ethnic entrepreneurs often need protection from government officials as well as from rival owners outside their ethnic communities. Government is dealt with in much the same way that businesses always have: bribery, paying penalties, searching for loopholes, and organizing protests.

Ethnic strategies, then, reflect both the opportunity structure within which ethnic businesses operate *and* the particular characteristics of the owner's group. Accordingly, we have placed ethnic strategies at the center of Figure 1.1, emphasizing their emergent character. As we discuss in Chapter 5, the strategies adopted by the various groups we have studied are remarkably similar.

CONCLUSIONS

This chapter has developed an explanation for immigrant enterprise that emphasizes the interaction between the opportunity structure of the host society and the group characteristics and social structure of the immigrant community. The demand for small business activities emanates from markets whose small size, heterogeneity, or susceptibility to flux and instability limit the potential for mass distribution and mass production. Because such conditions favor small-scale enterprise, they lower the entry barriers to immigrants with limited capital and technical resources. Opportunities for ownership result from the process of ethnic succession: Vacancies for new business owners arise as the older groups that have previously dominated small business activities move into higher social positions.

As for group characteristics, two factors promote recruitment into entrepreneurial positions. First, the situational constraints that immigrants confront sometimes breed a predisposition toward small business and further encourage immigrants to engage in activities — such as working long hours — that are needed to gain minimal efficiencies. Some ethnic groups have cultural norms that create a set of understandings about appropriate behavior and expectations within work settings. Second, resource mobilization is facilitated if immigrant firms can resolve problems by drawing on their connections with a supply of family and ethnic labor. While these factors lift the self-employment rate of the overall immigrant population, levels of business activity vary among specific immigrant groups. A group's success in attaining business ownership is determined by three characteristics — its premigration experiences, the circumstances of its migration and settlement, and its postmigration experiences — and how these characteristics interact with one another and with the local opportunity structure.

2

Trends in Ethnic Business in the United States

Roger Waldinger
Howard Aldrich

The history of ethnic business in the United States over the past century reveals the complex interplay between the two dimensions we identified in Chapter 1 — opportunity structures and group characteristics. As the U.S. economy evolved from an industrial to a postindustrial base, opportunity structures changed and immigrant groups at different times have found themselves facing very different market conditions. Markets in some business sectors have opened, while others have closed. In almost all markets, small businesses, once thought headed for inexorable decline, have shown remarkable resiliency and continue to attract immigrants. Many opportunities have been opened to ethnic minorities because groups previously dominating a market have left to seek their fortunes elsewhere. A succession of immigrant groups, differing in what we have called predisposing factors and in their capacity for resource mobilization, have cycled through the opportunity structures of U.S. cities and towns.

In this chapter, we turn our attention to the contemporary scene in the United States. We review recent trends in self-employment, and present national statistics on rates of business ownership among various ethnic groups. We use case histories of three groups — Afro-Americans, Asians, and Hispanics — to illustrate the intricate relations among market conditions, access to ownership, predisposing group characteristics, and a group's capacity for resource mobilization. Our accounts show that any explanation of ethnic business participation must, of necessity, emphasize the historically contingent nature of the process.

THE STATE OF SMALL BUSINESS

We begin with the opportunity structure of the United States today. As in other advanced societies, the 1970s marked a shift in the United States to a postindustrial economy. With the explosion of service employment, as well as sharp declines in manufacturing and changes in manufacturing markets, the environment for small firms changed drastically. Services have always been a sector in which small firms are prevalent, and thus the growth of services produced an increase in the small firms' share of employment. The postindustrial transformation provided additional impetus to the proliferation of small concerns: The most rapidly growing service industries, such as business services and health, were precisely those dominated by small firms (U.S. Department of Commerce 1987). Manufacturing took place within an increasingly competitive environment in which markets for standardized products were conquered by foreign producers. American manufacturers adapted by striving for flexibility, with a consequent lowering of economies of scale and therewith a decline in average plant size (Granovetter 1984; Piore and Sabel 1984).

In this context, small business, despite predictions of inexorable decline, became the engine of employment growth. Birch (1981) showed that small firms accounted for the bulk of new jobs created between 1968 and 1976; though his claim has given rise to considerable debate (Armington and Odle 1982), the evidence supporting the continuing contribution of small firms to economic growth seems compelling (Birch 1987). With dynamism centered in the small firm sector, the long-term decline in nonagricultural self-employment turned around, rising from 6.9% in 1972 to 7.8% in 1983, as shown in Table 2.1. Although nonwhites have shared somewhat in the increase, the gains were greatest for whites.

The disproportionate gain for the self-employed was fairly small and short-lived, however. Data show that the curve has once again turned around, as the proportion self-employed dropped back to 7.4% in 1986. The disproportionate change in the percentage of workers self-employed took place in the context of extraordinary job growth for the U.S. economy: While the percentage of Americans working for them-

Table 2.1 Self-Employment Rates, United States, 1972-1986 (self-employed as percentage of total employed)

Year %	Whites %	Nonwhites %	Total Population %
1986	7.9	4.1	7.4
1985	8.0	4.2	7.5
1984	8.2	4.3	7.7
1983	8.3	4.3	7.8
1982	8.0	4.2	7.6
1981	7.8	4.2	7.3
1980	7.6	3.9	7.1
1979	7.6	3.9	7.1
1978	6.8	4.0	6.8
1977	6.9	3.9	6.9
1972	6.9	3.9	6.9

SOURCE: 1972-1982: U.S. Bureau of Labor Statistics, labor force statistics derived from the Current Population Survey, Bulletin 2900; 1983-1986: U.S. Bureau of Labor Statistics, unpublished data.

selves may be declining again (and then only slightly), the fact remains that the number of self-employed increased by over 2.1 million between 1975 and 1986. Gains of such magnitude are difficult to reconcile with traditional expectations of small business decline, and they suggest that ethnic entrepreneurs may still find considerable opportunities in the small business sector.

THE STATE OF ETHNIC BUSINESS

The foreign-born have always been heavily overrepresented in self-employment. In turn-of-the-century New York, for example, the foreign-born were overrepresented not only in the petty trades of peddling and huckstering but also among "manufacturers and officials," "merchants and dealers," and other proprietary occupations. Small enterprise played an important role in the economic progress of a variety of immigrant groups — Jews, Italians, Greeks, and others — and their proportionally higher involvement in entrepreneurial activities continues to differentiate these groups from much of the population.

The renewal of mass immigration to the United States since 1965 has brought an infusion of new immigrant owners to the ranks of petty proprietors. Miami, New York City, Los Angeles, and many other centers of the new immigration contain flourishing enclaves of ethnic economic activity. As in the past, newcomers to the United States are overrepresented among the self-employed. In 1980, 9.2% of the foreign-born population in the nation's largest cities was self-employed, as opposed to 7.1% for the native-born (Light and Sanchez 1987). For many immigrants, small business appears to be an important part of the settlement process. Only the most recent groups of newcomers are self-employed at a rate below that of the native-born; after ten years in the United States, self-employed rates for the foreign-born exceed those for the native-born and continue to climb with length of stay.

The generally high level of self-employment masks a great deal of variation among ethnic groups. At the turn of the century, for example, the high rates of business activity among Russian Jews contrasted with much lower levels of entrepreneurship among French Canadians or among Poles. Today, similar disparities appear when we compare Koreans or Cubans — among whom business development has been rapid — with Mexicans or Haitians. Moreover, self-employment rates have been persistently low among Afro-Americans — a matter that has provoked considerable scholarly debate.

Limitations on Available Data

Though there is a wealth of data about ethnic businesses in the United States, using those data is complicated because the sociological definition of "ethnic business" — a business whose proprietor(s) has a distinctive group attachment by virtue of self-definition or ascription by others — and the official definition do not converge. The sociological definition covers persons of a multitude of possible national origins, whereas the official definition focuses on blacks and Hispanics. The federal government has specified a subset of ethnic groups to be designated as "minorities," and supportive policies and data collection efforts are directed toward this subset. What lies behind this focus on "minorities" rather than "ethnics" is the belief that the experience of Afro-Americans is qualitatively distinct from that of the country's other ethnic groups. Whether the same qualitative difference applies to the other ethnic groups classified as minorities — Cubans, Koreans, Asian Indians, Filipinos, and Japanese — is a matter of controversy among social scientists.

Official classifications have consequences for our ability to describe and analyze the state of ethnic business. As part of its economic censuses, the federal government conducts a census of minority-owned businesses every five years. The *Survey of Minority and Women-Owned Businesses* compiles valuable information about the operating characteristics of firms, but it contains relatively little information about the characteristics of individual minority entrepreneurs and nothing about "nonminority" ethnic groups. For such data, one must turn to population surveys conducted by the U.S. Bureau of the Census: the *Current Population Survey* (*CPS*), a monthly survey of 66,000 households; and the decennial *Census of Population.*

The sample size of the *CPS*, the basic source for tracking intercensal changes, is nonetheless too small to provide the finer disaggregations of interest to the analyst of ethnicity. Consequently, the most basic data source is the decennial *Census of Population*, from which considerable information about the attributes of self-employed individuals—including race, ethnicity, and nativity—can be extracted. However, the law forbids the census to ask questions about religion, and thus there are no official statistics about religioethnic groups—most important here, the Jews—that are significant to the understanding of ethnic business. Fortunately, community and academic surveys provide a viable alternative data source (Cohen 1983; Ritterband and Cohen 1984).

The disparity in coverage and definition among the various data sources makes a consistent and comprehensive description of ethnic business in the United States difficult. Nonetheless, one salient characteristic does emerge from virtually all of the data sources, namely, the extraordinary level of variation in business participation among U.S. ethnic groups.

Statistics on Self-Employment

Using the 1980 *Census of Population,* Fratoe (1986) cross-tabulated data on self-employment and income from self-employment with responses people gave to a self-identified ancestry category. He calculated a business participation rate for each ancestry group, shown in Table 2.2, by dividing the number of self-employed persons in the group by the total size of the group, and multiplying by 1,000. The national average was 48.9 self-employed persons per 1,000 members in an ancestry group.

Fratoe's calculation of business participation rates reveals several basic patterns. First, historic middleman minorities (Jews—who tend to report themselves as of Russian ancestry—Lebanese, Armenians, and

Table 2.2 Business Participation Rates of the 50 Largest U.S. Ancestry Groups, 1980 (ranked highest to lowest)

Ancestry Group	Business Participation Rate	Ancestry Group	Business Participation Rate
1. Russian	117.4	27. English	59.6
2. Lebanese	106.6	28. Finnish	53.3
3. Rumanian	104.3	29. French	51.9
4. Swiss	104.2	30. Polish	51.6
5. Greek	94.9	31. Yugoslav	50.2
6. Armenian	94.5	32. Irish	49.7
7. Danish	93.2	33. Canadian	49.2
8. Syrian	92.7		
9. Norwegian	88.2	National Average	48.9
10. Austrian	85.7		
11. Czech	76.9	34. Cuban	47.9
12. Swedish	76.2	35. Asian Indian	47.1
13. Belgian	74.7	36. French Canadian	45.6
14. Latvian	74.4	37. Portuguese	42.9
15. Welsh	72.4	38. Slovak	35.3
16. Dutch	72.2	39. American Indian	33.3
17. Scottish	69.7	40. Colombian	30.1
18. Korean	69.2	41. Ecuadorian	22.7
19. Hungarian	68.3	42. Filipino	22.4
20. Lithuanian	68.1	43. Jamaican	21.5
21. German	68.1	44. Hawaiian	20.3
22. Iranian	66.4	45. Mexican	18.6
23. Japanese	64.8	46. Vietnamese	16.5
24. Chinese	60.2	47. Haitian	15.5
25. Italian	59.9	48. Dominican	14.6
26. Ukrainian	59.7	49. Subsaharan African	13.6
		50. Puerto Rican	10.6

SOURCE: Adapted from Fratoe (1986): tabulations from the 1980 Census of Population and Housing, Public-Use Microdata Samples, Sample "A."
NOTE: "Business Participation Rate" = number of self-employed multiplied by 1,000 divided by total persons in group.

Greeks) are heavily overrepresented in self-employment, at double or more the national average rate. Second, Asian immigrants (Japanese, Chinese) have above- or near-average participation rates. Third, blacks (who are categorized as of "Subsaharan African" ancestry) and Mexicans and other Hispanic groups continue to have considerably below-average participation rates.

The incomes that the various ancestry groups earned from their activity in self-employment also ranged widely around the national

Table 2.3 Mean Income of Self-Employed Persons in the 50 Largest U.S. Ancestry Groups, 1980 (ranked highest to lowest)

Ancestry Group	Mean Income	Ancestry Group	Mean Income
1. Iranian	$31,370	National Average	18,630
2. Russian	30,270		
3. Asian Indian	29,800	27. Portuguese	18,570
4. Filipino	27,800	28. Korean	18,503
5. Rumanian	26,530	29. Dutch	18,470
6. Austrian	26,210	30. English	18,370
7. Lithuanian	25,900	31. Canadian	18,350
8. Lebanese	24,180	32. Irish	18,290
9. Lebanese	24,180	33. Colombian	18,170
10. Syrian	23,630	34. German	18,090
11. Hungarian	23,390	35. Czech	17,510
12. Ukrainian	22,170	36. French	17,320
13. Armenian	21,430	37. Cuban	17,510
14. Greek	21,140	38. Norwegian	16,760
15. Yugoslav	21,000	39. French Canadian	16,730
16. Polish	20,950	40. Slovak	16,400
17. Belgian	20,820	41. Jamaican	15,320
18. Scottish	20,520	42. Hawaiian	14,700
19. Welsh	20,450	43. Finnish	14,420
20. Italian	20,170	44. Ecuadorian	14,160
21. Japanese	19,680	45. Dominican	13,870
22. Haitian	19,100	46. Mexican	13,850
23. Chinese	18,980	47. American Indian	13,110
24. Danish	18,920	48. Vietnamese	11,500
25. Swiss	18,830	49. Puerto Rican	11,490
26. Swedish	18,660	50. Subsaharan African	11,260

SOURCE: Adapted from Fratoe (1986): tabulations from the 1980 Census of Population and Housing, Public-Use Microdata Samples, Sample "A."
NOTE: Income reported was for 1979, by persons who designated themselves as self-employed or employees of their own corporation; mean income was rounded off to the nearest $10.

average of $18,630. As one might expect, a group's business participation rate is strongly related to its average income. Visual inspection of the income rankings shown in Table 2.3 is consistent with what statistical analysis confirms: The higher the level of participation in business, the higher the income from self-employment (the rank order correlation between the two rankings was Spearman's rho = .61, significant at the .01 probability level). The income data also suggest that for those groups whose participation in business is considerably below average — including Mexicans and blacks — businesses tend to be marginal.

When one narrows the scope of interest to those groups officially categorized as "minorities," several patterns appear. In Table 2.4, mi-

Table 2.4 Characteristics of Minority-Owned Businesses

	Business Ownership as % of Group Size	Number of Firms (thousands)	Sales per Firm (dollars)	Firms with Employees (thousands)	Percentage of Firms with Employees	Employees per Firm
Total population	6.4	14,545.7	473.5	N.A.	N.A.	N.A.
Asians	5.5	255.6	70.1	49.3	19.3	4.7
Koreans	9.0	31.8	84.2	7.9	24.8	3.1
Asian Indians	7.1	25.5	65.0	6.3	24.7	3.2
Japanese	7.0	49.0	55.6	6.8	13.9	4.7
Chinese	6.6	52.8	115.0	14.1	27.7	6.5
Filipinos	3.4	26.4	28.2	3.0	11.4	2.7
Vietnamese	2.0	5.2	41.1	2.3	44.2	2.0
Hispanics	1.7	248.1	60.4	39.9	16.1	4.8
Cubans	4.6	36.6	58.7	5.2	14.2	4.3
Mexicans	1.6	143.2	50.1	24.1	16.8	4.4
Puerto Ricans	0.7	14.7	45.8	1.7	11.6	3.3
Blacks	1.3	339.2	36.7	38.6	11.4	4.3

SOURCE: *The State of Small Business* (1987); U.S. Department of Commerce, Bureau of the Census (1980, 1985a, 1985b, 1986).

norities are ranked by the proportion of persons in a group owning businesses; also shown are the total number of business firms, sales per firm, the number of firms with employees, and the average number of employees per firm. The first row of Table 2.4 reports figures for the entire U.S. population as a baseline against which to evaluate the figures for minorities.

As Table 2.4 shows, business participation tends to be highest among Asians and much lower among various Hispanic groups—with the notable exception of Cubans—and among blacks. On average, minority businesses tend to be small; indeed, they are much smaller than non-ethnic businesses. Sales per firm in all minority groups were considerably lower than average sales for all U.S. businesses. A much smaller proportion of minority firms had paid employees, and even those with employees tended to have considerably fewer workers per firm.

Of course, smallness can be seen as an attribute of the business development process in a community and of the life cycle of individual businesses. The most fertile fields of new business births are those where the barriers to entry, and hence size requirements, are low. Many businesses begin as part-time ventures related to a person's paid em-

Table 2.5 Industry Distribution of Minority-Owned and All Businesses, 1982
(percentage)

Industry	Total Population %	All Minorities %	Asians %	Blacks %	Hispanics %
Agriculture	3.6	2.8	4.5	1.4	2.9
Mining	1.6	0.2	0.2	0.1	0.1
Construction	10.7	7.4	4.8	6.8	10.8
Manufacturing	3.7	1.5	1.7	1.2	1.7
Transportation	4.0	5.3	2.9	7.2	5.3
Wholesale trade	4.1	1.4	1.7	1.1	1.5
Retail trade	19.6	25.5	28.5	24.8	23.5
Finance	14.5	4.9	6.0	4.4	4.5
Services	36.9	41.6	41.2	43.4	39.6
Total	100.0	100.0	100.0	100.0	100.0

SOURCE: See Table 2.4.

ployment, a phase during which there may be virtually no income at all.
Nonetheless, the lowest average sales and the smallest proportion of
firms with paid employees were again found among those minorities
with the lowest rate of participation in business.

In addition to being small, minority businesses differ from other
businesses in their distribution across industries. As Table 2.5 shows,
minority businesses are greatly overrepresented in the retail and services sectors and underrepresented in manufacturing and the finance-
insurance-real estate sector. Their concentration in retail and service
businesses reflects not only the small size of such establishments but
also the initial concentration of opportunities. Opportunities arise in
these industries because minority population growth provides the consumer base to which ethnic entrepreneurs sell. From this initial ethnic
consumer market, some groups have quickly moved on to serve nonethnic markets, whereas others have remained tied to their original
markets.

Data on industrial distributions also suggest that the restructuring of
the American economy has been of limited importance for the overall
opportunities facing minority business owners. Retailing is actually the
one small business industry where larger businesses have grown most
rapidly (U.S. Department of Commerce 1987). Even though minority
businesses are also overrepresented in the service sector, they tend to

be underrepresented in those particular service industries that hav
grown fastest in the past decade and that are most characterized by ver
small establishments.

CASE HISTORIES OF THREE GROUPS

We turn now to a review of the historical origins and current positio
of three ethnic minorities in the United States: Afro-Americans, Asian
and Hispanics.

Afro-Americans

The majority of America's black population consists of the descer
dants of slaves imported from Africa between the early seventeenth an
early nineteenth centuries, augmented by immigrants from the Wes
Indies and a growing trickle of newcomers from Africa. The history c
business in the Afro-American population dates back to the half centur
before the abolition of slavery, when a small base of businesses owne
by freedmen existed in southern and northern cities. Ironically, oppor
tunities for black enterprise were better in the South than in the North
Labor in southern urban centers was in short supply because white
disdained the manual jobs associated with blacks, and the supply o
urban slaves was inadequate to meet the demands of the South's late
growing industrial sector. Consequently, well over half of the fre
blacks in cities such as New Orleans or Charleston were employed i
skilled or artisanal jobs, often in trades such as barbering that involve
a skill originally learned on plantations.

Many black skilled craftsmen worked on their own, but historian
have also documented the growth of an entrepreneurial sector. Increas
ing black populations gave rise to black proprietors, who set up restau
rants, boardinghouses, and grocery and grog shops despite harassmen
and restrictions from white authorities (Berlin 1974). In northern cities
free blacks maintained themselves at the margins of the economy, a
legal prohibitions and societal restraints barred access to ownership i
more skilled lines of work. Just over 5% of the free blacks living in New
York in 1850, for example, were engaged in artisanal trades (Curry
1981: 260). In 1838, 80% of free black Philadelphians were laborer
and, of the 4% engaged in entrepreneurial occupations, almost al
were proprietors who sold food or secondhand clothing from pushcarts

(Hershberg 1981: 382). By contrast, artisans constituted more than two-thirds of the New Orleans free black population by the middle of the nineteenth century, and the businesses that black entrepreneurs in New Orleans maintained were far more substantial than those owned by their counterparts in northern cities (Curry 1981). One conservative estimate put the total value of property and businesses owned by blacks in New Orleans at over $9 million (Marable 1983).

Black businesses grew slowly after the abolition of slavery, initially developing along the patterns established prior to 1863, but eventually traditional specializations were broken under the combined impact of industrialization, immigration, and the changing climate of race relations. Early on, business was mainly the province of a small, often mulatto, elite who depended on connections to a white clientele. Such enterprises were concentrated in such lines as catering, tailoring, and barbering; in the last, blacks often constituted the majority of the trade. By the late 1800s, however, growing racism, status anxiety, and self-segregation among white elites broke the paternalistic ties that once linked them to black businesses. Increased desire among whites for both physical and social distance from blacks, combined with greater competition from immigrants, pushed blacks out of their traditional trades and back into serving mostly black customers. In Cleveland, for example, the proportion of blacks who were barbers slipped from 43% in 1870, to 18% in 1890, to less than 10% in 1900; the same trends were more severe in cities like New York, Philadelphia, and Boston (Kusmer 1976: 82). In the South, Reconstruction, "black codes," and the *Plessy v. Ferguson* decision of 1896 spelled the end of legal civil rights for blacks (Butler and Wilson 1988). In the North, increased immigration from Europe and subsequent increased competition for jobs also limited the opportunities open to blacks (Lieberson 1980).

While black business ties to whites attenuated, black populations grew in size and became more segregated, thus changing the market conditions for black enterprises. These twin developments gave rise to what DuBois (1907: 179) called the *group economy*: "a cooperative arrangement of industries and services within the Negro group such that the group tends to be a closed economic circle largely independent of the surrounding white world." Insurance agents, undertakers, real estate dealers, newspaper editors, and bankers — all of whom served a black clientele — were the leading entrepreneurs in the burgeoning black ghettos of Chicago, Cleveland, New York, and other major metropolises. Behind them stood a plethora of small shop owners selling necessities for the general market and items preferred especially by black cus tomers. For an account of black business development in the cities c Tulsa, Chicago, and Durham (North Carolina) during the early decade of the twentieth century, see Butler and Wilson (1988).

Despite the existence of distinctive consumer preferences, as well a a growing number of customers confined to the ghetto marketplace an a small network of black financial institutions (Butler and Wilso 1988), the potential of DuBois's group economy was barely realized By 1939, the proportion of blacks among the nation's retail dealers wa no greater than it had been in 1910. Myrdal (1944) estimated that blac merchants received only 5% to 10% of black trade. In their 1938 stud of Chicago's black ghetto, Drake and Cayton (1962) found that th numbers of black- and white-owned businesses were equal, but that th white businesses had ten times the sales of the black-owned stores. Mos black businesses were small and concentrated in personal service line like undertaking or hair care, where discrimination and whites' desir for social distance created a "closed market." A national survey of blac enterprises conducted in 1946 revealed a similar pattern: 15% of th businesses were service oriented, 85% were owned by one person, anc 81% were operated in ghetto neighborhoods (Pierce 1947).

Studies conducted in the 1960s, during the height of the civil rights movement, showed that not much had changed. A 1964 study of busi nesses in North Philadelphia discovered that one-third of the black businesses were engaged in hairdressing and barbering (Tabb 1971: 55). A survey of businesses in New York's Harlem area in the mid-1960s found that whites owned 37% of the businesses but employed 61% ol the workers in the area (Vietorisz and Harrison 1970). Disparities were even greater in the ghetto areas of Chicago, Boston, and Washington, where whites owned 55% of the businesses but employed 88% of the persons working in local businesses (Aldrich 1973). The basic pattern was for blacks to be concentrated in small retail and service businesses and for whites to own most of the construction, manufacturing, trans portation, and wholesale businesses and also to operate *all* businesses, including retail and service businesses, on a larger scale than blacks (Aldrich 1973: 1409).

In the 1960s, with the outbreak of unrest in the nation's black ghettos, economic development in black communities became a critical policy concern. The federal government became more concerned with black access to business ownership and with assisting blacks in mobilizing resources for business start-ups. Lending programs for black entrepreneurs began in 1965; assistance was further amplified in 1969 when President Richard Nixon announced his plan to foster "black capitalism." Government incentives available to black businesses were varied, and included loans and loan guarantees, provision of venture capital and technical assistance, and procurements of services that were "set aside" for minority entrepreneurs (Harrison 1974; Fusfeld and Bates 1984). Many of the incentive programs begun in the 1960s continue today, and these programs are reviewed at greater length in Chapter 7.

However, the face of black business has barely altered over the past two decades. In 1982, the average black-owned firm was a sole proprietorship, in the services industry, located in an urban area, with gross receipts of about $15,000 (U.S. Department of Commerce 1986). Between 1969 and 1982, the fastest-growing sector of black-owned business was services, accounting for 34.4% of businesses in 1969 and increasing to 43.4% in 1982. The relative proportion of manufacturing firms dropped over the same period, falling from 3.8% in 1972 to 1.2% in 1982. Only 6,106 black-owned businesses were incorporated, and only 11.4% had paid employees. Perhaps even more significant, rates of return to self-employment are substantially lower for blacks than for whites, when other differences are statistically controlled (Sullivan and McCracken 1988). In 1980, self-employment added nearly $2,200 to the earnings of black males, but over $4,500 to the earnings of white males. Returns to self-employment were insignificant for black women, and white women actually earned less if they were self-employed.

One important development has been the growth of a small sector of "big" black-owned businesses. *Black Enterprise,* a business-oriented magazine, first identified the "Top 100 Black Businesses" in 1973 and has been tracking the progress of this leading group ever since. These black businesses of the top rank achieved impressive growth, with sales up from $473 million in 1972 to $1.9 billion in 1982, producing an increase of 81% in constant dollars during a time when constant dollars GNP increased by only 24% (*Black Enterprise* 1982).

Notwithstanding these gains, the top black businesses remain a class of relatively small businesses, with limited employment potential — there were only 136 black-owned firms with 100 employees or more in 1982 (U.S. Department of Commerce 1986). Not one of the 1983 top black businesses came close to making the list of the *Fortune* 500 largest companies (Landry 1987). By 1986, the last company on the *Fortune* 500 list grossed two and a half times as much as the very largest black business; and the last five companies on the *Fortune* list together employed more than all the 100 top black businesses combined. More-over, a large proportion of the leading black businesses were still engaged in providing services to the black community. Only 12 manu-facturing firms were on the 1982 list — down from 27 among 1972's top 100 — and 5 of the 12 produced cosmetics and hair products for women. The single largest category of businesses was automobile dealerships, which suggests that these big businesses constitute a sort of "dependent sector," subordinate to larger white firms. The great majority of black businesses remain small, and the traditional pattern remains in place, as Table 2.4 shows, with black businesses considerably smaller in sales and employment than other minority concerns. Hair care contains by far the largest single number of black-owned businesses.

Explanations for Black Business Development

Accounting for the underdevelopment of black business has been a persistent scholarly concern. This chapter cannot review the entirety of this discussion, but the outlines of the main argument can be sketched, using the dimensions identified in Chapter 1. They include (1) the absence of strong predisposing factors, such as a business tradition; (2) the lack of a large protected market; (3) the fragmented social structure of black communities, which inhibits resource mobilization; and (4) intense prejudice and discriminatory behavior by the majority community against blacks, which limits access to ownership as well as necessary resources, such as capital and credit.

Perhaps the most common explanation is that of E. Franklin Frazier (1949), who contended that, because of slavery and severe discrimina-tion after emancipation, which confined blacks to the most menial jobs, blacks gained little experience in "trading and selling." However, Frazier's argument is not entirely convincing, because many European immigrants were former peasants without entrepreneurial backgrounds, and the extreme residential segregation of blacks should have provided a captive market, such as that enjoyed by South Asians in British cities (Aldrich, Cater, et al. 1985).

One differentiating factor between blacks and white immigrants, Glazer and Moynihan (1963: 33) suggested, was that "the Negro, while a migrant, was not like the immigrants, bearing a foreign culture, with special needs that might give rise to a market." This argument is not compelling either, because there are distinctive needs — such as for hair and body care — life-style differences, preferences for particular foods, and other differences, which should have provided black businesses with some shelter from competing white organizations (Wilson 1975).

Light (1972) proposed still another possibility: that the sources of business underdevelopment can be traced back to the social structure of black communities. Whereas immigrant groups like the Chinese, Japanese, or Jews generated scarce resources by mobilizing ethnic solidarity through close social ties to other immigrants and by using rotating credit associations, black communities were too riven by individualism, competition, and status differences (between northerners and southerners, middle class and lower class) to overcome barriers to business entry. Indeed, Light's analysis is consistent with black business owners' oft-recorded complaint about the failure of black customers to provide them with support. As one observer noted, in a comment that recurs in virtually every historical case study of black businesses (see Drake and Cayton 1962: 439-443; Pierce 1947: 181-193), black customers would "walk three blocks or more to trade with a white man, when there is a Negro store next to their door. They say the Negro does not have as good material as the white man. In all cases that is not true" (quoted in Higgs 1976: 91).

A forceful economic critique, however, can be made of Light's culturalist argument: The extraordinary discrimination encountered by blacks not only deprived black business owners of capital and skills, but impoverished their customers, who were, therefore, driven to buy at the lowest prices from white concerns. Therefore, even if social solidarity had been strong, black customers would not have patronized black businesses. Poverty also weakened the informal sources of support so badly needed in the provision of business information, capital, and labor. The distinctive characteristics of black urban households preceding and during the years of mass migration northward—many female-headed households, unrelated boarders, small families—reduced the supply of cheap yet trustworthy family labor (Zunz 1982).

These various explanations are ultimately arguments about first causes, and adjudicating among them is quite difficult. We simply note that the sources of black business underdevelopment are multiple, and many factors must be considered. More important, the adaptation of blacks, both to the weakness of the business sector and to their overall economic situation, has set in motion a vicious circle that impedes further development of black businesses. Given the paucity of entrepreneurial opportunities on the one hand and pervasive discrimination in private employment on the other, blacks' search for advancement has led them into the public sector.

Government has proven more susceptible to black political mobilization than has private industry. As a result, it is in the public sector that barriers to entry and to promotion have fallen furthest. Landry (1987), for example, in his 1976 survey of almost 1,200 middle-class blacks and whites, found that about half of all black males, compared with only about one-fourth of whites, held government jobs. Furthermore, black males in private industry earned lower incomes than whites. White middle-class males in the private sector earned an average of $2,000 more than those in government, whereas black middle-class males in the private sector earned $2,000 less than those in government. Landry's data are consistent with tabulations from the 1980 *Census of Population*, which showed that blacks were greatly overrepresented in government employment — government accounted for 27.8% of total black employment, in contrast to 16.6% of all (white and nonwhite) employed U.S. workers.

Government employment is consequential because it establishes an ongoing, self-feeding alternative to business as a mechanism of social mobility: Information flows, networks of informal support, organizational power centers as well as role models become increasingly anchored in the public sector. Of course, some movement into upper-level positions in private industry has taken place as well, and the ranks of black managers increased by 83% between 1972 and 1982. The dynamic of advancement in private industry is not dissimilar to that in the public sector: Many of the gains have taken place in large firms that are sensitive to government pressures for affirmative action and broader societal demands for fairness. Moreover, the proportional increase in black private sector managerial employment is far greater than the increase in self-employment.

Finally, the growing differentiation in the social structure of black America has had a negative impact on business development (Wilson 1987). The emergence of a sizable black middle class since the 1960s has been accompanied by the growth of an "underclass" of chronically unemployed men and poor, female-headed households. As middle-class economic status has improved for some blacks, their social and physical distance from lower-class families has increased, weakening the ability of lower-class blacks to find role models and make the connections needed to get started in business. The growth of the underclass has had an even more damaging impact, by disconnecting young people from the labor market and weakening connections to other blacks with employment or business know-how and contacts (Wilson 1987).

Asians

Asian immigration to the United States began in the 1850s. Until recently, the level of immigration was quite low, and thus the Asian population has been relatively small for most of the twentieth century. For most of the past century, Chinese and Japanese constituted the majority of the Asian population in the continental United States. The Chinese, and later the Japanese, were drawn to the United States by labor demands in the extractive and agricultural industries on the burgeoning Pacific Coast. But competition with white workers, small farmers, and petty entrepreneurs, fueled by racist sentiments, led to measures that sharply narrowed the flow of immigrants from the Orient. The first Chinese Exclusion Act, subsequently renewed several times, was enacted in 1882. In 1907, the United States and Japan concluded a "gentleman's agreement" whereby Japan imposed voluntary quotas on prospective emigrants. The Japanese government agreed not to send Japanese laborers, whereas the U.S. government allowed Japanese laborers to bring in their family members. The 1924 Immigration and Naturalization Act, which set up quotas by country for immigrants from Europe, barred any further immigration from Asia, with the exception of Filipinos, who were annually admitted in substantial numbers as U.S. citizens until 1935.

Some Asian immigration nonetheless continued at a very reduced level, as Asians learned to evade various exclusionary provisions. They succeeded, through litigation, in overturning statutes that prohibited the immigration of wives and children of Chinese American and Japanese American citizens. America's involvements overseas during World War II and the subsequent cold war period made American politicians pay more attention to the sensitivities of its allies in Asia (Briggs 1984), leading to a relaxation of some of the more restrictive provisions.

Large-scale Asian immigration did not begin anew until 1965, when the Hart-Cellar Act abolished both the country-of-origin quotas and the exclusions against Asian immigrants. A new system of allocated immigration entries was established, based either on close family ties to U.S. citizens or residents or on possession of scarce skills. Asians initially moved to the United States through the skilled labor preferences — the immigrants of the late 1960s and early 1970s tended to be highly educated professionals. These first settlers quickly built up a population base that enabled their close relatives to move to the United States on the basis of family preferences. Finally, the collapse of U.S.-supported regimes in Indochina, and the upheavals that followed, unleashed a massive flow of refugees from Vietnam and Cambodia.

The new immigration not only has involved a rapid buildup of the Asian population — Asians were the single largest group of legal immigrants coming to the United States in the 1980s — but has also brought diversification in settlement patterns across national origin groups. Chinese immigration remains substantial, but Koreans, Filipinos, Indians, and Vietnamese are now represented in large and growing numbers. The earlier Asian immigrants concentrated on the Pacific Coast and often lived in densely populated, homogeneous Chinatowns or Japantowns, but the newcomers are much more widely dispersed. They often skip over the ethnic neighborhood stage and move right to the suburbs (Reimers 1985).

Involvement in business has been a salient characteristic of America's Asian communities since the late 1800s. The new immigration has reinvigorated and amplified the Asian ethnic economy; there are large and burgeoning Chinese, Korean, and Indian business sectors in many American cities. Although Asian-owned businesses are similar to black-owned businesses in some respects (over 90% are sole proprietorships, and they are concentrated in the retail and service sectors), they tend to be larger and more profitable. The remainder of this section provides a capsule description of the business activities of Chinese and Koreans. Our main emphasis is on the current situation, though historical background is provided where appropriate to show the evolution of the various Asian communities.

Chinese

Chinese immigrants were originally imported to work as laborers on railroads and mines in the mid-nineteenth century. Chinatowns grew up to serve the market of coethnics created wherever concentrations of Chinese arose. Such population concentrations supported stores that not only sold merchandise but also served as social and communication centers. After violence and anti-Chinese legislation forced them out of the mainstream economy, the Chinese regrouped into a small business sector, confined to lines of trade that required long hours, hard work, cheap labor, and low profit margins, and hence posed little competitive threat to whites (Barth 1964; Boswell 1986; Lyman 1974).

Laundries were the single most numerous type of business. The restaurant trade burgeoned after 1900, as the invention of chop suey helped attract white customers who were lured by the prospect of a bland, mildly exotic dish served at a cheap price. The expansion of the restaurant business in turn created opportunities in related lines of trade (Light 1974).

Early Chinese immigrants were almost all males, and later exclusionary provisions made it extremely difficult for wives and fiancées still living in China to join their husbands in the United States. Consequently, the old Chinatowns were a "bachelor society," with few women and a very small native-born population. The needs of isolated single males gave rise to a sizable ethnic vice industry, which expanded as the Chinese discovered a profitable market among white males (Light 1977). As the "bachelor society" slowly declined after 1900, the local market for the vice industry weakened. The dependence of the restaurant industry and ancillary gift and curio trades on white tourists led to further dismantling of the various vice businesses.

The growth of Chinese businesses was facilitated by the social organization of the Chinese community, which expedited resource mobilization. Immigrants were bound together by lineage, clan, dialect, or locality ties, and these connections helped immigrants scratch together the resources needed to start a business and keep it going. Villagers patronized store owners from the same locality, found jobs with other villagers, and recruited labor from among newcomers from the same place (Lyman 1974). Out of these village or clan connections also sprung the *hui*, a rotating credit association. The *hui* enabled otherwise penurious newcomers to pool their savings and allocate the monies in sequence to participants who thereby gained the capital to set up a store. Villagers also organized themselves into district associations, which at times overlapped with the trade guilds that grew up in the main Chinese trades. Both types of organizations played an important role in regulating competition and labor relations (Light 1972).

The story of Chinese Americans from 1900 to the mid-twentieth century is one of population decline, very gradual sex-ratio normalization, and the emergence of a second generation. As the population declined and the second generation increasingly moved into the mainstream economy, Chinatowns dwindled in population and size. After World War II, job opportunities in the mainstream economy multiplied, and college-educated sons and daughters of Chinatown's small business families entered the developing white-collar and professional sector of

American society. College-educated Chinese became civil service workers, accountants, engineers, doctors, and businessmen (Nee and Nee 1973). The older generation of Chinese remained behind. As Nee and Nee (1973: 253) wrote in their history of San Francisco's China-town, the remaining people were "the owners of small groceries and laundry shops; the aging bachelors, a younger group of men who had entered Chinatown as "paper sons' during the forties, spoke no English, and depended for their living on employment in the restaurants, mar-kets, and small factories which served the community." Businesses that served the distinctive tastes of the Chinese community or the tourist trade remained active, but the institutional completeness of Chinatown was shattered.

San Francisco's Chinatown — and others like it throughout the coun-try — was rescued from eclipse by the new wave of immigration, which began as a trickle of refugees in 1962, and then swelled to almost 5,000 per year after the passage of the Hart-Cellar Act. The newcomers first crowded into the established Chinatowns, spilled over their traditional boundaries, and then established satellite Chinatowns in areas of New York or San Francisco where there had never been a sizable Chinese community before. The influx of newcomers also reinvigorated the ethnic economy, replacing the declining hand-laundry industry with a burgeoning restaurant industry. Much of this growth occurred because the influx of immigrants allowed Chinese restaurants to offer a rela-tively inexpensive meal just at a time when life-style changes in the broader American population led to a taste for more exotic foods and also greater shares of income being spent on meals made in restaurants rather than at home (Bailey 1987).

Another sector that expanded rapidly was the making of garments. Some garment manufacturing had always existed in the major China-towns, like San Francisco's or New York's, but by the eve of the new migration, the declining and aging populations could support only a handful of factories. After 1965, the rapid proliferation of garment shops was accelerated by the movement of family units in the new immigration, and by the rapidly increasing numbers of women who provided a ready supply of labor for the traditionally female-dominated garment trade. As we note in Chapter 6, clothing also had the advantage of being a field in which getting started in a business of one's own was possible with only a little capital and access to family and kin labor (*Chinatown Garment Industry Study* 1983; Waldinger 1986), and the

Chinese community's social organization facilitated such resource mobilization.

The restaurant and garment industries — the two main branches of the ethnic economy — generated growth in ancillary fields. The 1984 *New York Chinese Business Guide & Directory,* for example, listed 64 Chinese food wholesalers, 25 restaurant suppliers, 6 sewing machine dealers, 4 fabric shops, and 4 purveyors of silk and embroidered material. Population expansion had an even more dramatic impact on business activity, as businesses that sold to the new immigrants — from food vendors to professional services — multiplied rapidly.

The inflow of capital has affected American Chinatowns in a variety of ways. Capital was either brought over by wealthy individuals who moved to the United States or sent over for investment purposes by rich residents of Hong Kong or Taiwan who wished to remain in the Far East but preferred the United States as a safe investment for their funds. The influx of capital has strengthened, to some extent, the economic ties between the local, ethnic business sector and the homeland — numerous Hong Kong, Taiwanese, and Chinese banks maintain branches in Chinese areas in the United States. Much of the new capital has also gone into real estate, leading to a burst of speculative investment and rapid price increases in residential, industrial, and commercial real estate in and around the various Chinatowns. Much of the capital has also flowed into the hands of Chinese real estate developers who are energetically constructing new commercial and housing developments to meet the needs of the growing Chinese population.

Chinese immigrants have thus gone through several cycles of opportunities and market conditions in the United States, beginning as laborers in the nineteenth century and experiencing periods of expanding and contracting opportunities since then. Chinese business owners in larger cities have benefited from serving ethnic consumer markets, but in virtually every large city neighborhood, as well as in smaller cities and towns, the ubiquitous Chinese restaurant has clearly served a nonethnic market. The descendants of the early immigrants are economically assimilated into the U.S. economy now, but continuing waves of immigration have kept Chinatowns alive. Group characteristics, especially strong ethnic social organization and community institutions, have enabled the Chinese to survive and prosper in spite of often hostile treatment by mainstream institutions.

Koreans

The U.S. Korean population—which numbered 354,600 in 1980 and has grown since—is of very recent origin. For a few years at the turn of the century, Hawaiian sugar planters recruited Koreans to work on sugar plantations; 7,000 arrived in Hawaii before the Japanese cut off the flow. A very small proportion of these immigrants moved on to agricultural work in California, where a handful set up businesses or farms of their own (Kim 1980). Thereafter, virtually no Korean migration to the United States took place until the 1950s, when the United States took in over 20,000 Koreans, mostly the brides of American servicemen, with some orphans and war refugees.

With the 1965 immigration reforms, Korean movement to the United States increased drastically. Many of the early immigrants were highly skilled professionals—in particular, doctors and nurses—who filled vacancies in municipal hospitals serving minority populations and took jobs in lower-status, lower-earning specialties that could not attract sufficient numbers of native physicians (Kim 1981). Other early immigrants were skilled workers, such as mechanics. With this population base in place, subsequent Korean immigrants were able to move to the United States on the basis of the family preferences specified in the 1965 legislation, and most of them were also highly educated. Over 90% of adult Koreans living in the United States in 1980 had completed a high school education, and substantial numbers had four years of university education or more. About 45% of Korean immigrants with prior work experience who moved to the United States in 1985 had previously been employed as professionals or managers.

One other characteristic of Koreans' movement to the United States is their rapid dispersion to many different cities. Their pattern of settlement contrasts sharply with that of the Chinese, who have continued to converge on the old population centers of San Francisco, Los Angeles, and New York. In 1985, for example, the three principal U.S. destinations for Korean newcomers—Los Angeles, Washington, and New York—received only 28% of that year's arrivals (Immigration and Naturalization Service 1985). This dispersion clearly limits the chances of Korean businesses serving a geographically segregated coethnic market as Chinese merchants had.

Of all recent immigrants, Koreans have moved most quickly and visibly into the small business niche. In 1980, roughly a third of employed Korean males in New York, Chicago, Los Angeles, San

Francisco, and Atlanta were self-employed. In New York City, Korean-owned fruit and vegetable stores are ubiquitous, and Koreans are well represented in other retail lines such as dry cleaning, fish stores, and stationers. In Los Angeles, gas station franchising and grocery stores, rather than the fruit and vegetable trade, proved to be the main lines of entry into business. From these specializations, Koreans have since branched out into the liquor store business and the garment industry.

Kim (1981) suggested that Korean businesses can be classified along two dimensions: (1) the ethnic origin of the clientele (Korean or other) and (2) the source of demand (originating in Korea or in the United States). Kim cross-classified these two dimensions to produce four categories: (I) selling ethnic consumer goods, (II) importing Korean goods for sale to non-Korean customers, (III) providing services related to the problems of immigrant adaptation, and (IV) selling non-Korean products to non-Koreans.

Of the categories in Kim's taxonomy, the business lines in cells I and III involve commercial activities that generally accompany the process of immigrant settlement: the furnishing of ethnic consumer goods (cell I) and the provision of services related to the problems of immigrant adaptation (cell III). Businesses that fall into cell II provide an important ingredient in the success of the Korean ethnic economy in the United States. Korean business owners have profited from their ties to South Korea's export-oriented economy, which has given them privileged access to the low-priced consumer items in which the Korean economy excels.

Korea exported over $8 million in goods to the United States in 1983, accounting for about one-third of total Korean exports. Many Korean immigrants established import-export businesses, with about 150 Korean-owned import-export companies in New York in 1979 (Kim 1981) and more than 200 Korean-owned import-export companies in Los Angeles in 1983. Using extensive networks,

Korean importers distribute Korean-made consumer goods to other Korean wholesalers and retailers. When Korean immigrants start new businesses dealing in wigs, handbags and other Korean-imported merchandise, they have easy access to information and can very often purchase merchandise on a credit basis. In operating such businesses, they receive preferential treatments from Korean wholesalers in item selections, prices, speed of delivery and credits. (Min 1984: 20)

But it is cell IV that contains the greatest concentration of Korea businesses: The distinguishing mark of Korean business in America i the fact that growth has occurred by selling nonethnic products in th general market.

What accounts for Korean entrepreneurs' success in serving the nonethnic market? In older areas of the country, like New York, Chi cago, and Philadelphia, *occupational succession* has taken place among white ethnic groups that previously dominated retail trade. The children of Jewish and Italian merchants are now moving into higher management or the professions, and, therefore, Koreans have access to owner ship by replacing these older merchant groups (Kim 1981; Waldinge 1986, 1987). Koreans have also discovered a niche in low-income minority communities. Large retail chains and individual white merchants have gradually withdrawn from minority areas, where the costs of business are high, security risks are considerable, and income levels are too low to provide a market for the fancier items that provide a big markup (Light and Bonacich 1988). In Atlanta, where 60% of Korean businesses are located in the inner city or in areas that are at least half black, Min (1984) found that Korean business owners said that they would have much more difficulty competing in white areas than in black neighborhoods.

Group characteristics have also played an important role in Koreans' business success. Rather than a background in petty enterprise, the cultural resources that Koreans bring with them into business are a high level of education, prior exposure to the American standard of living, and a commitment to permanent settlement in the United States. But as middle-aged immigrants with poor facility in English, many Koreans find it difficult to reenter white-collar occupations; hence business has emerged as an alternative path of upward mobility. Education and home-country linkages aid Koreans in this pursuit.

Koreans also gain advantages from the ethnic networks in which they are embedded. Many Koreans emigrate with capital, and those who are cash-poor can raise money through rotating credit associations known as *gae*. Because Koreans migrate in complete family units, family members provide a supply of cheap and trusted labor. The prevalence of self-employment means that many Koreans have close ties to other business owners, who in turn are a source of information and support. The high organizational density of the Korean community — which is characterized by an incredible proliferation of alumni clubs, churches, and businessmen's associations — provides additional conduits for the flow of business information and the making of needed contacts (Kim 1987; Light 1980; Waldinger 1987).

Koreans thus entered the United States under conditions very different from those of early Chinese immigrants, filling positions for which there was high demand. They also came from different social strata and brought with them higher aspirations than the waves of Chinese immigrants who came earlier in the twentieth century. Blocked mobility in their original careers pushed many well-educated Koreans into self-employment, and many filled vacancies left for them by white shop-keepers in America's inner cities. As in the Chinese community, Korean resource mobilization has been aided by strong ethnic networks.

Hispanics

The Hispanic-ancestry population of the United States numbers over 17 million. While *Hispanic* is the term used by both census-takers and popular media to describe these people, it is not clear whether *Hispanic* is a meaningful category for social analysis or just a catchall term used for convenience's sake. The Hispanic population is made up of a variety of different groups: Mexican Americans constitute slightly more than half, Puerto Ricans make up a sixth, and Cubans add a twelfth (Moore and Pachon 1985). Among these major groups, there are significant differences in background, in geographical distribution in the United States, and in the circumstances of their incorporation into American society.

Within each segment, there are important lines of cleavage as well: The wealthy exiles who fled Cuba just after the revolution have little in common with the lower-class *Marielitos*. Similarly, the "Spanish Americans" of New Mexico (known as *Hispanos*) are descendants of sixteenth-century Spanish settlers of "New Spain" and think of themselves as quite distinct from the rest of the "Mexican-origin" population. In addition to these three major groups, one-fifth of the Hispanic population is categorized as "other Hispanic"—a residual category that includes Latinos from all over Central and South America.

The Hispanic population has grown rapidly in recent years as a result of high fertility and high levels of immigration. The cycles and patterns of immigration vary significantly among the major segments of the population. Mexicans move both as legal immigrants—who mainly benefit from the quotas set aside for the reunification of families—and as undocumented immigrants who illegally cross the U.S.-Mexico border in the Southwest. Most Mexican migration has converged on the Southwest, although newcomers are increasingly dispersing to other regions.

Cubans have mainly migrated as refugees in a series of sporadic bursts over the years since the Cuban revolution in 1959, with significant differences in background and experience characterizing the various waves. Though many refugees moved immediately to Miami, the U.S. government attempted to limit the local impact of the refugee flow and settle the immigrants in a number of different cities. Over time, however, the Cuban population has resettled itself in Miami.

Puerto Ricans, who are citizens of the United States by virtue of the status of Puerto Rico as a commonwealth of the United States, began a massive migration to the continental United States in the 1940s. Initially, they concentrated in New York, but they gradually fanned out to other areas, with New York now containing only 44% of the Puerto Ricans living in the United States. *Net* out-migration from Puerto Rico appears to have ceased, and secondary migration has altered the distribution of the Puerto Rican population on the continent.

The growth of the various Hispanic communities has spurred considerable business development. Hispanic *barrios* in major American cities all contain *bodegas* (grocery stores), restaurants, travel agencies, and other businesses that provide for immigrants' special tastes and needs in a familiar idiom and manner. However, population growth has provided only a limited base for ethnic economic development — most Hispanic groups remain underrepresented in business, as can be seen from the data on self-employment in Table 2.2 or on business/population ratios in Table 2.4.

According to the 1980 census, 83% of Hispanics of Mexican ancestry resided in five southwestern states: Arizona, California, Colorado, New Mexico, and Texas (Torres 1988). These states include 56% of the businesses owned by persons of Mexican ancestry, and Torres (1988) used the 1980 Public Use Microdata sample to analyze the determinants of self-employed income among such persons. Most were U.S. citizens, although a sizable minority were born in Mexico. He included only nonfarm, nonincorporated businesses. Several findings stand out. First, most were concentrated in the retail and service sectors, with the small fraction owning businesses in professional and related services making substantially more than other owners. Second, proficiency in English was strongly associated with higher income, possibly reflecting the positive consequences of being oriented toward the nonethnic market.

Third, a subanalysis of five cities showed that most businesses were located at the periphery of the central business district, rather than in it. Because Torres's data were cross-sectional, and he had no measures of resource mobilization (except for real estate taxes paid, which could be a consequence rather than a cause of business success), we must treat his results as tentative. Nonetheless, his analysis paints a picture of fairly marginal businesses that succeed to the extent they serve a market larger than their own coethnics.

Only the Cubans have attained notable success among Hispanics as ethnic entrepreneurs. We turn now to their experience.

Cubans

Prior to the Cuban revolution of 1959, the United States was home to a small community of Cubans, numbering little more than 30,000 (Portes and Bach 1985: 88). The overthrow of dictator Fulgencio Batista sparked the first outflow, dominated by his supporters and other wealthy individuals and families. In the next two years, as the social and class policies of the Castro regime crystallized, growing numbers of professionals and owners of large and small businesses fled the country as well. Since 1962, migration has occurred in sporadic bursts: Between 1962 and 1965, and then again from 1973 to 1979, the Cuban government clamped down tightly on the outward flow. Only between 1965 and 1973, and again in 1980, were substantial numbers of refugees able to leave Cuba. The possibility of any future migration was the subject of negotiations between the governments of Cuba and the United States in 1988-1989.

Between 1959 and 1980, about 800,000 Cubans left the island, of whom 85% went to the United States and Puerto Rico. Generally, more recent migrants have been of lower-class background than those who arrived in the earlier refugee waves. While the *Marielitos* resembled their predecessors in their occupational experience in Cuba, many lacked kinship ties in the United States, raising questions about their prospects for successful economic integration.

As a refugee population, Cubans have been directly affected by government policies to a much greater extent than the other ethnic groups discussed in this chapter. The U.S. Cuban Refugee Program, created in 1961, attempted to divert many refugees away from the Miami area, providing sponsors if the refugees had no family ties in the community as well as job contacts and temporary assistance (Pedraza-Bailey 1985). Though over 450,000 refugees were eventually resettled

outside of Miami, an unprecedented wave of secondary migration ha
brought many Cubans back to South Florida. In 1980, just over half o
the Cuban population lived in the greater Miami area, and the Sout
Florida share has undoubtedly grown since.

The development of the Cuban community in Miami has been ac
companied by the growth of an "ethnic enclave": The number o
Cuban-owned firms grew from 919 in 1967, to about 8,000 in 1978, t
almost 21,000 in 1982 (Portes and Bach 1985: 89; U.S. Department o
Commerce 1986). As with so many other immigrant settlements, ser
vicing the needs of coethnics has been a fertile field of immigran
growth. As of 1980, for example, two geographers counted approxi
mately 700 Cuban groceries and over 400 Cuban restaurants (Boswel
and Curtis 1984).

Manufacturing has also been a growth area, accounting for 30% o
the receipts of Cuban-owned firms in 1982. The Cuban-owned manu
facturing sector includes a shoe factory employing 3,000 people, doz
ens of transplanted cigar factories, and a thriving garment industry i
which, according to an industry source cited by *Time* magazine, "Al
most 100 percent of the small manufacturers are Cuban, almost 10(
percent of the contractors, big and small, are Cuban, and almost all th
top management is Cuban" (*Time* 1985: 73).

Two main patterns of development have emerged in the Cubar
business community. First, very small businesses have proliferated
with the number of firms almost tripling between 1977 and 1982, while
per-firm receipts fell by half (Sanders and Nee 1987). Second, a tier o
"large" businesses, mainly independent of the ethnic market, has begun
to emerge. Though Miami is home to only 5% of the Spanish-origin
population in the United States, it contains close to half of the 40 larges
Hispanic-owned industrial and commercial firms (Portes 1987: 349).

The growth of the ethnic enclave has altered the integration of Cuban
immigrants into the Miami economy in significant and noticeable ways.
Portes and Bach's longitudinal study of the experience of 580 Cuban
refugees from 1973 to 1979 traced the profound effects of ethnic
enterprise on labor market experience. During these six years, the
proportion of refugees who ran businesses of their own rose from 8%
to 21%, and the single most important predictor of self-employment at
the end of the study was employment by another Cuban three years
before. About 37% of the refugees who were still *employees* in 1979
worked for other Cubans, and working in an ethnic firm provided a
better return on experience than Cubans received in comparable non-

ethnic firms (Portes and Bach 1985, chap. 6; but see Sanders and Nee 1987). The spread of Cuban businesses has meant that newcomers enter a pervasively ethnic milieu. Portes's more recent work on the *Marielitos* in Miami found that "86 percent lived in Cuban neighborhoods, 75 percent patronized mostly stores owned by co-nationals, and 82 percent read exclusively Spanish-language newspapers" (Portes 1987: 351).

Considerable controversy exists over the sources of Cuban entrepreneurial success. Perhaps the best review of existing interpretations is offered by Portes (1987), who argues that a concatenation of unexpected, unintended factors laid the groundwork for the growth of the Cuban enclave. Many of the early refugees came with considerable capital, but only a minority chose to funnel their monies into business, with the rest buying real estate and opting to live as rentiers.

After the failure of early attempts to overthrow the Castro regime, Cubans began to perceive the circumstances of their migration as a situation of "no return," which in turn stimulated the investment of productive resources. Organizations of various types — religious, occupational, regional — proliferated among the refugees, providing a network for the exchange of business information and contacts and the mobilization of resources. Aspiring entrepreneurs leveraged their capital by using contacts with lenders that dated back to a shared Cuban experience as well as by using ties to Latin American investors seeking a safe investment harbor in Miami. Finally, class differences within the immigrant community and the successive waves of migration furnished a ready flow of low-wage workers, many of whom were willing to work at low rates with the expectation that they would in turn learn how to run their own firms.

The Cubans thus have found niches in the opportunity structure that go beyond the ethnic market. Historically, they have benefited from the government's foreign policy, but group characteristics have proved much more important than internal American politics. Raising capital was apparently not a problem for the more ambitious Cuban entrepreneurs, and close ties to coethnics, ethnic social organizations, and ethnic career ladders have combined to spur Cuban economic success.

CONCLUSION

In this chapter, we presented recent trends in self-employment and national statistics on rates of business ownership among various ethnic groups in the United States. The entrepreneurial record of Koreans, Chinese, and Cubans is a story of exceptional success, but the experience of economic integration through small business is common to most of the latest wave of immigrants to the United States. The prevalence of petty entrepreneurship among the new immigrants reflects the continuing, indeed enhanced, importance of small business in the immigrant economy — the structural transformation of the American economy has expanded business opportunities, making small business an increasingly viable niche. Moreover, the newcomers have enjoyed the opportunities created by ethnic succession, as the withdrawal of white ethnics from petty retailing and manufacturing activities has created vacancies that the new arrivals — as seen in the case studies of Koreans and Chinese — have been quick to exploit.

Among Afro-American communities there is no parallel to the growth of immigrant enclave economies — the self-employment rate among Afro-Americans remains far below the national average. New immigrants, rather than native-born blacks, have emerged as the successors to whites as the suppliers of goods and services in black ghettos.

Our three case studies show the complex interaction between the two dimensions we identified in Chapter 1 — opportunity structures and group characteristics — that were shown in Figure 1.1, and the different strategies pursued by different ethnic groups. Changing opportunity structures have presented immigrant groups with very different market conditions, depending upon when they arrived in the United States. Opportunities have become available because groups previously dominating a market have left or have been economically assimilated (such as the Japanese). A succession of immigrant groups, differing in predisposing factors and in their capacity for resource mobilization, have risen and fallen in visibility in the business sector. Our review indicates that any explanation of ethnic business participation must take account of the historically contingent nature of the process.

3

European Trends in Ethnic Business

Jochen Blaschke
Jeremy Boissevain
Hanneke Grotenbreg
Isaac Joseph
Mirjana Morokvasic
Robin Ward

In western Europe, businesses run by persons from minority ethnic groups have always been present, but three changing historical circumstances have increased their salience and visibility in the past few decades. First, massive immigration from former colonies, southern Europe, and North Africa has led to the growth of sizable ethnic communities, especially in large urban areas. Many of the jobs that attracted them have since disappeared in the wake of industrial restructuring. Second, industrial restructuring has been accompanied by rising unemployment, as traditional large-scale employers (for example, iron and steel, automobiles) have closed down plants and laid off workers. Large firms have felt the full force of increasing competition from low-labor-cost countries, and large firms' perceived need to reduce labor costs has accelerated the transfer of labor from labor- to capital-intensive production. Where firms have survived, they typically employ a much smaller, more highly skilled work force carrying out a narrower range of economic activities within the business. Immigrants and their children have had to look elsewhere for employment, and many have found it in ethnic enterprises.

Third, the opportunity structure for ethnic business has become more favorable as Europe's changing industrial structure has led to a resurgence of smaller and middle-sized enterprises, a development similar to that in the United States. In this chapter, we review the effects of these forces on ethnic business in Europe and provide information on trends in Great Britain, Germany, the Netherlands, and France.

BACKGROUND

Ethnic entrepreneurship in Europe today is a result of huge immigration processes accompanying the expansion of labor markets during the economic boom of the 1950s and 1960s. Ethnic business began to develop after the decline of traditional small entrepreneurship, when the big retail chains and the industrial production of consumption goods took over the craft and small trader markets. On a smaller scale, the decline of traditional small business is still going on in countries with a standard pattern of industrial development, such as Austria.

The new mushrooming of small businesses in western European countries is closely associated with an increase in unemployment associated with a new form of economic development, described as the coming of "postindustrial society" or the "microelectronic revolution." Unemployed people are looking for new economic opportunities, and highly qualified people now consider self-employment more attractive than employment in high-tech firms. Between 1970 and 1985, self-employment rates turned upward in many European countries, although not all (Eurostat 1984, 1987). Many immigrants and their children have had few opportunities in the labor market because they arrived as unskilled or semiskilled laborers. Accordingly, many have turned to small business enterprise, some in new ethnic enclaves and others in businesses that draw on the immigrants' economic traditions.

Many small firms in Europe today act as subcontractors or franchises under the continuing control of large companies. Others are responding to the switch in consumer preferences away from standard commodity-like products to specialized, more differentiated goods and services, where the low volume of sales puts smaller firms in a strong competitive position. Thus firms supplying ethnically distinctive goods and services are just one category within the growing small firm population.

Immigration and industrial restructuring have had a profound effect on the kinds of economic activity open to ethnic minorities. First, they have been disproportionately affected by structural economic decline, as they were concentrated in traditional sectors of industry that were labor-intensive and threatened by increasing international concentration. Second, their relative lack of current technological skills, together with the continuing practices of racial and ethnic exclusion, has severely disadvantaged migrants and their children (Jenkins 1986; Jenkins and Solomos 1987).

Immigrants and ethnic minorities have become increasingly dependent on the small firm sectors of their economies, whether as owners or as employees. Ethnic enterprises have focused initially on the consumer demands of their ethnic communities because of their specialized knowledge and access through social networks to these markets. However, in recent years, ethnic ownership of businesses serving wider markets has grown. Just as the scale of contraction in the labor market has been too great for newly created firms to soak up all the resulting unemployment, so too have the market opportunities for ethnic business owners been insufficient to accommodate all those looking to business as a way of making a living. In particular, low barriers to entry have frequently resulted in gross overcompetition among enterprises (Aldrich et al. 1983).

The broad processes we have described have occurred in all the industrial societies of northwest Europe, with significant contextual differences. Economic restructuring has not followed a single pattern, as the size and character of immigration have varied greatly across countries. Significant variations in political processes across countries have also affected the opportunities for small firms and the rights of nonnationals to take advantage of them. Nevertheless, sufficient commonalities exist to warrant our treating all countries within the framework of the model presented in Chapter 1.

Our concentration on Great Britain, the Netherlands, Germany, and France in this chapter reflects the greater research attention paid to immigrant businesses in these countries than in other nations of Europe. Even for these countries, data are still not complete and academic research is in its early stages—the material we present is more or less the state of our knowledge of ethnic business development in Europe. Growing attention to business development in other nations suggests that material soon will be available on other societies—such as Switzerland, Belgium, or the Scandinavian countries—in the near future.

GREAT BRITAIN

Ethnic business in the United Kingdom has a long history. For centuries, Jewish-owned businesses have played an important part in commercial life (Pollins 1984), and immigrant groups such as the Huguenots have stimulated economic development by using their skills and knowledge to set up businesses in their new surroundings. However, not all long-established immigrant groups in Britain have a reputation for entrepreneurship. For example, the Irish have been migrating to Britain for many generations but are still widely identified as employees rather than employers, even though the construction industry — which is still dominated by Irish labor — has provided opportunities for the establishment of ethnic enterprises, both large and small.

Growth of the Ethnic Business Sector

After World War II, immigration to Britain increased as people were needed to fill jobs in the rapidly expanding economy. Immigrants from the New Commonwealth (chiefly the Indian Subcontinent, East Africa, and the Caribbean) became, with the Irish, the largest body of immigrants in Britain. However, relatively few set up their own businesses as long as regular full-time employment was available. For example, in 1971, nine years after the British government stopped free immigration from the New Commonwealth to Britain, only 6.7% of men born in India were self-employed or running businesses, 5.1% of those from Pakistan, and 2.4% of those born in the Caribbean, compared with 9.3% for the whole population (Reeves and Ward 1984).

By 1977-1978 the proportion of Asian heads of household (i.e., those of Indian, Pakistani, and Bangladeshi ethnic origin) in business was about the same as that for the total population, while that for Afro-Caribbeans lagged well behind. Asian businesses emerged as a significant phenomenon only in the 1980s. Smith (1984), using a more comprehensive definition of business/self-employment, showed that, in 1982, 18% of males of Asian ethnic origin in work were business owners, compared with 14% of whites and 7% of West Indians. Average figures recorded by the Department of Employment in 1988 (p. 167) showed that the percentage of white males who were business owners remained at 14%, whereas it was 24% for Indians and 22% for Pakistanis/Bangladeshis. (In all these data sets, the proportion of white and ethnic minority women in business has been far below that for men from the same groups.)

The movement of migrant workers into business has varied greatly by ethnic origin and area of settlement. Unlike some Continental countries that have relied largely on "guest-workers" to provide an additional source of labor during this period, much of the immigration to the United Kingdom was of Commonwealth citizens who exercised their right to immigrate, until the Commonwealth Immigration Act closed the door in 1962. This legal situation led to immigrants coming from a wider range of socioeconomic backgrounds than was typical on the Continent—doctors and shopkeepers, for instance, as well as manual workers and small farmers (for a statistical analysis of the economic background of immigrants to western Europe, see Castles et al. 1984).

New immigrants, because of their terms of entry, were free to settle wherever job opportunities were best. Consequently, the distribution of the New Commonwealth population over urban areas in Britain was highly uneven, particularly among those from South Asia. In areas of long-term economic decline, there were few jobs and thus few settlers. In Liverpool, for example, only 0.1% of the population in 1978 was born in India, Pakistan, or Bangladesh (Ward 1984: 212). At the other extreme, in areas with high rates of job vacancies, settlements were much more extensive. In Birmingham, for example, 6.4% of the population in 1978 was born in the Subcontinent. A similar pattern is found among those coming from the Caribbean: In Liverpool and Birmingham in 1978, 0.3% and 4.8%, respectively, of the population was born in the Caribbean.

Their terms of entry also gave immigrants the right to start up businesses in the same way as the local population. Those wishing to set up on their own in Britain are not normally required to demonstrate any technical, commercial, or linguistic skills, qualifications, or experience, because there is no question of needing official approval to begin trading. Hence the characteristics of those entering Britain and the terms on which they have been allowed into the country have combined with an official laissez-faire policy to ease the entry into business of immigrant minorities substantially.

The Asian business stratum began to emerge by 1978, as shown by the proportion of Asians in different areas who were *own account workers*—working for themselves with only the help of their families and not engaged in business involving professional services. In areas where fairly well-paid jobs were still available, the proportion of Asians in such businesses was very low; for example, 2.3% in Birmingham and 2.9% in Coventry. In areas where jobs were less well paid, a higher proportion of Asians moved into own account businesses; for example 5.4% in Bradford and 7.8% in Bolton. In regional commercial centers particularly those with fewer job opportunities, Asians working on their own account were an even greater proportion of the total Asian work force; for example, 10.0% in Nottingham, 14.9% in Manchester, and 31.0% in Newcastle.

Thus, as our model in Chapter 1 suggests, the movement of ethnic minorities into business is strongly associated with the relative availability (and attractiveness) of jobs in areas of settlement. The timing of the rapid extension of Asian business during the late 1970s and early 1980s — when unemployment was increasing dramatically — supports this view, as do the variations among local areas.

Differences Among Groups in Great Britain

Ethnic business should not be understood simply as a response to constraints in the labor market, however. On the contrary, there are significant differences between the levels of Asian and Afro-Caribbean business that cannot be explained simply by opportunity structure characteristics, and we also need to take group characteristics into account. We take up this issue in Chapter 5, where we argue that various predisposing factors and the resources available to prospective entrepreneurs in different ethnic groups have greatly affected the kinds of businesses established and the ways they have developed.

Historical conditions have had an important effect on the opportunities of the various ethnic communities in Britain. They experienced substantial variations in the market conditions for business and employment when they came to Britain at different periods and in different circumstances. Thus we must be cautious about generalizing to "all ethnic businesses." Before large-scale immigration to Britain from the New Commonwealth, for example, there were communities of Poles and Ukrainians who came as "European voluntary workers" at the end of World War II, when the economy was recovering from the effects of wartime devastation. In the early years, the Poles and Ukrainians were concentrated in jobs in specific industries (such as textiles and the mines), but eventually they were assimilated into the mainstream economy.

Much of the early Asian immigration, particularly among Muslims, was of males, with families being left in the country of origin (Bangladesh, India, and Pakistan). Jobs were easily available between 1955 and 1962, but in the absence of other family members, there was little demand for ethnic goods and services. When families were reunited (and expanded) in Britain, jobs were beginning to dry up, but business opportunities in the ethnic market were expanding because of an increasing demand for goods and services by ethnic minorities.

The other main source of Asian immigrants was East Africa, where decolonization was threatening the economic dominance of the Asian community, particularly their hold on the business sector. Those coming to Britain from Kenya in the mid-1960s onward, and the refugees from Uganda who arrived in 1972, came as families and from a background quite different from that of those who came directly from South Asia. Many of them were not engaged in business in East Africa, but they included a significant commercial stratum whose experience and attitude toward business were an important influence on the way they adapted to the British economy.

The largest group of New Commonwealth migrants in Britain have come from the Caribbean. Their level of business development has been limited by a variety of factors, not least the migration of those with higher qualifications and incomes to the United States and Canada, where opportunities for both business and high-income employment have been much greater (Foner 1979).

Data from the Department of Employment's 1984 Labour Force Survey (Barber 1985) provide information on the extent of self-employment among a variety of ethnic groups, although the relatively small size of the samples suggests fairly large confidence intervals for the precise point estimates. As shown in Table 3.1, all Asian groups sustain a much higher self-employment rate than whites, with the Asian/white disparity highest among females. Not all Asian groups fare equally well, as high levels of self-employment among persons of Pakistani/Bangladeshi backgrounds coincide with very low levels of labor force participation. About one in three are out of the labor force, compared with only about one in eleven of the East African Indians. Persons from West Indian backgrounds seem to do worse on both counts: There is considerably less self-employment among West Indians than among whites, with West Indian women particularly unlikely to be working on their own; West Indians also experience a depressed labor force partic-

Table 3.1 Ethnic Origins and Self-Employment, United Kingdom, 1984

| | Whites | West Indies | East Indians | | | | Other Ethnic Groups | All Employed Persons |
			All East Indians	East African-Indians	Pakistani-Bangladeshi			
	%	%	%	%	%		%	%
Males:								
Percent who are								
employee	85.7	89.1	75.2	73.1	74.8		81.1	85.4
self-employed	14.3	10.9	24.6	26.9	25.2		18.4	14.5
Total	100.0	100.0	100.0	100.0	100.0		100.0	100.0
Females:								
Percent who are								
employee	93.2	98.2	87.9	80.7	79.5		92.1	93.3
self-employed	6.6	1.8	12.1	19.4	20.4		7.8	6.6
Total	100.0	100.0	100.0	100.0	100.0		100.0	100.0

SOURCE: Adapted from Barber (1985).

86

ipation rate, comparable to that of the Pakistani/Bangladeshi adult population.

Extrapolating from the results of earlier censuses and surveys (Brown 1984), Ward (1987) produced rough estimates of the business lines in which ethnic firms are found. About two-thirds of all Asian-owned firms in Britain are in distribution and catering, compared with one-quarter of white firms and one-fifth of those owned by Afro-Caribbeans. These firms are very unevenly scattered over the country. Ward (1987) has estimated that at least one-half of convenience shops in inner urban areas are now in Asian hands. The contrast between Asian and Afro-Caribbean business would appear even greater if firms involved in retailing and wholesaling had been kept separate. In particular, local surveys carried out in North and South London, Birmingham, Manchester, Leicester, and Cardiff have shown that Asian firms are heavily concentrated in retailing, but there are few Afro-Caribbean retail establishments (Brooks 1983; Creed and Ward 1987; Soni et al. 1987; Ward 1987; Wilson and Stanworth 1983). Many of the Afro-Caribbean retail outlets do not follow the practice of Asian shops in selling to the public items that they have bought wholesale (Ward 1986). Instead, they are "make and sell" businesses, with the goods (bread, shoes, clothes, and so on) often being made on the premises.

By contrast, almost half of all Afro-Caribbeans in business are in the construction industry, compared with just over a quarter of white firms and one in fifty of Asian businesses. An identical figure was obtained in an earlier national survey carried out in 1974 (Smith 1977). These figures, together with the more detailed descriptions available in reports of local area surveys, indicate that Asian businesses are concentrated in retailing and clothing manufacturing, whereas Afro-Caribbean businesses are concentrated in services.

Characteristics of Asian and black businesses are broadly similar, but there are important local variations. Businesses in each sector are small, compared with white firms, a feature closely related to their recent establishment. Indeed, work carried out in Leicestershire showed that Asian firms have been growing significantly faster than white firms of a similar size in the same industries. Afro-Caribbean firms in Leicester also matched white firms in their rate of growth, but, as in other areas, they are still very young and very small.

Asian entrepreneurs draw heavily on ethnic networks in establishing and running their businesses. They derive great benefit from access to start-up finance and to labor from within the community, and the terms on which they gain access to these resources allow them to reduce costs and to make their businesses more responsive to the demands of the market. Frequently, too, they buy supplies from Asian firms and sell to Asians (either Asian firms or individuals). Increasingly, however, they use ethnic resources to run small businesses that sell petty commodity items to the general public.

Afro-Caribbean firms, like typical small, white-owned businesses, are not closely involved in community networks. Paradoxically, the availability of funds from within the community gives Asians an advantage in going to the bank for additional finance, because the bank is not being asked to bear a very high proportion of the risk. Afro-Caribbeans, who are more dependent on banks for start-up finance, are less able to obtain it. Their different experience with the banks can be related in many cases to basic lending principles, such as expecting the owner to bear as much of the risk as the bank. However, bankers' well-developed stereotypes of the success of Asians in running businesses and lack of success among Afro-Caribbean are in many instances a substitute for a realistic appraisal of the particular circumstances. As a result, Afro-Caribbeans depend far more than Asians on business advice agencies to assist them in effectively presenting applications for loan finance. They often use such financing to build businesses around the application of skills that allow them to sell products on the basis of their distinctive appeal rather than their cost (Ward 1987).

Changing opportunity structures in Britain, especially in large urban areas, have thus played a major role in the business participation rates of immigrants. Residential segregation has created ethnic neighborhoods that have provided a base for Asian and Afro-Caribbean businesses. Predisposing factors have shunted most Afro-Caribbeans into paid employment, whereas an increasing fraction of the Asian community has entered self-employment. Resource mobilization has also been more effective in the Asian than in the Afro-Caribbean community, with financial institutions magnifying the advantages of Asians.

WEST GERMANY

Germany has always been a multicultural region, and ethnic boundaries have frequently determined areas of industrial development. When the Prussian-dominated German Reich was constructed in the nineteenth century, an ethnically unified nation was created that promoted homogeneous economic development. However, ethnic and religious minorities remained, and they were active in politics and economics; for example, a tradition of entrepreneurship characterized the Huguenots as well as the Jewish and Polish populations (see the writings of Sombart and Schumpeter). Other established minorities, such as the Italians, have also contributed to the development of small business in Germany.

The characteristics of ethnic business in the Federal Republic of Germany today are a result of the new waves of migration since World War II. In the 1950s and 1960s, immigration was based mainly on contract labor organized by state agencies to fill vacancies in a booming economy. These "guest-workers" were recruited in the Mediterranean countries, first from southwestern Europe and later increasingly from Turkey.

During the 1970s, the earlier male-dominated immigrant population was expanded through family reunification and by the immigration of high-skilled and professional workers, such as religious leaders, teachers, and businessmen. Institutionally complete ethnic communities were reconstructed by an inflow of political refugees, who formed — together with members of the ethnic intellectual and business elite — the political leadership of the immigrant groups, especially of the Turkish immigrant population.

Statistics on Business Participation

Data on the business participation of foreign nationals in the Federal Republic of Germany are very difficult to evaluate. Sources include (1) the micro-census, a survey far too small to give any accurate data; (2) statistics of the "Central Register for Foreigners," which are not very reliable because they are based on forms filled out at the Immigration Registration Office; and (3) other data bases for several regions in Germany, also not systematically researched by various public bodies. However, independent of their reliability, all these sources have one feature in common: The number of businesses run by non-German nationals is increasing disproportionately to the ethnic population size. According to the Federal Office of Statistics in Frankfurt, in 1985 more than 100,000 business establishments were run by foreign nationals. In addition, there are tens of thousands of ethnic businesses that are run by immigrants who have obtained German passports.

In 1972, the number of foreign nationals in Germany increased to 3,457,100, and the number of the foreign population occupationally active was 2,592,102. Less than 1% of this population was engaged in business. Until 1980, the number of foreign nationals remained relatively constant, despite major ethnic and demographic changes in the composition of the population (Blaschke 1985). The economically active population of foreign nationals varied substantially over time: Their numbers increased until 1973 — when the government's immigration policy came to an end — declined over the 1970s, increased again for a very short period, and have since stabilized. Today, the economically active population of foreign residents in Germany is smaller than in 1972. However, the number of foreign nationals who are self-employed grew continuously by 1980 to around 240% of its size in 1972.

Between 1972 and 1985, the number of Turkish nationals in the Federal Republic doubled. The Turkish population included increasing numbers of families and refugees, and its demographic and social profile changed. The number of Turkish nationals and the proportion who are economically active have been stable since the early 1980s. However, the number of self-employed Turks increased around tenfold between 1972 and 1985.

In contrast to the Turkish case, the growth in self-employment among Greeks, Italians, and Yugoslavs can be traced back to the 1960s. The number of nationals from these three countries has been more or less constant since 1972, while their employment rates actually decreased because of families being reunited in Germany and an increase in the number of children. However, their rates of self-employment have increased significantly. Spaniards and Portuguese, whose number and employment rates have decreased since the beginning of the 1970s, have also increased their representation in business ownership.

As in the United Kingdom, the trend toward ethnic self-employment dramatically increased around 1980. The statistical data are not precise, but the various sources agree on this point. The Berlin Project (Blaschke and Ersoz 1986) also found that, by the early 1980s, ethnic business covered a wider range of activities, probably caused by the rising insecurity of migrants' economic situations. Opportunity structures changed because of the growth of sizable ethnic communities, and, therefore, ethnic markets, especially in the Turkish population. The new communities contained a wider range of cultural and political institutions and larger numbers of women and children, and hence generated ethnic niches for new goods and services, especially food and clothing (Blaschke et al. 1986-1987).

Rates of business participation differ widely across the various ethnic communities. Italians have been active in small business during the course of the twentieth century, and they have become more active since the end of World War II. Italians prospered in ice cream production and distribution, which flourished during the 1960s and 1970s when the catering and retail food industries expanded. The 1985-1986 Gelsenkirchen study found that, out of 73 Italian premises observed, 24 were active in the ice cream business, 24 in restaurant or bar catering, 5 in the fast-food sector, and the rest in other lines of business. The Berlin data show a similar pattern. Today, Italian small businesses are well established in serving the tiny Italian communities and the German middle class with "Italian specialties."

Portuguese and Spanish small business participation is not as widespread as among other groups. With the return of migrants to Portugal and Spain, and the decline of Portuguese and Spanish subcommunities in Germany cities and towns, there are fewer ethnic retail and service premises serving a strictly ethnic market than in the early 1970s. Instead, flourishing Spanish and Portuguese restaurants mostly serve the native German population in nearly all West German cities.

The Greek and Yugoslav populations have also increased their participation in small business, notably in the restaurant trade. Even in small German residential areas, one is likely to find a Yugoslav restaurant next to an Italian pizzeria. Yugoslavs and Greeks are still running many enterprises serving their own communities. However, with the decline in size of the ethnic populations, these services are no longer flourishing. More and more, business owners serve the needs of the native German population. Greeks have a tradition of running small tailoring shops (*Anderungsschneidereien*), an area of enterprise increasingly taken over by Turks (Morokvasic-Muller n.d.). Greeks are also known for their prominence in the fur trade.

New settlements of migrants from other European countries have been followed by new business starts, especially South Asians from Great Britain and refugees from Indochina and the Middle East. Indian, Pakistani, and Vietnamese restaurants have appeared in many German cities, as have Lebanese groceries.

Data from the Berlin and Gelsenkirchen studies, confirmed by micro-census data (Korte n.d.), show a concentration of ethnic businesses in catering. Trade and craft enterprises serving the ethnic communities or German neighborhoods show a similar concentration, such as in tailoring. Economic activity by immigrant groups in other sectors, notably construction and transport, is increasing but is still marginal.

The Turkish Community

The Turkish community in West Germany has been observed by two separate research projects in Berlin and in selected German towns (Sen 1986). In the Turkish community, there are various motives for starting a small business: (1) family tradition; (2) economic security considerations in view of rising unemployment rates, particularly among second-generation Turks; and (3) the increasing demand for special goods and services among the growing Turkish communities (Blaschke and Ersoz 1987a).

Legal factors play a central role in explaining the increasing proportion of self-employed Turks. Most Turks now have the legal right to open a business, the prerequisite being a residence permit issued after more than eight years of labor migrant status in West Germany. The liberalization of formal requirements for starting craft and trade firms in various branches has also increased Turkish self-employment (Blaschke and Ersoz 1987b).

Turkish businesses have been a characteristic feature in the growth of residentially distinct Turkish communities. Businesses are an integral part of these communities and they benefit from community networks. They serve community demands, with growth especially noticeable in community-oriented sectors such as video distribution and groceries. However, another trend is visible — that of establishing small firms that provide cheap services to the wider economy in such sectors as greengrocers, fast food, construction, and transport.

Thus changing opportunity structures in Germany, especially in the political and legal status of immigrants, have played a major role in ethnic groups' business participation rates. Residential concentration of some minorities, such as the Turkish community, has also played a role in creating ethnic enclaves, which has spurred business development. An increasing fraction of the Greek, Italian, and Yugoslav populations has entered self-employment. Resource mobilization has also been more effective in some groups than in others, although further research is required to determined why this has occurred.

THE NETHERLANDS

Immigration to the Netherlands took place on a considerable scale in the period following World War II. The wavelike nature of immigration was determined by political circumstances, by conditions of the decolonialization process (persons repatriating from the Netherlands East Indies, Moluccans, Dutch nationals of Surinamese and Antillean origin), and by developments in the Dutch labor market (in the case of migrant workers). Large immigrant groups of non-Dutch origin have settled in the Netherlands (Penninx 1979), creating a population of around 640,000 immigrants (see Table 3.2), which is about 4.5% of the Netherlands' total population. Most of them settled in the old nineteenth-century urban quarters of the large cities (Penninx 1979).

Ex-colonial subjects make up the largest ethnic minority, estimated at 279,000, with Surinamese the largest single group. Immigrants from southern Mediterranean countries are the second largest grouping, with those from northern Mediterranean countries a less significant number. About 25,000 Chinese were present in 1979, along with 10,000 political refugees. A large proportion of these minorities are expected to stay permanently, especially migrants of Surinamese descent and migrant workers from the Mediterranean region.

Unfortunately, studies of ethnic businesses in the Netherlands are scarce, but ethnic entrepreneurs have recently received more attention. The scale of their activities is growing, and they are also receiving attention because of concern over the assimilation of immigrant outsiders into Dutch society. Assuming that about 50% of the ethnic population in the Netherlands is employed, some 2.2% are active as entrepreneurs (Instituut voor Toegepaste Sociologie 1986).

The various ethnic groups differ in their rate of entrepreneurial participation. Among the Surinamese, approximately 2%-3% of the working population is self-employed; among Antillean immigrants, the proportion is also 2% (Reubsaet and Kropman 1985). For the Turkish working population, the rate of self-employment is considerably higher at approximately 5%-6% (Tap 1983). Few Moroccans are entrepreneurs (Bakker and Tap 1984) and an entrepreneurial tradition is almost completely absent among Moluccan immigrants (Veeman 1984), most of whom came to the Netherlands following careers as professional soldiers in the former Royal Netherlands Indies Army. In addition to these differences in the rate of business activity, there are also differences in the level of economic success and in the distribution by business sector.

Table 3.2 Estimates of Ethnic Minority Population Size in the Netherlands

Main Groups	Country of Origin	Population Size	Regional Total
Southern Mediterranean countries	Turkey	154,000	
	Morocco	102,000	256,000
Northern Mediterranean countries	Italy	21,000	
	Greece	4,000	
	Spain	23,000	
	Portugal	8,000	
	Yugoslavia	14,000	70,000
Ex-colonial subjects	Surinam	190,000	
	Antilles	38,000	
	Molucca	40,000	
	Indonesia	11,000	279,000
Other categories			
	China (including Hong Kong)	25,000	
	Refugees (Vietnam, Chile, and Poland)	10,000	35,000
Total			640,000

SOURCE: Instituut voor Toegepaste Sociologie (1986).

Chinese and Hindustani immigrants from Surinam are more active in business than are Creoles. Fieldwork in Amsterdam (Boissevain and Grotenbreg 1986) in 1983 found 214 businesses, which were classified by the ethnicity of the owner and type of business, as shown in Table 3.3. Hindustanis form only 28% of the Surinamese population in Amsterdam, but they control 40% of the enterprises. The Chinese are even more active, relative to their population size. Hindustanis are most strongly established in retail, while Creoles and Chinese are concentrated in catering, as are Javanese. These three ethnic groups came from the same country of origin at about the same time, and their starting positions appear to have been more or less equal. What accounts for their unequal rates of entrepreneurial participation?

The Chinese conform most closely to the ideal type of middleman minority described by Bonacich (1973). Many Chinese emigrated to Surinam or were recruited to work as self-employed (Heilbron 1982: 232). As a trading minority, they dominated the distributive sector of

Table 3.3 Surinamese Business Activity in Amsterdam by Ethnic Group

Business Type	Creole	Hindustani	Chinese	Other	Total
Tropical greengrocers	0	27	6	1	34
Record/video	6	7	1	—	14
Barber	10	1	—	—	11
Goldsmith	1	2	3	—	6
Butcher	—	4	—	—	4
Garage	—	2	—	—	2
Tailor	2	2	—	—	4
Coffee shop	24	3	—	—	27
Café	17	—	2	—	19
Restaurant/snack bar	11	14	16	6	47
Travel agency	6	5	—	—	11
Miscellaneous*	15	19	1	—	35
Total	92	86	29	7	214

SOURCE: Fieldwork by Jeremy Boissevain and Hanneke Grotenbreg.
*Includes diverse shops and market stalls.

the Surinamese economy. Chinese associations were active in Surinam and played an important role in organizing rotating credit associations, which gave members access to capital. On the national level, these associations acted as pressure groups, representing the interests of more powerful Chinese to government and influencing trading practices, including pricing. Important patronage and kinship links existed between the small neighborhood grocers and the wealthy merchants (Vermeulen 1984: 92-96).

Chinese immigrants in Amsterdam are not heavily involved in retail trade. They left Surinam relatively late, and upon arrival found their traditional economic niche already occupied in Amsterdam by the Hindustanis. The Chinese turned, instead, to the restaurant field, where Indonesians and Hong Kong Chinese were already active, and their activities are now expanding.

Hindustanis were originally imported to Surinam as contract laborers for the plantations. On termination of their contracts, they were offered a chance to remain and become land-owning peasants, and many did remain. The first Hindustanis to become active in trade, however, were not descendants of contract laborers. Many British Indians came to Surinam as traders, and they recruited other Hindustanis to assist them (Heilbron 1982: 149). The growth of Paramaribo — the capital city of Surinam — is paralleled by the movement of Hindustanis to the city and

its environs. Hindustanis produced vegetables and fruit for the city'
market and organized transport between rural areas and the city. Trades
men, transport owners, and small farmers are entrepreneurs par ex
cellence. They are accustomed to independence, making decisions
coordinating the family enterprise, and, above all, saving to protec
themselves against unforeseen events. The activity of Hindustanis i
Amsterdam in the fruit and greengrocer sector is simply an extensio
of their activities in Surinam.

The experience of Creoles was very different. After failing as peasan
farmers following their manumission, Creoles increasingly becam
involved in wage labor and crafts. Though at first active as marke
traders, they were gradually replaced by the Hindustanis, who ha
closer links with rural suppliers (Kruijer 1977: 69). In Surinam ther
are far more Hindustani and Chinese than Creole shops. Creoles ar
more active in the civil service and as white-collar workers in large
firms, and especially as skilled and unskilled wage laborers with th
big companies exploiting Surinam's bauxite and timber wealth. Man
Creoles are also unemployed and are obliged to *hossel* (hustle) i
Paramaribo to survive. The male Creole custom of spending a good dea
of time outside the home with friends played an important role i
Creoles' choosing to establish cafés and coffee shops in Amsterdam.

Although the immigration of Surinamese to the Netherlands has a
long history, until the 1960s their numbers were limited. After that they
increased slowly until 1968 and then more rapidly, reaching a peak in
1974-1975. After the independence of Surinam in 1975, migration
declined sharply, to rise briefly again toward the end of the 1970s.

The entrepreneurial activity of Surinamese in Amsterdam reflects
their migration history. The first *tropica* shops were established in the
1960s. These sold a variety of Surinamese fruit, vegetables, and groceries. The market for fresh tropical vegetables and fruit expanded with
the stream of Surinamese migrants, and *tropica* shops multiplied rapidly. During the 1970s, Surinamese entrepreneurial activity diversified.
Travel agencies, small restaurants, barbershops, butchers, cafés, driving schools, and record and, more recently, video shops joined the
tropicas. Development of Surinamese businesses has been extremely
rapid, especially during the past five years.

In 1983, there were approximately 250 Surinamese enterprises in
Amsterdam. The average age of their owners was 38 — an average age
quite similar to that found in most studies of small business owners —
and they had been established for an average of five years. Entrepre-

Table 3.4 Number of Greek Businesses in Four Cities 1983, in the Netherlands, by Type

	City			
Business Type	*Utrecht*	*Rotterdam*	*Amsterdam*	*Nijmegen*
Catering	24	43	14	5
Import-export	1	10	5	1
Retail trade	10	4	1	5
Miscellaneous	8	14	—	1
Total	43	71	20	12

SOURCE: Adapted from Vermeulen (1985).

neurial activity was concentrated in retailing, catering, and crafts. Most enterprises were located near the open-air markets in the older sections of Amsterdam, where real estate is relatively inexpensive; hence many immigrants have also settled in these areas.

Greek businessmen are predominantly concentrated in catering (60%) and in the retail trade (30%). The development of Greek businesses started around the 1930s; some Greeks started as furriers employed by others and later established their own stores, as they did in Germany. Other Greeks became active in shipping services and in the import of Greek products. Through these first establishments, other Greeks — mostly family members — were invited to join the firms, and gradually their businesses expanded. Other businesses, such as catering services, were founded in the 1960s, and they expanded as the number of Greek laborers in the Netherlands increased.

Most Greek businesses are established in urban centers and the big cities (see Table 3.4): Fieldwork in 1983 found 43 Greek businesses in Utrecht, 71 in Rotterdam, 20 in Amsterdam, and 23 in Nijmegen (Boissevain and Grotenbreg 1986). In recent years, Greek restaurant keepers have also located in small towns in the country.

The Greek merchant service in Rotterdam has grown over the years, as Greek-owned shipping companies established important relations with Greek shipowners, and a considerable part of their business receipts results from trade with Greek ships. Greek pubs near the harbor have undoubtedly profited from sales to Greek seamen on shore leave there.

Because of the protected market, and probably also because of relatively little competition, the most successful Greek companies can

Table 3.5 Turkish Business Activity in Amsterdam

Business Type	Estimate of Number
Textile-industry	80
Coffee shops	50
Snack bars	40
Pizzerias	25
Butchers	20
Import	10
Miscellaneous	32
Total	257

SOURCE: Adapted from Tap (1983).

be found in shipping services and deliveries and in import/export firms, especially the older companies established around World War II. Greek entrepreneurs are successful not just because the demand for their products is growing but also because of a number of group characteristics, such as favorable predisposing factors and strong ethnic social networks. They are willing to work long hours, are able to draw on family labor, and have a positive attitude toward economic mobility.

In Amsterdam, there is a concentration of 14,500 Turks, representing 2% of the population of the city. Turkish businessmen in Amsterdam are active in a variety of sectors. Table 3.5 gives estimates of the number of Turkish businesses by business type, based on fieldwork in 1983.

Many Turks in Amsterdam have become involved in the "rag trade." An important factor favoring the increase of smaller Turkish enterprises is decentralization. Larger enterprises favor little *ateliers* because they want to minimize labor costs and they need quick, flexible suppliers for small lots of clothing. Many of the Turks active in the rag trade were previously involved in tailoring in Turkey and many others had worked in the clothing industry. Moreover, it is relatively easy to start a clothing workshop. No license is required and little capital is needed for second-hand machines, and premises are also easily acquired. As we show in Chapter 6, this pattern is replicated in the clothing industries of Paris, London, and New York.

Predicting the future is difficult. In the long run, the differences among the various ethnic groups that have been highlighted here will diminish somewhat. For the Surinamese, we may expect the Chinese among them to expand their activities to other areas, in part because of their prior experience and the considerable capital to which they have access. The children of Creole businessmen will have been socialized in some of the values—such as hard work, saving, and especially the desire for independence—that have been important for their parents' economic survival as self-employed workers.

Ethnic differences will continue to influence the style of entrepreneurship, but the different groups of Surinamese immigrants are linked in symbiotic relations to each other. Hindustani shopkeepers and Chinese restaurateurs depend largely on Creole clients. A Creole wholesaler supplies products to a series of Hindustani shops on which he, in turn, relies for his survival. Because he has been established in Amsterdam for years, he is also a source of advice for his customers. An active Creole entrepreneur employs both Hindustanis and Creoles in his travel agency and draws customers from both ethnic groups. The ongoing internal exchange among the three groups, as well as the interaction with Dutch culture, ensures that differences in style will probably diminish. Their interdependence is a source of mutual strength.

FRANCE

France has a long-standing tradition of immigration. Parents and grandparents of many French citizens come from various parts of the world, and some 18 million French are of the first, second, or third generation. Around 1930, decades of immigration had resulted in about 3 million foreigners in France. Immigration slowed considerably during World War II but surged again in the 1950s, and Paris remained the pole of attraction for about one-third of all immigrants. Immigration was encouraged by demographic conditions in France and by postwar economic need. France had a lower birthrate than any other European country at that time and it badly needed workers in agriculture and industry. Immigration was the most obvious solution to both problems.

The international political scene also produced numerous refugees, and France received many who had escaped conflicts and persecutions in their own countries—Russians, Armenians, Jews from various parts of Europe, and, in the 1930s, those who escaped the fascist regimes of Germany, Spain, and Italy. By 1982, there were 4.3 million foreigners in France—8% of the total population.

The self-employed population can be estimated by deducting the wage-earning and salaried from the total economically active (unemployed excluded) population. Such calculations show that the self-employment rate of French nationals is three times that of foreign nationals in France (18% versus 6%). Self-employment has always been lower among foreigners than among natives. For instance, in 1931, of the economically active foreign population, 9.6% were self-employed, compared with 40% among the French (Schor 1985: 47). Current census data indicate the presence of 111,760 foreigners in retailing, which is 4.4% of the total employed in retailing, and 234,560 in services, which is 5.8% of the total employed. In both sectors, the immigrants' share ranks below their proportion (6.6%) of the total economically active population (INSEE 1984). Among foreigners in retailing, Italians represented 10%, Spanish 10%, Portuguese 20%, and North Africans (including Algerians, Moroccans, and Tunisians) about 30%. In the category "services," of which one-quarter are hotels, cafés, and restaurants, half are owned by North Africans.

Among foreigners, only 4% were in the category of craftsmen, retailers, and entrepreneurs (i.e., the category including self-employed only). However, the percentage of self-employed persons is larger for long-established minorities among the North Africans, and among some other recently arrived immigrant groups. Practically one of ten artisans, retailers, or entrepreneurs is a foreigner. This proportion would certainly be higher if the foreigners who have recently taken French citizenship or their children (who are French by birth — roughly 100,000 persons a year) were included. Such individuals tend to patterns of residence and employment similar to those of their ex-compatriots and have comparable access to resources and labor.

France has accepted foreigners of many socioeconomic levels — workers, refugees, intellectuals, artists. Of the Spanish refugees crossing the French border in 1939 (500,000 of them within three months), most stayed in France. Armenian refugees settled in the Parisian region and in the south of France. They were successful in business, running food stores and entering the garment trade, where persons of Armenian origin were well-known French manufacturers in the 1980s.

Some small nationality groups have markedly influenced the French way of life and thought. A case in point is that of the Russians between the two world wars. Russians numbered fewer than 100,000 persons, but among them were many well-known artists, writers, and other intellectuals. Cabarets, restaurants, tearooms, and gambling places mushroomed in the 1920s in Paris and at the Côte d'Azur. Some Russians became successful in business, such as the owners of *haute couture* houses, whereas many others remained socially obscure and economically disadvantaged.

Jews in France

Between 1880 and 1925 some 100,000 Jews, victims of persecutions and pogroms in eastern and central Europe, immigrated to France either to settle or as a first stage on the way to the United States or Britain. France was relatively near, and it was one of the first Western countries to have emancipated Jews (1791). It had kept its reputation of being a *terre d'asyle* in spite of anti-Semitic countercurrents. According to some estimates, 80% of Jewish immigrants came to Paris, the center of French clothing production (Green 1986).

Jews found employment in production and in retailing. Petty trade was for the newly arrived, which was often the only means of economic survival for those not knowing French and without any formally recognized skills, and frequently also a first step in the accumulation of capital for an independent business. Many immigrants brought prior skills as tailors (Klatzmann 1957), furniture makers, shoemakers, or fur specialists (Green 1986), and in these industries they represented a large proportion of the labor force. In clothing, Jews made up about a quarter of workers and contractors. In such specialized clothing trades as ladies' clothing and fur, their share of employment reached 80%.

At the turn of the century, almost two-thirds of the Parisian Jewish population worked in skilled jobs, 6% in unskilled, and more than one-quarter in retail (Green 1986). A small percentage (4%) were lawyers or translators or had opened various information bureaus, catering to the needs of their own community. In the category "skilled worker," the distinctions among dependent worker, independent home-worker (the status that Jewish tailors usually had), and petty entrepreneur were blurred. This ambiguity about immigrants' status in the complicated hierarchical structure of production still remains (as is discussed in Chapter 6).

Immediately after World War II, foreigners and naturalized citizens represented about one-half of the active male population in the garment industry — the *patrons* and entrepreneurs (Klatzmann 1957: 81). The most heavily represented nationalities were Polish, Italian, Armenian, Russian, and Rumanian. Among Poles, Russians, and Rumanians, the proportion of Jews was 60%. According to the 1946 census, their propensity for entrepreneurial enterprise was the same as that of the

French, and it was considerably higher for the naturalized group
(Klatzmann 1957: 83).

North African Immigrants

In 1979, 2,370 of 38,655 retail shops in the Parisian area were owned
by North Africans (Alain 1980). One out of five grocery stores and one
out of ten café-restaurants held by foreigners are North African. In some
districts, up to half of the grocery stores and cafés are held by North
Africans, such as in the 10th arrondissement of Paris. Algerians typically run coffee bars; they are among the few national groups who do
not need professional cards for this industrial sector.

Tunisians are the smallest of three national groups of North African
origin but are the most oriented toward self-employment. Running a
food store or a restaurant is the aim of many Tunisians who arrive in
France as wage workers. Before national independence, many Tunisians
went to Egypt or Algeria as traders; after independence, they have
mainly gone to France. In 1975, 140,000 Tunisians were residents of
France, more than one-third of them concentrated in the Parisian area
(Boubakri 1984; Simon 1979). Approximately one-third of the total
were Jewish and the rest were Muslim. According to Boubakri's estimate, there are about 180 Tunisian restaurants in Paris, with an average of three self-employed persons and four employees per restaurant
(1,260 persons altogether). The restaurants are strongly concentrated in
several districts, having either an ethnically homogeneous or a mixed
clientele, depending upon the district.

Most Tunisian restaurant owners rely on a century-long tradition of
doughnut making and on a network of shops in Tunisia and elsewhere.
People from the south of Tunisia have established a monopoly on these
shops (Boubakri 1984). Each shop traditionally employs members of
the same family or the same ethnic group exclusively, and outsiders
are rare.

Chinese

One of the most visibly successful ethnic groups in business is the
Chinese, especially in Paris. In the nineteenth century, the Chinese were
not associated with French immigration, which was marked primarily
by immigrants from the Mediterranean, North Africa, and southern
Europe. Today, Paris has its own Chinatown.

The Chinese in France are mostly refugees from Indochina. The majority hold passports from Cambodia, Laos, and Vietnam. Census data show sizable increases in the population of Indochinese immigrants from all three countries. Between 1975 and 1982, the following increases were recorded: people of Cambodian origin, from 3,115 to 4,960; of Laotian origin, 4,520 to 35,880; and of Vietnamese origin, 11,380 to 35,160. No other immigrant group has had such an increase in numbers within such a short period in recent years (INSEE 1982). Indeed, the trend in other groups is rather toward stagnation or decrease, especially among traditional immigrant groups.

Chinatown in the 13th arrondissement of Paris owes its name not to residential exclusivity of a cultural group but to the business presence of Chinese merchants: 40% of the shops in the area are owned by Southeast Asians. In addition to supporting strong commercial activity, Chinatown is also a dynamic production center in textiles. Though only a few Chinatown entrepreneurs belong to big business families, most of them were entrepreneurs in their countries of origin. In Vietnam, they monopolized the food trade and restaurants, and they dominated the textile industry and finance.

In addition to the know-how they brought along, the Chinese also rely on the same networks and resources that they used effectively in their countries of origin. As in the United States, they have established rotating credit associations (*tontine*) and they rely on cheap, clandestine labor. Their success as entrepreneurs is related to an absence of negative discrimination toward them — unlike in the United States — and the presence of legal assistance for refugees.

Other Immigrant Groups

Another group that has only recently become visible in France is of black African origin. Senegalese traders started coming in the early 1970s, and the first settlers served as a base for later arrivals. Their network spreads all over France, in particular in the bigger cities and in the border towns toward Italy and Germany (Salem 1984: 8). They are engaged in petty trade, selling peanuts, sponges, toys, and especially handmade wooden objects as *art negre* in the streets. In some parts of Paris in the 1980s, trendy hairdressing shops have been created with flashy names like Afrostar, which offer their clients "a new way of expressing their personality." Most customers are black.

Another relatively new Asian group in Paris is the Japanese, with over 10,000 of them resident in the early 1980s (Holzman and Guidicelli 1983). In the 1960s, a Japanese restaurant was a rarity, but now there are Japanese restaurants all over Paris. Indeed, the opera district could be described as "Japanese," with its numerous restaurants, stores, and bars. Japanese residents and tourists can even buy French pastries in a Japanese-run bakery in the center of Paris.

Yugoslavs represent a relatively small group with low visibility that is highly concentrated in Paris and the Parisian region. Though many of them are recent immigrants, they are also part of a long-established immigration chain. The majority of Yugoslavs who came to France did not have work contracts, but rather found work through informal networks in the community. Yugoslavs have primarily gone into garment production. They have set up businesses and employed their compatriots, often undocumented workers. In addition to cheap labor as an ethnically based resource, they have relied on in-group networks for various financial transactions (Morokvasic 1986). Yugoslavs have opened food shops, restaurants, a bookstore, a driving school, a real estate office, and a travel agency, primarily catering to the needs of their own community.

France has thus attracted one of the most diverse populations of immigrant entrepreneurs, and their characteristics are only slowly being documented by research. Some groups have settled into vacancies left by the withdrawal of natives, such as in the garment business, grocery stores, and cafés. Others have found an ethnic market niche in which they serve both coethnics and the native French population. Preliminary evidence indicates that most mobilized resources through close ties to coethnics, building on ethnic social networks.

CONCLUSIONS

Our review of trends in four western European societies suggests three generalizations about the fate of minority immigrant groups in businesses, building on the model developed in Chapter 1. First, a group's position and success depend very much on the period during which it immigrates to a host society. Opportunities are continually opening (and closing) as the economies of Western nations develop. Many groups found opportunities first in serving coethnics, and subsequently in carving out a market in the native population. We will address this issue in Chapter 4. Second, a group's position depends, in part, on the cultural, social, and economic resources it brings with it. However, lacking such resources, groups can often fashion strategies to compensate. Success with such strategies depends heavily on the nature of ties among coethnics and the shape of the social networks in which immigrants are embedded. We will address this issue more fully in Chapters 5 and 6.

Third, a group's position is heavily influenced by the legal and political restrictions it confronts. Some immigrants are welcomed; others are merely tolerated. Some migrate to societies where business start-ups are simple and cheap, whereas in other societies, would-be business owners face a nightmarish tangle of bureaucratic regulations. In this respect, the United States stands out as a business environment in which legal-political restrictions on immigrants are minimal after the migrant is settled in the country. By contrast, immigrants in many western European nations must resort to a variety of creative subterfuges to evade legal constraints on their economic activities.

4

Spatial Dimensions of
Opportunity Structures

Roger Waldinger
David McEvoy
Howard Aldrich

In this chapter, we examine the spatial relationship between businesses owned by members of an ethnic group and the residential pattern of that group. We show that the relationship is complex, differing by type of business, and varying over time. We argue that the spatial characteristics of different types of business lines may operate either as opportunities or as constraints on the overall level of business development. After reviewing differing spatial business-population arrangements, we show that there is a succession of business stages linked to changes in ethnic communities.

OVERVIEW

The ethnic neighborhood looms large in the popular iconography of the American ethnic experience as well as in its scholarly interpretation. The high-water mark of immigration to the United States, at the turn of the twentieth century, was accompanied by the creation of distinctive ethnic enclaves. Most of the nation's cities were dotted with ethnic "colonies" — Germantowns, Little Italys, Chinatowns, and the like — where immigrants concentrated for sustenance and support. Over time, the immigrants and their descendants moved on to newer, better neighborhoods, but the original areas of settlement often remained a concentration of ethnic stores and services, and thereby a symbol of common ethnic identity.

In the new neighborhoods to which the immigrants and later generations dispersed, they continued to live in considerable isolation from the native population. The "urban village" of the mid-twentieth-century American city, as Gans (1962) showed in his classic portrait of Italian Americans in Boston, was a world circumscribed by the converging contours of class and ethnicity, in which everyone knew everyone else. The centrifugal forces of the American city have since emptied many of these older "urban villages," but even as attachment to the old neighborhood has waned, a new set of immigrant groups has arrived. In turn, they have placed their own stamp on the urban landscape, seeming to replicate, in burgeoning Chinatowns, Koreatowns, and extended *barrios*, such as East Los Angeles, the experience of their European predecessors.

The experience of migrant groups in Europe often mirrored the American pattern, although frequently with differences of scale or intensity. The Jews of Britain, like those in the United States, have moved in the twentieth century from ghetto to suburbs. The South Asian population in Britain is heavily concentrated in clusters, which, some would argue, also deserve the title "ghetto" (Jones and McEvoy 1978). In continental Europe, contemporary lower-status migrants from Northwest Africa, Asia Minor, and southern Europe occupy the older, less desirable quarters of cities such as Berlin, Frankfurt, Rotterdam, Brussels, Paris, and Bordeaux (White 1984).

In many cases, the more recent communities follow in the footsteps of a variety of predecessors, and the symbols of this ethnic succession are apparent. In London's Brick Lane, the Bengali community is served by a mosque that served as a synagogue from 1898 to 1975, and was built in 1744 as a church for French Huguenots. In Bradford, Yorkshire, the first center of migration from Pakistan (Dahya 1974), Howard Street is within a hundred yards of the late-nineteenth-century German Evangelical Church and of the church of Our Lady of Czestochowa, serving the post-1945 Polish community.

Despite the attention paid to the ethnic neighborhood, the relationship between ethnic settlement patterns and the development of an ethnic economic base has not been adequately explored. Classic accounts of immigrant ghettos noted how population concentration gave rise to specialized businesses serving their coethnics, and the employment of a ethnically based manufacturing labor force was also noted.

However, these factors were seen as a natural outgrowth of the pattern of settlement, and hence not as issues worthy of close examination.

ETHNIC NEIGHBORHOODS
AND BUSINESS CONCENTRATIONS

Most newcomer groups have begun by clustering in distinctive areas and have kept some spatial isolation from dominant, established populations, even as their original area of settlement has been abandoned and new neighborhoods have been established. Opportunities for ethnic business owners first arise in such ethnic neighborhoods. As noted in Chapter 1, ethnic communities often have a special set of needs and preferences that are best served, and sometimes can only be served, by those who share their needs and know them intimately — the members of the ethnic community themselves. As newcomers cluster together for sustenance and support, they build up a critical mass of customers needed to support businesses that cater to these distinctive ethnic tastes.

The Jewish quarter in Manhattan, for example, burgeoned from a small "nondescript colony," very much overshadowed by Irish and German residents as late as 1880, into a dense center of Jewish life by the turn of the twentieth century. As early as 1890, ethnic proprietors serving the local Jewish trade did quite well. A private survey, commissioned by the Baron de Hirsch, found 413 butchers, 370 grocers, 307 dry goods dealers, 120 restaurant keepers, 83 shoe dealers, 80 coal dealers, and 58 booksellers concentrated on the Jewish East Side.

Almost a century later, commercial activity in the same area reflects the transformation produced by the influx of newcomers from China. Whereas a small Chinese population had always bordered the Jewish Lower East Side in one section of a census tract known as "old Chinatown," by 1980 there were four contiguous tracts with populations more than one-half Chinese, another four with populations more than one-quarter Chinese, and rapidly growing Chinese concentrations in the adjacent tracts. In turn, this burgeoning population has made Chinatown a hotbed of ethnic commerce, both large and small.

Wherever they live, New York's Chinese immigrants are drawn back to downtown Chinatown to work and shop, creating an atmosphere of an old city market, with hundreds of entrepreneurs tending their own stalls or shops. Bushels of live blue crabs, crates of bok choy, and hordes of intense shoppers crowd the sidewalks of Canal Street, the central business district of Chinatown. Shopkeepers hawk wares from every available nook: batteries and audiotapes, scarves, T-shirts, jewelry, and food of every description, from lobsters to doughnuts. As of 1989, there were hundreds of Chinese businesses located in the Chinatown area; indeed, the pull of the ethnic market was so great as to make commercial rents higher than any in other business areas, save the most prestigious downtown locations.

Neither population concentrations on the scale of the nineteenth century nor the presence of groups as entrepreneurially active as Jews or Chinese are necessary to support a cadre of ethnic business owners serving a local, ethnic market. In Providence, Rhode Island, where Italian immigrants and their children made up 14% of the city population by 1914, a local retail enclave developed that eventually provided employment to more than a tenth of the male immigrants in the city's major Italian enclave (Smith 1985). The relatively small Italian community of St. Louis, with a population of 7,500 in 1915, supported 557 pasta factories in 1919 (Mormino 1986: 99). Similar evidence about Italian business activity was reported for Pittsburgh, Cleveland, and other American cities in the first part of the twentieth century (Barton 1975; Bodnar et al. 1982).

In contrast to immigrants, black Americans have not prospered in business, as we have seen in Chapter 2. However, one can still observe a significant relationship between black population concentrations and the emergence of a black business enclave. Starting in the 1900s, blacks from the southern United States moved north in growing numbers and crowded into areas like Chicago's South Side, New York's Harlem, and Cleveland's Hough District. As they did so, black business enclaves also emerged, although on a smaller scale than in immigrant communities.

In 1899, W.E.B. DuBois found only 63 black-owned businesses in New York, but soon after, businesses proliferated to service the tastes of the new arrivals from the South (Scheiner 1965). "The great influx of Afro-Americans into New York has made ... possible a great number and variety of business enterprises," editorialized the *New York Age* in 1907 (cited in Osofsky 1966: 32). In 1909, a decade after DuBois's study, George Haynes counted 300 black-owned businesses in New York (Henri 1976). Osofsky (1966: 32) noted how many businesses, "saloons, barbershops — the plethora of small businesses necessary to satisfy a community's need — catered to the newcomers. Restaurants advertised special "southern-style' breakfasts and dinners. Negro grocers specialized in Virginia fruits, vegetables, and chickens. Migrants asked friends to send them special southern delicacies."

Black business growth was greatest in the first-settled and most densely black area of Harlem: In the late 1930s, two-thirds of the businesses in this section were black-owned (Frazier 1937). In Chicago, rapid growth of the black population after 1915 created a "black market." Whereas there had been only 500 black businesses on the eve of the great migration, by 1938 the South Side counted 2,600 black-owned commercial establishments (Spear 1967). In Cleveland, the number of black retail dealers increased almost tenfold between 1910 and 1930, and the city's growing, highly ghettoized population provided a base for new ventures among newspaper publishers, undertakers, real estate operators, and other entrepreneurs (Kusmer 1976). Blacks pouring into Detroit during and after World War I congregated in a rapidly growing ghetto that provided a market for a small but growing group of black entrepreneurs. The first directory of Detroit's black community listed 11 undertakers, 37 real estate dealers, and a score of small retail establishments of new or secondhand goods (Zunz 1982).

In Britain, the business experience of Afro-Caribbeans reveals a clear echo of the experience of American blacks. Afro-Caribbean businesses rely heavily on the custom of coethnics and are heavily concentrated in areas with substantial black populations (Brooks 1983; Sawyer 1983; Wilson and Stanworth 1983). Lines of business also show substantial concentration: construction firms, beauty and hairdressing salons, entertainment, the motor trades, and travel businesses. Service activities are characteristic and there is a dearth of nonfood retailers, other than record shops.

In contrast with West Indians in the United States, whose entrepreneurial achievements are often favorably compared with those of American-born blacks, West Indian business in Britain is frequently seen as restricted in scope and lacking in dynamism. The usual comparison is with the rapid proliferation of South Asian enterprises in the past two decades. Reeves and Ward (1984) suggested that one reason West Indian businesses in Britain are not more numerous is that the West Indian community is not segregated *enough*. West Indians share their residential areas with South Asians (especially in older, terraced housing areas) and with whites (especially in public housing areas). Various factors, including greater numbers and distinctive ethnic tastes, give Asians a competitive edge over West Indians in the terraced districts. In the public housing estates, there are relatively few and relatively expensive retail sites available, and those are ones for which white owners compete. Exclusively West Indian areas in British cities would not guarantee West Indian business success, but would certainly increase its chances.

Ethnic Residential Succession

The ethnic market provides a powerful stimulus to the growth of ethnic business, but other conditions — unrelated to the existence of distinct ethnic tastes — also further the development of a spatially concentrated ethnic economic enclave. Recent research in the United States and Britain shows that a critical factor for ethnic minorities is that they rarely start out in new areas, but instead inherit older neighborhoods previously inhabited by whites. Increases in the ethnic minority population do not necessarily lead to white flight, but whites prove reluctant to move into neighborhoods where the nonwhite proportion is on the rise. Because a high proportion of the population naturally moves in any one year, whites' refusal to settle in racially changing areas inevitably leads a neighborhood to turn from white to nonwhite (Aldrich 1975).

Changes in the composition of the residential population gradually lead to complementary shifts in the ranks of local entrepreneurs. Perhaps the first noticeable impact of succession on small businesses is that personal-service businesses begin to segregate by the identity of their clientele: Taverns, for example, might cater either to whites or to blacks. Eventually, an entire local shopping area may be taken over by the expanding group. Because the new population has different tastes, and, very likely, lower income, demand drops for particular kinds of goods and services. Specialty shops and stores carrying high-quality goods lose their market, especially as white middle-class shoppers refuse to come back into the area. Highly specialized stores go out of business, while more flexible stores change their products and prices. Patterns of recruitment into local business simultaneously change. The proportion of whites decreases, not because of whites leaving, but because a changing neighborhood can no longer attract new white owners, who instead establish businesses in areas that are predominantly white. Given a naturally high rate of failure among all small businesses, vacancies arise and they are filled by businesses started by members of ethnic minority groups (Aldrich 1975).

Studies of white, black, and Puerto Rican businesses in the United States, and of Asian and white businesses in Britain, have documented the impact of changes in ethnic residential composition on the opportunities for minority business owners. The pattern is for the proportion of native white businesses to diminish at a fairly constant rate across industry types in the early stages of succession, with retail and service businesses slightly more likely to leave; in the latter stages of succession, the loss of retail and service businesses is substantial and disproportionate, compared with other kinds of business. Much of the change over time in the industry distribution of white-owned business is due to a decline in retail consumers' goods and food sales businesses. It is not surprising that much of the gain in the minority business population occurs in precisely these industries, as minority entrepreneurs take advantage of newly vacated niches (Aldrich and Reiss 1976; Aldrich et al. 1989).

Neighborhoods may be the starting point of ethnic business, and remain an important magnet for ethnically oriented services and customers, but expansion beyond the neighborhood or the ethnic market is critical if businesses are to grow. The problem in communities where business is strictly neighborhood-linked is that the ethnic market can support only a limited number of firms, in part because it is quantitatively small, and in part because the ethnic population often lacks sufficient buying power.

The constraining impact of the local ethnic market is highlighted by the situation in many American black communities, where the low incomes of residents restrict the range of possible business activities. The fact that white-to-black succession occurs in the oldest neighborhoods means that the commercial infrastructure is so old and out of date that it attracts only marginal producers (Harries 1971). Black shopping areas also lack the goods and prices that consumers desire. Neighborhoods with large black populations have higher prices; a poorer selection of brands, prices, and sizes; dirtier stores; and poorer quality of fresh products (Hall 1983). As areas turn from white to black, the number and variety of goods-supplying businesses declines while the number of service activities increases, making it difficult for black consumers to supply their needs from their local shopping centers (Rose 1970). Consequently, the departure of white businesses generally does lead to some increase in the black-owned business population, but the increase is too small to occupy all the businesses left by whites. The result is a slowly increasing vacancy rate, creating a scene familiar to ghetto residents: broken storefronts, shattered glass, and boarded-up or burned-out business sites (Aldrich and Reiss 1976).

Effects of Business Concentration
upon Subsequent Growth

Initial concentration of ethnic businesses in the ethnic neighborhood may stimulate further business expansion. Three consequences of business concentration are of particular importance: (1) the generation of agglomeration economies spawning further business development, (2) the promotion of ethnic identity through cultural dominance of an area, and (3) the development of an export platform from which ethnic firms can branch out into the larger market.

Agglomeration Economies

First, economies of agglomeration occur when ethnic firms proliferate and attract additional customers who are drawn by the size and diversity of the physical marketplace. Thus commercial enclaves anchored to a densely settled neighborhood ethnic market later become regional ethnic shopping centers. The Parisian Chinatown in the 13th arrondissement, for example, serves local Chinese customers, but it is also a center of commerce and services for the whole regional and even for the national Chinese population. Indeed, the Parisian Chinatown seems to be more a commercial center than a residential community (White et al. 1987). Similarly, Asian businesses in the Belgrave Road area in Leicester attract Asian and white shoppers from the local area but also lure so many Asian shoppers from outside the Leicester area that a regular bus service brings Asian shoppers from North London and the Continent (Ward 1987). In London's Soho, many of the Chinatown businesses — travel agencies, printing and book shops, sellers of kitchen equipment — provide for an essentially Chinese clientele coming from throughout Britain and Europe. On a more local scale, the same phenomenon is repeated in the smaller and less prosperous Chinatown in Liverpool.

Cultural Dominance

Second, these agglomeration economies spur additional growth. The size of the ethnic market now provides a scope for specialists whose services would otherwise not be in sufficient demand; greater customer traffic strengthens a group's dominance of an area, which in turn leads to high visibility for goods and services with a strong ethnic component. Thus the ethnic market becomes a place that ethnic shoppers frequent both for the goods they find available and for the role it plays in maintaining ethnic identity.

Miami's Little Havana commercial district is an example of an enclave dominated by one culture. The advertisements, posters, and billboards are mostly in Spanish, and neon store signs announce *Joyeria, Ferreteria,* or *Muebleria.* Cuba, Havana, or other place names are often included in a business's title. Small Cuban flags or stickers are prominently displayed in the shop windows. "Maps of Cuba, posters of Jose Marti with inspirational quotes by the Cuban patriot . . . and campaign posters for local politicians . . . are also found on many windows. Wall murals in the district depict other aspects of Cuban culture" (Boswell and Curtis 1984: 94).

As the concentrated, most visible center for ethnic goods and services, the enclave retains its customer base even after residential dispersion has occurred. The immigrant Jewish enclaves of Manhattan's Lower East Side, Paris's *Pletzl* (the *Marais*), and London's East End, for example, remained important cultural and commercial centers for Jews long after Jews had scattered to other areas. As of 1989, New York's Chinese population was rapidly spreading out to parts of the city beyond its historic Chinatown, as well as to the suburbs, but Chinatown continues to attract Chinese customers from all over the New York metropolitan area. Not only have service businesses proliferated, but the extraordinary street traffic supports hundreds of peddlers selling ethnic delicacies.

Branching Out

Third, the ethnic market may also serve as an export platform from which ethnic firms can expand. In the 1900s, Greek immigrants in the United States constituted an almost all-male community; the immigrants gathered in restaurants not just to find inexpensive meals, but for company and a familiar environment. This original clientele provided a base from which the first generation of immigrant restaurateurs could branch out. More important, the immigrant trade established a pool of skilled and managerial talent that eventually enabled Greek owners to penetrate beyond the narrow confines of the ethnic market and specialize in the provision of "American food" (Fairchild 1911; Saloutos 1964).

In the 1980s, Dominican and Colombian immigrants active in the construction-contracting business in New York City appeared to be enacting a similar development. Most of these immigrant business owners were engaged in additions and alterations work for an immigrant clientele. Immigrant customers patronized coethnics not only to search for savings, but also because they sought reliability, guaranteed by immigrant contractors' reputations in the community to which they were linked. These initial jobs are important in two respects: (1) They are small and, therefore, allow immigrants to start out at a relatively low level, and (2) they support immigrant contractors in assembling a skilled labor force and gaining efficiency and expertise, qualities that are gradually allowing them to expand into the broader market (Gallo 1983).

MANUFACTURING'S IMPORTANCE IN CONCENTRATING ETHNIC RESIDENTIAL POPULATIONS

The typical ethnic enclave is an emporium of retail trade. The ethnic population constitutes the market for the business: The concentration of coethnics in a single area provides the customer base from which local ethnic firms then grow. Ethnic firms also flourish in competitive, low-barrier manufacturing industries such as clothing. But in manufacturing the causal relationship between business locations and residential locations is no longer the same: Now the business locations are the cause, and the patterns of residence are an effect.

Perhaps the best example of this linkage is the evolving locational relationship between the New York clothing industry and the mainly Jewish immigrant workers and business owners who made their livelihoods in this trade. In the late nineteenth century, Jewish immigrants clustered in the Lower East Side at the edge of the factory and warehouse districts. The immigrants settled in a dense concentration because there was not yet a mass transportation network to move workers cheaply from home to work. Low wages and the instability of employment kept workers within close walking distance of nearby factories. In their heavily settled neighborhood, the immigrants found that information about job opportunities circulated rapidly. In turn, the tremendous immigrant population concentrations created a thriving ethnic enclave. As Kessner (1977: 136) argued in his study of Jewish and Italian immigrants in turn-of-the-century New York: "Congestion also produced economic dividends. The peddler, for instance, prospered as a result of the large concentrations; so did the many specialty shops that catered to an ethnic clientele. Moreover, the narrowly confined pattern of settlement made the "sweating system' possible."

At first, only those members of the community least dependent on employment in the needle trades could afford the move to newer neighborhoods beyond the central business district. Harlem, for example, gained a sizable Jewish population in the 1890s, but newcomers were more likely to be manufacturers, managers, professionals, clerks, or small business owners. Clothing workers were still underrepresented in this area as of 1900:

> The only major group of ghetto workers who could not easily live and work uptown were those employed in the needle trades. In their case, the absence of both local industry and efficient rapid transit linking workers with downtown factories may have been the determining factor limiting their numbers in the uptown settlement. (Gurock 1979: 40)

By contrast, the Brooklyn communities of Williamsburgh and Brownsville grew up as factory towns when elevated railway lines joined these Brooklyn areas to the Lower East Side. Lower land costs led Jewish factory owners to build their plants along these transportation links; workers recruited along ethnic and hometown lines then followed. The influx of jobs and workers created a real estate boom; small Jewish builders profited, building houses with commercial space on the ground floor. In turn, a self-enclosed enclave developed. In Brownsville, "shopping areas within the neighborhood, including a commercial "strip' on Pitkin Avenue and an open-air, pushcart market on Belmont Avenue, offered community residents a degree of self-sufficiency" (Zukin and Zwerman 1984: 5).

After 1905, rising wages and a burgeoning mass transit network allowed Jewish workers, as well as their bosses, to escape the Lower East Side. However, the locational requirements of the clothing industry exercised an important, though changing, influence, on the pattern of Jewish settlement. Up to 1910, the clothing industry was clustered on the Lower East Side, constrained from moving elsewhere by the need to find a pool of available labor. Gradually, between 1910 and 1930, the industry moved to a new area at the heart of the central business district known as the garment center.

The key factor in relocation was a change in the mode of selling. Prior to World War I, most garment manufacturers did most of their selling through a road force of traveling salesmen. After the war, stores sent buyers who visited the manufacturers in their showrooms and who were interested in comparing offerings without much loss of time. Consequently, the industry moved out of its original home into a newer district, adjacent to railroad and hotel facilities. The rest of the industry moved in the manufacturers' wake, because both contractors and suppliers needed a location close by for quick deliveries and frequent on-site, in-person consultation.

The Jewish geography of the 1920s reflected the locational linkage to the newly established garment center. The most successful entrepreneurs moved out of the older, middle-class community of Harlem and settled in Manhattan's Upper West Side. This close-in, high-rent area was first linked to the new garment center by subway in 1918 and gained another connection in 1925. Thus in 1915

> men who listed themselves as manufacturers of clothing or the sundries used by the garment trade comprised less than 3 percent of a sample of Jewish West Side household heads. A decade later, they represented a startling 51 percent of a similar sample of the same kind of households. (Berroll 1987: 21)

As for workers, they too dispersed along transportation routes that tied them directly to the garment center. Having lower incomes than their bosses, they spilled out into areas that were more distant from the garment center and, therefore, less expensive than the Upper West Side.

Manufacturing is no longer a thriving activity in the urban industrial economies where today's immigrants work. For those ethnic minorities active in the clothing industry, however, the linkage between work and residence remains an important influence on the location of the ethnic community. Indeed, the situation of New York's Chinese immigrant garment industry parallels the story recounted above.

Chinese Garment Manufacturers in New York City

In the early 1960s, there was no Chinese garment industry in New York City, just a handful of small shops. Starting in the late 1960s, however, their numbers grew quickly: By 1970, there were just over

100 shops; five years later, the number had more than doubled; by 1980, there were 430; by 1986, the count stood at 460. Four factors, in addition to the large influx of new immigrants resulting from the 1965 change in U.S. immigration laws, account for this phenomenal growth: (1) Garment shops were a viable alternative to traditional Chinese businesses; (2) suitable premises were available at cheap rents; (3) residential concentration provided a near-at-hand Chinese labor force; and (4) the areas of Chinese garment manufacturing were near enough to the traditional garment district that subcontracting arrangements were feasible.

First, in the garment industry, the newcomers found a viable alternative to the limits of the traditional ethnic economy. The old Chinese ethnic economy was rooted in restaurants, laundries, and the tourist trade. Laundries, however, were a dying business — there were only so many tourists to be attracted to Chinatown, and setting up a restaurant required considerable skills and capital. A garment shop, by contrast, required little in terms of initial investment. The exodus of older ethnics from the ranks of small entrepreneurs created opportunities for newcomers to take their chances.

Second, local circumstances produced attractive low-rent opportunities for shop owners. Chinatown bordered on an old industrial district, filled with antiquated loft buildings occupied by the machinery and printing trades. As New York's manufacturing sector crumbled in the late 1960s and early 1970s, these spaces emptied out. Their old occupants either went out of business or modernized, which meant a move to better, larger quarters. As lofts became vacant, rents tumbled, and Chinese garment factories became the inheritors. Throughout the 1970s, this filtering-down process continued, making low-cost space available at advantageous lease terms.

Once in place, the immigrant garment industry quickly acquired a dynamic of its own. The demand for labor to staff the local garment factories affected the stream of newcomers to New York; compared with other cities, New York received a disproportionate number of low-skilled newcomers from China, Hong Kong, and Taiwan. Moreover, while many of the newcomers to New York moved to Queens or Brooklyn, those immigrants who gravitated to the garment industry during the late 1960s and 1970s were far more likely to settle in Chinatown. In 1980, for example, just under half of the roughly 20,000 Chinese members of the largest local of the International Ladies' Garment Workers' Union lived in Chinatown, whereas only a quarter of the city's Chinese population made Chinatown their home.

Third, for the immigrants, residence in Chinatown provided the convenience of being able to walk to work. Proximity to the area's concentration of jobs was also a sort of unemployment insurance, because if any one employer went under or laid workers off, there was likely to be another job vacant in one of the scores of factories close at hand. Employers also gained from this arrangement: A nearby source of labor provided a constant supply of workers looking for jobs, and proximity kept teenagers, mothers of young children, and older workers, who might not have commuted long distances to work, readily available for work in a local factory.

Fourth, the area's concentration of garment factories provided a convenient production base for manufacturers needing a local contracting shop. Though not adjacent to the garment center, Chinatown's contracting facilities were sufficiently near for the type of regular, person-to-person interaction that New York manufacturers need. Shops could be visited daily; shipments could be sent frequently, even in small quantities; and a manufacturer's production supervisor could be kept rotating from one close-by factory to another on a full-time basis.

Of course, since the early years of Chinese garment manufacturing, both garment jobs and garment workers have scattered widely over the New York metropolitan area. Nonetheless, as with the Jewish-dominated needle trades, the pattern of Chinese dispersion is linked to transportation networks providing connections with the main center of Chinese garment manufacture. The new Chinese population concentrations in Queens and Brooklyn have grown up along the subway lines that link these second areas of settlement to the original Chinatown community. Now that the buildup of people and commercial businesses has pushed up rents beyond a level that garment contractors can afford, Chinese clothing factories are sprouting in the newer neighborhoods of Chinese settlement.

ETHNIC ENTREPRENEURS AS MIDDLEMEN

In the dense ethnic settlements like Chinatown, Little Havana, London's Brick Lane, or Paris's *Goutte d'Or*, ethnic business owners serve members of their own populations. There may also be a viable niche for ethnic proprietors whose market is the majority population, and ethnic groups that specialize in trading with the majority population can be characterized as "middleman minorities." Traditionally, middleman minorities have been associated with precapitalist societies, where they often dominated trading and commercial activities. Spanish Jews, for example, played a critical role in international commerce in the Middle Ages, and Armenians controlled the overland trade between Europe and the Middle East well into the nineteenth century. Today, Lebanese Christians are found in middleman positions throughout the Near East and Africa, while in Lebanon itself, the small Armenian community remains disproportionately engaged in small and large industry (Armstrong 1976).

Though attenuated and confined to peripheral economic activities, the role of the middleman minority persists in advanced industrial societies. Jews, Koreans, Indians, and Chinese, in particular, exemplify those ethnic minorities whose overrepresentation in self-employment results from their success in finding customers outside their limited ethnic markets.

Doing business outside the ethnic community alters the distribution of ethnic businesses, because ethnic firms must now locate where their customers live. As businesses spread out across a wider territory, ethnic owners tend to follow — especially in those lines where the business demands long hours or personal attention. Evidence from various studies underlines the distinctive spatial characteristics of middleman minority groups. The Chinese in Britain "are associated with the family restaurant trade and therefore dispersed in urban neighborhoods, suburbs, and small towns throughout the country" (Watson 1977: 181). They live and work in areas where they have easy access to a large middle-class clientele. Watson (1977) claimed that, around 1970, the market for ethnic restaurants became saturated, and this led to a re-migration of Chinese restaurateurs from Britain to continental Europe, with the small towns of West Germany — along with the cities of Scandinavia — becoming the new frontiers of Chinese restaurant development.

Similar cases of a dispersed minority population serving majority customers are to be found in the *Sylheti* (Bangladeshi) restaurant owners and workers in Britain's urban areas (Carey and Shukur 1985-1986). Residentially dispersed Lebanese Muslims of Toledo, Ohio, operate bars, liquor stores, and restaurants in the city and clearly serve a mainly non-Muslim clientele (Zenner 1982). In Puerto Rico, Cuban refugees are overrepresented in business but are scattered across a series of business sites, in contrast to the situation in Miami, where Little Havana contains an extraordinary concentration of Cuban firms (Cobas 1987).

The centrifugal pull of serving a broader market is perhaps best illustrated by the case of Korean immigrants in the United States, as we discussed in Chapter 2. These newcomers have reported very high levels of self-employment. In 1980, 11.5% of the economically active Korean adults who had moved to the United States in the prior decade were self-employed. Tabulations from the 5% Public Use Sample for the cities with the largest Korean population show that self-employment rates for Korean immigrant males ranged from a low of 19% in Chicago to a high of 35% in New York. Despite these extraordinarily high levels of self-employment, the Korean population has not clustered in dense, homogeneous settlements. Though they are recent arrivals, a high proportion of Koreans live in the suburban areas that surround the central cities of the metropolitan areas. Data for the five SMSAs with the largest Korean population show that, in each SMSA, the proportion of Korean immigrants living outside the central city is close to or even greater than the average for the total population of those SMSAs.

More detailed analysis of Korean residential patterns have also uncovered a pattern of dispersion and frequent geographic mobility (Light and Bonacich 1988). An analysis of Koreans in Los Angeles showed that almost half (46%) of the Korean population lived in central Los Angeles, but that no zip code area in the very densest areas of Korean settlement contained more than 15% of the total Korean population. Similarly, analysis of mobility patterns based on telephone listings for individuals with common Korean surnames found that only 11% of the listings in the core Korean area survived over a five-year period during the 1970s; telephone interviews suggested that the core Korean area served as a short-term base of settlement for new immigrants, who then rapidly moved on to much less heavily Korean areas in the suburbs. Korean businesses are equally dispersed in their locations. For example, in Los Angeles County, California, there is a sizable concentration of businesses in Koreatown (Light and Bonacich 1988). But the Los Angeles Koreatown contains only one-third of the Korean firms in the county, and there are Korean businesses in 87% of the almost 10,000 postal districts in the county.

Middleman minorities often disperse, but their pursuit of market opportunities frequently takes them into areas different from those of the majority population. In the United States, black and Hispanic communities provide a particularly important market for middleman minority groups such as Koreans, Indians, Arabs, and Chinese, who have adapted their business locations to the residential concentrations of blacks and Hispanics. Minority communities lack the buying power needed to purchase higher-value items that in turn attract retail chains, and greater security costs make poorer minority areas unattractive to individual owners. The processes of ecological succession, discussed earlier, further diminish the supply of potential native white proprietors. When chain operations and native-owned stores shun such areas, middleman minority entrepreneurs often will serve them.

Japanese Americans in pre-World War II Los Angeles, for example, moved outward from the old Japantown by dispersing into areas of recent black population growth, as these areas also provided the customer base for Japanese businesses. After 1945, Chinese immigrant entrepreneurs replaced, to some extent, the Japanese, whose properties had been confiscated during the war. These Chinese business owners also sought to widen their markets beyond the ethnic enclave by gaining a black clientele. In 1970, the bulk of Chinese groceries in Los Angeles were in poor, mainly black neighborhoods.

Black and Hispanic markets are particularly important for Korean merchants. In Los Angeles County, half of the Korean businesses located outside of the main Korean enclave were concentrated in the mainly black and Hispanic sections as of 1977. In Atlanta, a city where the Korean population is too small to support an ethnic Korean economic enclave, almost 60% of Korean businesses in 1982 were found in the inner city or in areas that were at least half black (Min 1988).

THE EVOLUTION OF ETHNIC BUSINESSES

Thus far, our discussion has proceeded as if particular ethnic groups catered exclusively *either* to the population of coethnics *or* to a population of other ethnic groups. Such polarization is rarely wholly complete. In the first place, market linkages shift over time: An enclave business pattern may evolve into a middleman minority situation, and, conversely, a middleman business practice sometimes gives way to ethnic exclusivity. Several examples illustrate the range of permutations that ethnic businesses might undergo.

The history of Chinese and Japanese businesses in California is one of progression from reliance on primarily Oriental trade to heavy penetration of the majority market. During the California Gold Rush,

Chinese enclaves in California cities functioned as service, retailing, and entertainment centers for the much larger number of immigrants working in the hinterlands as miners or construction laborers. As mining and railway building receded, the Chinese drifted back to the cities; many took up the laundry trade. Profits in the laundry business were too narrow to support an extensive delivery network, and clients were also reluctant to travel long distances to bring in their clothes. Consequently, the laundries dispersed out of the Chinatowns. They moved first into the central business districts, and once these areas filled in, they spread out into white residential districts (Ong 1981).

Similarly, Japanese immigrants in Southern California at the turn of the twentieth century flocked to Los Angeles's Little Tokyo from the railroads and other seasonal jobs where they had originally found work. With the arrival of the immigrants came a bunkhouse system of labor contracting, with the owners of the boardinghouses doubling as labor contractors. Labor contracting bound the Japanese community together: "To achieve such organization, as for recruitment and outfitting, the close proximity and clear communications offered by Little Tokyo were crucial" (Modell 1977: 63). Several streets in Little Tokyo had few, if any, non-Japanese residents; in turn, concentration gave rise to businesses, such as billiard halls and express and forwarding companies, that serviced the immigrant workers. But as laborers became proprietors, Little Tokyo's population thinned out. Most Japanese business owners found their customers outside the ethnic community. Entrepreneurs who continued to serve their coethnics found that their businesses grew slowly and in proportion to the overall growth of the Japanese population.

Other groups have moved in directions different from those of the Californian Chinese and Japanese. In Britain, early South Asian migrants performed middleman minority functions as peddlers, and subsequently opened shops catering to their kinsmen who arrived in the mass migration of the 1950s (Ballard and Ballard 1977). Bangladeshi involvement in British retailing appears to have derived from their nineteenth-century employment in galley work in the British Merchant Navy, many of whose ships were crewed by Asian seamen of various nationalities. Bangladeshi galley workers subsequently established shore-based cafés in dockland areas. In the 1960s, a congregation of cafés was established in the Brick Lane area of Tower Hamlets as a response to the growth of the Bangladeshi population. Since then, many of these establishments have developed into restaurants aimed specifically at the white middle-class market stemming from nearby medical and educational institutions. Meanwhile, the expansion of the local Asian population has allowed the creation of a local infrastructure of food and clothing stores, travel agencies, and other services for the minority population.

The succession of new for old populations — as in Brick Lane, where Bangladeshis replaced Jews — may also convert an ethnic enclave into a middleman minority situation. For example, the Jewish businesses on Chicago's South Side, in New York's Harlem, and on Detroit's East Side started out as establishments serving a local Jewish clientele. When the Jewish population moved out and the areas became dense concentrations of black migrants, Jewish merchants found themselves selling to blacks. Wirth (1928: 237), who found that the Jewish peddlers on Chicago's Maxwell Street did a substantial business with a non-Jewish clientele, argued that "the prosperity of the ghetto fluctuates with the employment and earnings of the immigrant and Negro laborers in the industries of Chicago."

The sudden exodus of Jews from Harlem after 1925, and their virtual disappearance from the area after 1930, left the community with a large infrastructure of Jewish businesses that only grudgingly adapted to their new clientele (Osofsky 1966). A contemporary counterpart can be found in several of New York's immigrant Hispanic neighborhoods: These areas served as Cuban refugee enclaves in the 1960s, but later lost their Cuban populations as the refugees prospered and moved to better-quality neighborhoods. Cuban businesses, however, remained behind to serve an immigrant clientele of Dominicans and other Latin Americans.

Stages of Change

Despite varying permutations, there is a logical sequence of ethnic business patterns: The succession of business stages is linked to the changes occurring in ethnic communities. This sequence is suggested by Ward's (1984) study of South Asian self-employment in British cities, where he defines five types of business involvement. Two of these are "nonsettlement," essentially the absence of both Asian residents and Asian business, and "general," a situation where all of the remaining types occur in the same city. The other three types are "replacement labor," "ethnic niche," and "middleman minority."

These types can be conceived of as an ideal-typical developmental sequence: The sequence of stages may apply both to the ethnic commu-

Table 4.1 Business-Settlement Patterns: Developmental Sequence

		Population Concentration	
		High	Low
	High	Ethnic Niche	Middleman Minority
Business Specialization			
	Low	Replacement Minority	Economic Assimilation

nity as a whole and to the careers of individual entrepreneurs. As shown in Table 4.1, by cross-classifying the two dimensions of (1) ethnic population concentration and (2) the extent to which ethnic owners specialize in a narrow or broad range of business types, four patterns are derived: (a) replacement labor — a highly concentrated residential population and a small, specialized business population offering a narrow range of goods and services; (b) ethnic niche — a residentially concentrated population specializing in a wide range of jobs and business types; (c) middleman minority — residentially dispersed ethnic populations in which business owners provide a broad range of goods and services to groups other than their own; and (d) economic assimilation — an ethnic population that is widely dispersed, with business owners offering goods and services typical of the majority business population.

For immigrants incorporated into the secondary labor market, the sequence unfolds as follows. At the community level, the replacement labor phase involves new migrants occupying otherwise unwanted jobs in the lower tiers of the white economy — jobs in declining manufacturing industries, such as clothing, or menial jobs in service industries, such as restaurants and building cleaning services. At this stage, immigrants will typically live close together in the inner city for reasons of ethnic solidarity and economy. Few migrants have either the capital or the motivation to enter business. Because many newcomers see themselves as temporary migrants, the situational pressures are likely to impede their pursuit of business opportunities. Temporary migrants are so preoccupied with making money for their return trip that they become isolated socially and are slow to acquire the contacts and skills needed to start a business.

A second stage may be called the "ethnic niche." As time passes, the scale of the immigrant population grows, often associated with the arrival of wives and the birth of children (Piore 1979). The size of the minority market is now sufficient to sustain the development of businesses that cater mainly to an ethnic clientele. Immigrant business owners gain clients because immigrants have special tastes and needs that lead them to patronize their coethnics' shops. In addition, a substantial amount of business involves goods or services that have no ethnic content because of opportunities opened by ecological succession—immigrants emerge as replacements for white owners whose shops close because of failure or retirement.

The third stage emerges when immigrant owners in the ethnic niche use their developing skills, contacts, and capital and begin serving the population at large. Service to the majority population often begins with newsstands, grocery stores, and restaurants, which require long opening hours and where the return to investment in skills and capital is too low to attract native labor. The development of businesses that place an immigrant group in a middleman minority relationship to its customers, in turn, leads to a more dispersed pattern of settlement, as the distribution of the group's businesses now increasingly resembles the distribution of the general population.

While the growth of the ethnic niche creates the potential for business involvements outside the ethnic community, this stage may be realized only to a limited extent. In many instances, ethnic businesses remain confined to the residential concentrations from which a mainly coethnic clientele is drawn (Aldrich, Cater, et al. 1985).

An alternative sequence may occur in which the replacement labor phase is of limited duration, because the middleman minority stage is rapidly entered. This sequence could arise when a short initial *replacement labor phase* is followed by rapid entry into entrepreneurial positions being vacated by native whites. Under these circumstances, a significant immigrant business sector catering to another population arises before their own ethnic residential population is large enough to support an ethnic niche of its own. Because the general population constitutes the market, and the long hours demanded by shopkeeping add to the costs of commuting, middleman minorities will settle close to their customers rather than in proximity to one another. Thus, under these circumstances, we would expect only a slight relationship between ethnic residential patterns and the location of ethnic businesses.

Over time, the demand for replacement workers for the general economy and replacement entrepreneurs for the middleman minority niche produces that critical mass of coethnics needed to support a spatially concentrated ethnic business niche. Owners in this niche, however, are not totally dependent on locally residing coethnics for their clientele, because the concentration of ethnic businesses may serve as a "central business district" for the immigrant group at large, attracting coethnics from a broader geographic area.

One final permutation might be added to the sequence of stages mapped out thus far: economic assimilation. In this stage, there is a complementarity between the spatial and occupational dimensions of ethnic assimilations: As ethnic minorities take on the residential pattern of the host society, they become more similar to the "others" among whom they live. The Japanese of California appear to fit the entire sequence particularly well, with manual work in agriculture, followed by businesses catering first to the minority itself and then to the population at large, and in the third generation abandoning business for the professions. The pattern for the Japanese coincides with the experience of other U.S. ethnic groups whose rates of self-employment have declined steadily over the generations.

Arrested and Accelerated Development

This sequence can be most generally applied if we recognize not only a developmental sequence but also the possibilities of arrested or accelerated development. In the late nineteenth century, blacks living in U.S. cities tended toward a dispersed residential pattern, reflecting both their occupational attachments to white households (e.g., as domestics) and the integration of the small black elite with whites. As we noted in Chapter 2, black businesses were mainly in personal services — catering, barbershops, and express services. These service businesses had grown out of the personal and domestic trades in which blacks were concentrated and served a mainly white clientele. Increased competition from the foreign-born, the rising tide of racism, and the tightening color line pushed blacks out of these traditional trades by the late nineteenth century and forced the growing number of blacks, recruited to replace the labor flows shut off from Europe, into tightly confined ghettos. Consequently, both the nature and the location of black businesses changed.

Black barbershops, one of the more important black business lines, served a white public and were often located in downtown areas. When European immigrants replaced black barbers, who in turn opened up hair parlors catering to a black clientele, the businesses moved into ghetto locations (DuBois 1899; Katzman 1973; Meier 1962). In Detroit, black professionals and businessmen were relatively dispersed in the last two decades of the nineteenth century, but found themselves entrapped in the ghetto by 1920. Studies of Raleigh, North Carolina, and Birmingham, Alabama, show that prior to 1900, black businesses were interspersed among white establishments in the downtown area, but thereafter were pushed onto a "Negro Main Street" (Carter 1960; James 1975). Before 1900, Chicago's black market was small and served only by the less lucrative restaurants, barbershops, and small stores in the city's scattered black enclaves, and most businesses were oriented toward a white clientele (Meier 1962). Once the Great Migration gathered steam, black business became strictly a ghetto affair.

Though greater numbers and concentration have produced some business growth in black ghettos, the size of the black business enclave has remained permanently stunted. Even in the densest black neighborhoods, black owners have never achieved dominance over the local business area, nor have their establishments garnered more than a small share of the purchases made by black clientele. Ironically, black business owners have been too undercapitalized to take advantage of the black population base massed in the ghettos and hence have had to settle for inferior locations. De A. Reid (1940), who undertook one of the battery of supplementary studies prepared for Myrdal's *American Dilemma,* noted that black grocery stores were isolated even within the black community. Black householders complained that black establishments were inconveniently located.

Another survey of black businesses conducted in the 1940s found that most black businesses were located off the main ghetto shopping streets, in small business clusters serving nearby customers or in isolated locations where no other commercial stores were to be found. Ultimately, competition from other entrepreneurs, lack of skills, weak ties to coethnics who might have provided capital and other forms of support, and the impoverished state of the customer base kept black business arrested in an early phase of the ethnic niche stage.

Just as business development might be arrested in the ethnic niche stage, so too is it possible that ethnic concentration in business and self-employment might persist even after a group has lost much of its geographical distinctiveness. Thus Jewish Americans have moved away from the pattern of concentrated settlement characteristic of the first and second generations. Jews began by clustering in areas of extraordinarily dense Jewish population — in 1892, approximately 75% of New York's Jewish population lived in the Lower East Side — but then dispersed from this first area of settlement, adopting a multinucleated pattern in which they lived in a number of spatially distinct, yet heavily Jewish, areas.

With the advent of the third and fourth generations, however, more Jews have chosen (and have had the incomes) to live in suburban areas with lower Jewish populations. A 1975 survey of Jews in the Boston area, for example, found that "most Jews (65%) lived in census tracts classified as medium in Jewish concentration, with twice as many living in areas of low Jewish concentration as in areas of high Jewish concentration" (Goldscheider 1985). Returns from the 1981 New York Area Jewish Population Survey showed that almost half of the Jewish population lived in the suburbs, that the Jewish population was growing most rapidly in areas of low Jewish population, and that the proportion of Jews living in areas of dense Jewish concentration declined steadily with subsequent generations (Ritterband and Cohen 1984).

Despite geographical dispersion, Jews remain disproportionately self-employed. Population surveys in Jewish communities, large and small, old and new, declining and expanding, show that high levels of self-employment continue to characterize settlements that are now quite distant from the original immigrant generation. Indeed, concentration has persisted despite a shift from business to the professions; the data indicate that Jews are more likely than other ethnoreligious groups to be working for themselves, even when compared with their counterparts in such fields as medicine, law, or accounting (Goldscheider 1985).

CONCLUSIONS

To recognize a sequence of different minority business involvements is not to deny the possibility of their simultaneity. On the contrary, business development is likely to be uneven, and businesses catering to a minority population are likely to coexist with those aiming for the majority market. The problems of immigrant adaptation are quick to give rise to "adjustment entrepreneurs" (ethnic real estate agents, ethnic professionals, and so on) early on in the replacement labor stage. Later, an ethnic business enclave may develop in incipient form, but provide neither the bulk of business services nor substantial local employment to a population mainly engaged in ethnic labor. Even in the most vibrant enclaves, business development will sooner, rather than later, reach its ceiling unless it can branch off into the broader market, given the limited size of the ethnic population. Thus even a highly encapsulated community, like the Chinese in New York, maintains an enclave economy in Chinatown and in newer Chinese settlements, and middleman-type establishments in areas of little or no Chinese settlement (in business lines such as laundries, restaurants, and variety stores).

Any culturally distinctive group will generate demands for specific goods and services not demanded by the general market. Such tastes cannot be met in shops with locations selected to serve a nonminority population. Hence, if ethnic tastes are to continue being served, specialist centers of ethnic businesses for middleman minorities must emerge. And finally, the waning of ethnicity, occurring in the last stage of the sequence, is likely to be tempered by the persistence of old, if attenuated, ethnic enclaves. If, as Gans (1979) has argued, ethnicity is largely "symbolic" for the third and later generations of white ethnic Americans, the symbols of ethnicity may be kept alive by aging ethnic populations and the distinctive cultural tastes that they maintain.

5

Ethnic Entrepreneurs and Ethnic Strategies

Jeremy Boissevain
Jochen Blaschke
Hanneke Grotenbreg
Isaac Joseph
Ivan Light
Marlene Sway
Roger Waldinger
Pnina Werbner

In this chapter, we explore the *strategies* ethnic entrepreneurs employ to meet problems related to their enterprises. Strategies emerge from the interaction of group characteristics and opportunity structures, as entrepreneurs mobilize resources to meet market conditions, adapting to or creating solutions to problems. Many entrepreneurs from minority groups began their careers as immigrants, often lacking the skills and capital necessary to begin a business. They arrive as strangers in a new country, in time carving out for themselves an entrepreneurial niche in an ongoing economic system, using distinctive strategies. Although predisposing factors make each group unique to some extent, our research discovered a strong element of similarity across all the groups we studied.

The evidence presented is derived from research conducted separately among seven groups of minority entrepreneurs in Britain, France, the United States, West Germany, and the Netherlands. The groups studied are Gypsies in the United States (Marlene Sway), Koreans in

131

Los Angeles (Ivan Light), Chinese in New York (Roger Waldinger), North Africans in Lyon (Isaac Joseph), Pakistanis in Manchester (Pnina Werbner), Turks in West Berlin (Jochen Blaschke), and Surinamese — composed of immigrants of Afro-Caribbean ("Creole"), Hindustani, and Chinese descent — in Amsterdam (Jeremy Boissevain). Using an actor-oriented rather than an institution-oriented approach, we focus on the individuals who form businesses and on their embeddedness within their ethnic groups (Granovetter 1985; Long 1977: 153).

ETHNIC RESOURCES AND ETHNIC STRATEGIES

Although based on the observation of disparate groups in diverse national settings, our results nevertheless converge around the claim that ethnic entrepreneurs utilize similar strategies and sociocultural resources in the resolution of business problems. Quite apart from the socioeconomic resources they may possess, especially their wealth and human capital, ethnic entrepreneurs also draw upon their group characteristics, which we label "ethnic resources," in the context of strategy formulation. Ethnic resources are sociocultural features of a group that coethnic business owners utilize in business or from which their businesses passively benefit (Light and Bonacich 1988: 178). Ethnic resources characterize a group, not just its isolated members. Typical ethnic resources include *predisposing factors* — cultural endowments, relative work satisfaction arising from nonacculturation to prevailing labor standards, and a sojourning orientation — and modes of *resource mobilization* — ethnic social networks and access to a pool of under-employed coethnic labor.

Ethnic business strategies reflect the effective disposition of each ethnic group's social, cultural, and economic resources. As such, ethnic business strategies are conscious and centralized at the level of the individual enterprises whose owners/operators assess and exploit resources they individually control. However, ethnic strategies are also collective in two other senses.

First, ethnic trade associations are sometimes in a position to channel ethnic commerce in one direction rather than another. This direct influence can affect how ethnic minorities perceive niches and then open them for their own commercial exploitation. Second, because the resources most available to individual entrepreneurs are those common to the whole ethnic group, individual entrepreneurs independently

Table 5.1 Seven Common Business Problems That Confront Ethnic Entrepreneurs

---

1. How do ethnic or immigrant entrepreneurs acquire the information needed for the establishment and survival of their firms?

2. How do they obtain the capital needed to establish or to expand their business?

3. How do they acquire the training and skills needed to run a small business?

4. How do they recruit and manage efficient, honest, and cheap workers?

5. How do they manage relations with customers and suppliers?

6. How do they survive strenuous business competition?

7. How do they protect themselves from political attacks?

---

adopt similar strategies. Thus if a strong family structure represents a resource of a group, individual entrepreneurs from that group will exploit their family structure in business. They will seek/select a niche where family structure represents an important resource. Although no coordinated master plan exists, parallel decisions of the ethnic entrepreneurs push the ethnic group into selected niches. In this sense, a collective ethnic strategy develops without conscious, centralized coordination as long as ethnic entrepreneurs have access to sociocultural resources that are different from those of mainstream entrepreneurs.

These "outsider" strategies and resources distinguish ethnic entrepreneurs from mainstream entrepreneurs (Wilken 1979: 22) — ethnic or immigrant entrepreneurs are more than just mainstream entrepreneurs who also happen to belong to a legally, ethnically, or phenotypically distinct population subclass. Hence the study of ethnic entrepreneurship represents a theoretical specialty within the broader field of entrepreneurship research. This chapter focuses on seven problems with which all entrepreneurs must contend, attempting to show that ethnic entrepreneurs bring distinctive resources and strategies to the solution of these common business problems, as listed in Table 5.1.

Information

Information and advice are essential for entrepreneurs. Before starting their enterprises, entrepreneurs need information about markets, the availability of premises, and laws. Once established, they need information about supplies, prices, warnings of market fluctuations, successful products, industrial trends, and so forth. They also must locate reliable specialists who can help them with fiscal problems and provide legal advice, capital, and labor.

Direct ties in their own personal networks are of value (Aldrich and Zimmer 1986), and beyond these, ethnic entrepreneurs rely upon information received via various indirect ties within their ethnic communities. The structuring of networks differs from person to person and also among ethnic groups. For example, among the Surinamese entrepreneurs in Amsterdam, those of Chinese and Asian descent have more hierarchically organized families and a clearer sense of family loyalty and joint responsibility than those of Afro-Caribbean (Creole) descent. Hindustanis in Amsterdam generally have a more wide-ranging set of relatives in the Netherlands than Afro-Caribbeans, and they also consult a larger range of business contacts, such as lawyers, financial specialists, and accountants (Boissevain and Grotenbreg 1986).

Not all members of a person's network provide equally valuable or trustworthy information. Acquaintances and distant relatives can be utilized for information, but intimate, stronger ties can be relied upon for personal loans, labor, preferential deals, or crucial services in times of emergency. Thus large networks with a range of assorted links are an essential part of the assets of successful entrepreneurs, who spend considerable time building their networks, testing them, and, especially, servicing them.

We found that ethnic entrepreneurs used a number of ritualized occasions to exchange information as well as to service their networks. Alumni associations and churches, for example, brought Koreans in Los Angeles together for purposes unrelated to business. After the meetings, the participants adjourned for an informal round of conversation during which they exchanged information about business conditions and techniques (Light and Bonacich 1988: 192-203). Kinship and friendship links provided the supporting linkages by which church members or fellow alumni referred one another to someone in a position to help. Thus if Kim asked Lee, a member of the same church congregation, for tax advice, Lee could refer Kim to Lee's cousin, an accountant, in whom Kim could repose his confidence. Kim trusted Lee because he is a member of the same religious congregation, and Kim trusted Lee's cousin because he is related to Lee. In this manner, the mesh of voluntary and ascriptive social ties greatly expands the personal relationships of trust available to individual Korean entrepreneurs, thus enhancing their ability to obtain reliable information (Light and Bonacich 1988: 192-203).

Large-scale domestic ceremonial occasions, such as weddings or funerals, allow entrepreneurs to incorporate new acquaintances into their current social networks while formally continuing to sustain their prior relations. We found that our entrepreneurs were particularly conscious of how they used these occasions to further both business and status interests (Werbner 1984, 1985a, 1985b).

Ethnic entrepreneurs also gather information from specialized associations and media. For example, in 1980 about 100 local Pakistani manufacturers in Britain set up the Northwest Clothing Association. They met twice a month and exchanged information about prices, costs, customers, and new orders. There was also a less effective Traders Association, founded by Pakistani wholesalers. Korean real estate developers and traders in Los Angeles set up the Koreatown Development Association, and Koreans involved in the garment trade established the Korean Sewing Contractors Association.

The Surinamese community in the Netherlands had not, as of 1985, founded specialized associations to service the interests of entrepreneurs, but some Surinamese magazines have featured articles on the various business activities in which members of the community are engaged. So, too, the Los Angeles Korean newspaper *Hankook Ilbo* ran a series on 16 successive dates that provided detailed information about selected enterprises. The articles covered retail shoe stores, real estate, florists, laundries and dry cleaners, grocery stores, jewelry stores, construction, architecture, auto body repairs, nightclubs, liquor stores, food wholesaling, restaurants, automobile dealerships, printing, and gift shops (Light and Bonacich 1988: 187-188). Korean associations also sponsored seminars on business problems, often with the collaboration of interested government agencies such as the Minority Business Development Administration or the franchise tax board.

Turkish entrepreneurs in West Berlin tried to develop association networks brought from their homeland, with political organizations the most stable. Early in the 1980s a left-wing *kemalist* group organized and attempted to mobilize Turkish entrepreneurs. Since then it has provided advice, particularly on taxation and law, and organized regular meetings. At one meeting, plans for a Turkish bank in Berlin were discussed. An association of Turkish motor mechanics was organized, based on an existing network of left-wing activists who came to Germany as students or political refugees, and their network was used for such things as the training of apprentice motor mechanics. A politico-religious association of businesspeople attempted to establish a chain of shops in Berlin dealing in foodstuffs prepared according to Islamic law. In the 1970s, large numbers joined this plan, but the chain quickly went bankrupt. Nevertheless, special contacts exist among the mosque associations, and business matters are often discussed in mosques (Blaschke and Ersoz 1986, 1987a, 1987b).

Government agencies in Britain and the Netherlands have also attempted to reach ethnic businessmen through various advisory services, with varying levels of success. In the Netherlands, for example, Surinamese entrepreneurs were poorly informed about the services, subsidies, and advice the government provided to small businessmen. This communication failure was primarily due to the reluctance, and often the inability, of specialized bureaucrats to reach immigrant entrepreneurs (Boissevain et al. 1984).

Aside from ethnic or governmental channels, considerable scope exists for individual initiative in obtaining information. Robert, an Afro-Caribbean travel agent, explained how he located business premises in Amsterdam:

> I didn't know one street from the next. I still remember: I arrived in Amsterdam early in the morning and saw several window washers. I went over to them and asked if they wanted a couple of beers that evening in exchange for noting empty premises suitable for a travel agency. That evening I obtained several addresses.

Much of the information essential to entrepreneurs is gathered through ethnic channels. The ability of an ethnic community to provide the full range of information and services essential to the success of an enterprise depends in part on the size of the community and the length of time it has been established. Pakistanis have been trading in Manchester since the early 1950s, starting as market traders, and they have branched out into wholesaling and manufacturing. Their children have moved up in the professions, achieving a high degree of horizontal and vertical integration so that virtually all information essential to the success of the various enterprises is obtained from within the Pakistani community. Surinamese Asian entrepreneurs have been active in Amsterdam for less than ten years, and thus the range of services and information that members of this community can provide is far more restricted, although it is growing.

Capital

All entrepreneurs require a certain amount of capital to establish their enterprises, and the range of starting capital we observed was considerable. We also observed variations in how such resources were mobilized. Gypsy fortune-tellers, along with Manchester market traders, required the least capital. All a Gypsy fortune-teller required to set up a business was access to a front room for her *ofisa* and a few beads and trinkets, including a saint's statue to set the scene. The initial capital outlay a Pakistani needed to open a market stall was about 3,000 pounds. At another extreme, Koreans had to mobilize considerable capital in Los Angeles to open a gasoline station ($100,000) or a restaurant ($300,000). Intermediate between these were the 50,000 guilders ($19,000) Asian Surinamese invested to establish a tropical fruit shop, whereas Afro-Caribbeans and North Africans needed to mobilize only about $10,000 to open a small café in Amsterdam or Lyon.

Most of our informants told us that they had acquired the bulk of their capital through their own savings, a universal finding in studies of small business foundings. Some had arranged loans within the ethnic community, and a few had acquired bank loans, usually to expand the business. Very few had brought capital with them when they immigrated.

Cultural factors, differing across ethnic groups, affected how entrepreneurs saved and were able to arrange loans. Afro-Caribbeans have a more diffuse kinship system with less pronounced hierarchy and loyalty among family members, and they did not like borrowing money from each other. Seven out of ten of our Afro-Caribbean informants in Amsterdam told us that they were reluctant to borrow money from family or friends. One remarked proudly that he had established his business "without the help of my brothers! I've got my pride. You wait as long as you can. My brothers do the same. They don't ask for help until it is absolutely necessary." The attitude of the Amsterdam Afro-Caribbeans was in very marked contrast to those of other entrepreneurs — Chinese, Hindustanis, Pakistanis, Koreans, Gypsies, and Turks all stressed mutual help among kinsmen.

All our informants noted the importance of their personal savings in providing their initial capital. They accumulated this by wage labor, often at the cost of long hours and sometimes multiple employment and, always, Spartan living. The willingness of budding immigrant entrepreneurs to work extremely hard is a substantial asset. Fouad, a 21-year-old Lyon café owner, provides an extreme though not wholly unusual example. When he was saving for his business, he led a double life:

> I started working like a mad man. Sometimes I used to laugh at myself. Everybody was complaining about unemployment and I was sometimes able to work 36 hours at a stretch. I worked as an extra at the hotel where my mother was a part-time accountant, at the "Eighties" cinema, where I sold tickets, and occasionally I sold musical instruments. During the 18 months that I owned the "Miramar" I continued to work at the hotel. It was odd to meet my cafe clients as a blue-collar worker. They didn't understand! (Joseph 1986)

Usually one member of a Turkish family works for a wage to establish credentials that a bank will accept as a loan guarantee. Overworked female members of the family often take jobs in factories to guarantee credit and also help out in their husbands' businesses. Another important source of capital is credit from distant relatives. During the early settlement phase of the Turkish community in Berlin, a distant friend or relative was often brought in as a business partner. Such partnerships are rare today: Capital is now usually provided and guaranteed through a network of close relations.

Membership in rotating credit associations greatly facilitates saving and borrowing. The Korean *kye* and the Pakistani *kommitti* provided examples among our informants. The *kye* operates as an informal club whose members, from 9 to 90, agree to rotate their periodic contribution around the group until all have received the whole sum of money. Koreans in Los Angeles made extensive use of it for social and business purposes. The *Los Angeles Korea Times* estimated that there were at least 1,000 *kyes* in Los Angeles in 1983, approximately 1 for every 80 Koreans. The Korean newspapers also ran stories about big *kyes,* some of which went bankrupt owing $500,000 to more than 100 creditors. These stories demonstrate that *kyes* could generate very large sums of money, quite enough to permit a *kye* participant to pay the $250,000 needed for a complete restaurant or the $100,000 for a gasoline station with service bays (Light and Bonacich 1988: chap. 10).

The *kye* was useful to Koreans for at least three reasons. First, the institution permitted them to borrow a lump sum without collateral as long as they could convince organizers of their honesty and ability to repay. Second, arrangements were flexible, thus permitting participants to shape timing and mode of payment to their exact needs. Third, and most important, *kyes* made saving a festive event, thus stimulating Koreans to save more than if conventional savings deposits were their only vehicle. The Pakistani *kommitti* operated in a similar fashion, although the weekly share and thus the capital available ultimately was more modest. Obviously, where such saving associations exist, they greatly facilitate the access of entrepreneurs to capital.

We provide an extended example of the customs surrounding loans between kinsmen or close friends, as they are often cited as an important source of finance for business start-ups. Our example is of loans among Pakistanis, which are commonly extended on the basis of a verbal agreement and are rarely witnessed. They do, however, follow a set of explicit rules. These rules were explained by a factory worker (now a very successful factory owner):

> If a Pakistani needs money he can go to a relative or friend and ask him for 200 or 300 pounds. He cannot be refused, even if the friend has to borrow money in order to lend to him. Say he wanted to open a business, only the time would be fixed — at one year. After a year he could ask to extend that for another year. The lender would not go to him and ask for his money. It is up to the debtor to go to the creditor. The money is interest-free (because this is our religion). If a friend needs money he gives warning in advance that he will need money sometime in the future for some purpose. [According to this migrant there is a limit to the sum a man will agree to lend.] A man can tell his friend frankly that he cannot afford 1,000, only 300. Lending and borrowing goes on not only between brothers but also between friends. It could be someone a man has worked with side by side for a number of years. It is a matter of trust. If a man dies, his debts will be repaid by his son.

Similar loan conditions were observed among Turks in Amsterdam. This gave rise to considerable misunderstanding when Turks borrowed money from private Dutch lenders. The Dutch assumed that Turks were trying to cheat them when the Turks informed them they were not repaying on the agreed-upon date but were extending for another period.

Thus there are a number of important sources of capital for ethnic entrepreneurs outside the official lending institutions of the host society, and these channels all lead into the ethnic community. Hard work is the most basic financial resource making saving possible, and this is made possible only by the support of other members of the community.

Training and Skills

Business-relevant skills and training are often acquired through an apprenticeship in another coethnic's shop (Waldinger 1986). As one Dominican garment factory owner in New York pointed out, "I worked mainly for other Dominicans. I think that it's easier to get ahead if you work for a compatriot." In fact, three of every ten Hispanic garment factory owners surveyed in New York had previously worked for another Hispanic, and, of those with supervisory experience, two-thirds had been employed in immigrant-owned firms (Waldinger 1984).

These observations suggest the hypothesis that participation in the ethnic enclave may take the form of a career line: "a collection of jobs in which there is a high probability of movement from one position to another on the list" (Spilerman 1977: 560). Careers in the ethnic enclave range from entry-level jobs as dishwashers or cashiers, to some higher-level jobs as headwaiter or manager, and finally to ownership of one's own firm. Such career mobility in small business industries is at first counterintuitive: These industries typically fall into the secondary sector, where there are few established mechanisms of labor market information or structured mobility ladders.

However, the social connections among employers and workers in the ethnic enclave mold and give structure to the ways in which immigrants learn relevant skills (Bailey 1987). Ties within the ethnic economy widen workers' contacts and, therefore, increase the probability that they will move through the variety of jobs and firms that allow the acquisition of appropriate skills. The reciprocity implicit in network hiring reduces the likelihood that workers will quit and, therefore, enhances an employer's willingness to engage in training. As one immigrant factory owner in New York explained: "I won't provide training to unknown workers who come in looking for a job. When I need somebody, I ask the workers to bring in a relative. That way one worker helps another; and I don't have to worry about training someone who will find work in another shop."

No less important than skill is the motivation to go out on one's own. One Chinese garment contractor explained his decision to set up his own plant by saying, "My boss was making money, so I decided to go into business by myself." His explanation suggests that successful entrepreneurs serve as potential role models, reinforcing the drive for mobility through self-employment. Business activity, it appears, follows an imitative pattern: Initial business success signals the existence of a supportive environment, thereby encouraging other, less adventurous entrepreneurs to follow suit (Kim 1981).

Working for a small ethnic firm allows immigrants to learn nearly all aspects of business management, a goal that entry-level workers in large native-owned firms can rarely attain. Thus coethnic employees' participation in management is possible not only because of ethnic trust but also because of small firm size.

Thus the expansion of immigrant businesses in an ethnic community provides both a mechanism for the effective transmission of skills and a catalyst for the entrepreneurial drive (Waldinger 1986). From the standpoint of immigrant workers, the opportunity to acquire managerial skills through a stint of employment in immigrant firms both compensates for low pay and provides a motivation to learn a variety of different jobs. For employers who hire coethnics, the short-term consideration is lower-priced labor. Over the long term, immigrant owners can act on the assumption that the newcomers will stay long enough to learn the relevant business skills. Moreover, a new entrant's interest in skill acquisition will diminish the total labor bill and increase a firm's flexibility. Thus one can trace out a sequence of developments that shape the behavior of workers and entrepreneurs alike: first, the development of a distinct business niche; then a communitywide orientation toward business; finally, an understanding that newcomers will seek to go out on their own.

Labor

The ethnic enterprises we examined were overwhelmingly of small scale. When they were not one-person operations, they were often "mom-and-pop" enterprises. Many had grown from very humble origins, but virtually without exception they were family affairs. Ethnic entrepreneurs rely heavily upon family, kin, and coethnics for the cheap, loyal labor essential for their survival and success. All the Gypsy fortune-tellers, eight out of ten Korean businesses, three-quarters of the

Surinamese entrepreneurs, and most of the Pakistani and Turkish owners rely heavily upon the labor of their immediate family and other relatives. The only exceptions we found were Korean, Hispanic, Chinese, and Pakistani garment manufacturers whose high demand for labor obliged them to recruit labor outside kin networks, although even they had a clear preference for coethnic employees.

Family labor is important not only for ethnic businesses but for small businesses in general. Research on Asian and white small businesses in four English cities found that the proportion of spouses working in the shops was nearly identical for the two groups, and the proportion with children working in the shops was also similar (Aldrich et al. 1983). Asians made greater use of their extended families as workers, and this was due primarily to their employing greater numbers of brothers, sisters, cousins, and so forth.

Why is family and ethnic labor so important? The answer is simple: Family labor is largely unpaid, and relatives and coethnics, while not always paid excessively low wages, are prepared to work longer hours and at times that outsiders find unacceptable. Although the concept of wages is not foreign to family firms (particularly in relation to Pakistani daughters, for by custom Pakistani parents do not take from their daughters), labor input is fundamentally based on production demands. During seasonal high-demand periods, families may work late every night, seven days a week.

Few successful ethnic businesses are sustained without the labor of at least two family members, particularly during the businesses' formative years, unless owners have access to large-scale capital or specialized expertise. Even market trading, apparently relying on the labor of a single individual, requires an additional income to boost and support traders for several years until they establish themselves. More complex enterprises, such as manufacturing, tend to rely initially on a labor force that is at least partly composed of family members.

In the labor structure of a fortune-telling business, a fortune-teller is the most visible member of the work team. Behind the scenes are members of an extended family, all helping to make her business successful (Sway 1984: 90). Most fortune-telling parlors are family enterprises comprising three generations of fortune-tellers, with fortune-telling providing a family's basic livelihood. The most senior fortune-teller is the grandmother, the next in line is the wife of her son, and then the wife of her grandson in addition to any unmarried granddaughters. The women take turns telling fortunes in the same parlor. On busy days, two or three fortune-tellers work simultaneously.

Fortune-telling is ostensibly a one-woman business, but it is essential for the fortune-teller to have a related male at hand for protection. In addition to providing protection, this man can supplement a family's income by performing odd jobs: picking fruit; collecting scrap metal; servicing driveways; buying, selling, and repairing cars; and generally exploiting resources ignored by the host society. Gypsy men also assume the responsibility of maintaining the fortune-telling parlor, advertising, obtaining customers, and paying rent, license fees, and bribes to officials. Male members of the work team care for younger children, cook, clean, and provide general relief for the fortune-teller so she can devote her time to her business. This absence of a sex-typed division of labor in the household promotes the success of the enterprise.

Thus the viability and durability of small ethnic businesses results, in part, from familial perseverance rather than mere profitability. The long hours, low wages, and uncomfortable working hours characteristic of many ethnic businesses are often regarded as exploitation of family members and coethnics. However, "family" itself can be viewed as the exploitation of whatever resources are available to move ahead. As long as Koreans, for example, utilized kin and coethnic labor, their industrial despotism was tempered by reciprocal social relationships that imposed certain restraints upon employers.

Finally, another aspect of family labor must also be stressed: its loyalty. Having close male relatives within reach enables Pakistanis in Manchester, and Hindustanis and Chinese in Amsterdam, to expand their businesses. They can thus set up new branches and begin new ventures with younger brothers and sons who are willing to accept their authority and give them their loyalty. Afro-Caribbeans apparently have a more egalitarian ethos and are consequently much less willing to accept the authority of relatives in supervisory positions (Benedict 1979; Boissevain and Grotenbreg 1986).

The demand for family labor also generates obligations. Fathers and elder brothers who have benefited from the labor of younger family members are under obligation to provide opportunities for those who have helped them, when they become of age, so that they, in turn, can support their own dependents. Hence family maturation generates a tendency toward vertical and horizontal extension. In Manchester, as families mature, the labor of wives and teenage sons and daughters becomes available. A market trader may then open a wholesale or manufacturing concern, depending also upon his information network, his supply contacts, expertise, and the demographic composition of his familial work force.

The ethnic enterprise is thus a family mode of production for three reasons: First, it contains an in-built dynamism keyed to the development cycle of the domestic group. Second, it is a unit of production ideally poised to exploit open resources in an expanding market. Third, because it can call on loyalty and sacrifice through lower incomes and longer working hours, it can also cope successfully with periodic market recessions.

Customers

One of the essential problems facing entrepreneurs is their relations with customers and suppliers. Self-employed retailers and artisans are tied to their place of work through the pressure of business and the long hours they must put in. Thus, more than most occupational groups, they depend on customers and suppliers to satisfy their need for friendship and sociability (Boissevain 1981; England 1980: 269-313). Nonetheless, customers first and foremost mean business—how are they attracted and held?

Retailers use a variety of methods to gain customer loyalty, with their personalities often playing a role too. The success of an enterprise (particularly hotels, restaurants, cafés, and exotic boutiques) frequently depends on an entrepreneur's ability to negotiate different public images: (1) in the face of bureaucratic authorities, who demand legal compliance; (2) in the face of coethnic customers, who tend to take possession of the premises; and (3) in the face of nonethnic customers, who demand better services. These multiple roles are demanding and occasionally create formidable problems.

Entrepreneurs provide credit, small gifts, and special prices to win customer loyalty. General services are also important, such as finding the time to chat and joke with customers or to listen and advise them on serious problems. Robert, an Afro-Caribbean Surinamese travel agent, explicitly noted that aside from giving travel advice and selling tickets, he provided his customers with a variety of counseling services. When entrepreneurs' customers come from outside their own ethnic community—as do those of Gypsies and Pakistani market traders—

their relations with their customers are more straightforward and thus less charged with ambivalence.

Problems arise when entrepreneurs deal with members of their own ethnic groups, and most of our entrepreneurs relied heavily upon such customers. Yet, here lies the rub. Friends and kinsmen are never treated anonymously, as they expect special favors. Hindustani shopkeepers in Amsterdam were explicit about their dislike of fellow Asians as clients, and pictured them as stingy, haggling, and mean. A restaurateur said, "In our Hindustani restaurants they only eat soup, the cheapest item on the menu." Another shopkeeper maintained he "could not survive on only Hindustani clients because they often purchased only one item, tried to argue the price down, and were extremely stingy."

Turkish entrepreneurs in West Berlin as a rule speak of their non-Turkish customers with respect but dislike their Turkish customers' bargaining over price and quality, and increasingly are attracted by the fixed prices of their German colleagues. Nonetheless, they are still largely dependent upon their Turkish clientele and, therefore, practice a mixed customer policy, although they are increasingly reluctant to give credit. An Asian travel agent remarked that under no circumstances would he do business with fellow Hindustanis: "You can be sure then of having to be content with a small profit margin. A Hindustani cannot find his own shadow. He allows himself nothing!" (Boissevain and Grotenbreg 1986).

These Asian businessmen told us in no uncertain terms that they preferred the Afro-Caribbean customers from Surinam, who, they said, were much more enthusiastic shoppers, were less inclined to worry about the prices, and were less interested in bargaining. Similar feelings were reported by black businessmen in the United States, who complained that blacks expected special favors from them (Aldrich and Reiss 1970). Research on Asian shopkeepers in three English cities found similar results (Aldrich et al. 1983).

Pakistani local corner shops are likely to fail if they rely on small-scale purchases from kinsmen and friends. Small debts are often left uncalculated, or are regarded as repayment for prior services in a different transactional sphere, while credit is expected as a right, on an almost indefinite basis. Debts and credit are treated differently where the scale of transactions is much larger and where, most important, traders are able to allow long-term credit without thereby undermining their businesses.

The difference in credit practices seems to lie in both the form of trading and the time span allowed for credit. Pakistani wholesalers, manufacturers, and market traders buy and sell to one another *in bulk.* Whether the items bought or sold are numbered in dozens, hundreds, or thousands depends on the size of the two firms involved and the transaction. The commercial sphere dominates bulk trading. Sometimes it is underpinned by friendship and kinship and is paralleled by ceremonial gift giving, but the two are not confused. By contrast, basic transactional rules underlying kinship relations can affect small, over-the-counter retail sales in shops, cafés, and restaurants.

None of the retailing entrepreneurs we studied relied exclusively on customers from their own ethnic groups. Gypsies told the fortunes of blacks and especially of Hispanics; Koreans sold gasoline, alcohol, and served food to an ethnic kaleidoscope of customers; North African café owners served French as well as Moroccan, Tunisian, Algerian, and Armenian customers; Pakistani market traders dealt primarily with non-Pakistani customers; West Berlin Turkish shopkeepers served a wide spectrum of non-Turkish customers; and, in Amsterdam, Hindustani shopkeepers sold their tropical specialties primarily to Afro-Caribbeans, while Creole café owners served an ethnically mixed clientele, as did the Chinese. Notable exceptions were Pakistani wholesalers, whose customers are predominantly, although not exclusively, other Asians, thereby confirming the principles set out above.

As a general principle, minority or immigrant business owners can serve nonethnic customers more easily than coethnics in lines of trade that require impersonal transactions. For example, Korean small shopkeepers apparently do better than black shopkeepers in black American neighborhoods (Min 1984).

Competition

Intensive internal competition usually occurs when large numbers of immigrants open similar types of business. Immigrants are often followed into the same ethnic niche by others with similar skills and plans for mobility. Competition is thus often structured into an ethnic entrepreneur's situation, and this competition has been aggravated in recent years.

In his study of Asian businesses in the London borough of Wandsworth, Aldrich (1977) found that Asians in competition with other Asians were open longer, worked more hours per week, were open more

Table 5.2 Ethnic Entrepreneurs' Strategies for Coping with Competition

---

1. Self-exploitation: work longer hours, pay oneself lower salary

2. Horizontal or vertical expansion: move forward and/or backward in the chain of production, and/or open more shops of the same type

3. Create/join formal trading associations

4. Use marriage to join formerly competing families

---

often on Sundays, made deliveries and extended credit to a greater extent, and were more likely to employ their children than Asians *not* in competition with other Asians. Only two of these six results were statistically significant, but the pattern is nonetheless instructive. Competition with other Asians — but not with whites — was a spur to more intensive competitive behavior.

Ethnic entrepreneurs have developed at least four strategies for coping with competition from coethnics who replicate their activities, very often in the same neighborhoods, as shown in Table 5.2.

The first, most obvious, strategy is to cut overhead costs by working harder, putting in longer hours, and cutting employees' wages. This form of competition is, in the long run, suicidal, as the cycle of cost-cutting and increasing hours is never ending. Such effects have been particularly pronounced in the manufacturing and garment industries.

The second strategy involves horizontal and vertical expansion. Most often, aspiring entrepreneurs begin with modest enterprises, usually in an industry where friends or kinsmen have gained some expertise. This process generates intense competition, and one response by a small number of firms to this form of competition, especially for enterprises that are no longer marginal, is expansion. Enterprises can either expand vertically, by opening up complementary wholesale or manufacturing businesses, or expand horizontally, by opening up several businesses of the same type at different locations.

Pakistani immigrants in Manchester utilized both horizontal and vertical expansion. Market trading is the least costly enterprise to start, and new entrants often started there, thus bringing about a rapid multiplication of the number of traders. The vertical expansion of wholesaling resulted from the enormous expansion of market trading that

began in 1950. As competition in markets increased, the more successful traders opened wholesale warehouses, supplying themselves as well
as the new entrants into market trading.

Intensive competition at the wholesaling level also propelled firms
to expand in manufacturing, thus creating vertical integration within a
single firm on a very small scale. Although manufacturing appears to
be the most difficult, and least profitable, sector of the trade, it has the
greatest potential for penetrating into the home market. Several Pakistani manufacturers have, indeed, managed this transition.

Horizontal extension is typical of the various economic portfolios
successful entrepreneurs develop (Long 1979). In the rag trade, for
example, traders run several markets and retail outlets, usually in
widely separated localities, thus minimizing the risk of a single enterprise. An outstanding example of horizontal extension in Manchester is
that of an Indian family business that has five separate retail outlets
along a 50-yard stretch in the inner-city shopping area: a restaurant, a
travel agency, a sari shop, a grocery store, and a wholesale grocery
store. The family controls, in effect, about half the shops on the block.

Bonacich (1973) argued that "middleman minorities" engage in trade
in preference to manufacturing because trade products are more liquid
and travel more easily. The evidence in the garment industry suggests
that sometimes manufacturing constitutes an "invisible" part of immigrant enterprise, with manufacturers linked to their suppliers in
satellite-type relationships. The most prominent success tales are usually those of traders who have incorporated manufacturing firms or
extended into manufacturing as part of a larger trading enterprise.
Manufacturing, in other words, rarely exists as a discrete, large enterprise. Even though it is a less public form of business, often located in
back streets and large warehouses, manufacturing is nevertheless an
essential basis for the formation of an independent economic community (see Wilson and Martin 1982).

A third strategy for dealing with competition was observed in several
locations in response to undercutting at all levels of the trade: the
formation of *formal trading associations*. The most effective organization was the Manchester Northwest Clothing Association, founded
around 1980, with a membership of about 100 local Pakistani manufacturers. The manufacturers met twice a month and exchanged information about prices, costs, customers, and new orders, ensuring their
members did not undercut each other. Another association founded by
Pakistani wholesalers, the Traders Association, is not as effective yet,

but its foundation is nevertheless part of a general trend toward formalization and the regulation of competition.

Turkish business organizations in Berlin were not able to reduce competition in the early 1980s. Wholesalers and food manufacturers, however, constituted an oligopoly controlling import, export, and distribution of certain items. In no sense was there an open market for Turkish food. The members of this oligopoly, for the most part, were recruited from families that managed large concerns in Turkey. They had little or nothing to do with the small business people.

Los Angeles Koreans and Amsterdam Surinamese are faced with similar competitive pressure but have been less successful in establishing lasting associations to regulate competition. In most cases, Korean trade associations failed because individual Korean proprietors were unwilling to invest the time or money needed to make the associations viable, even though they understood the advantages that would accrue to all if their attempts were successful. For example, the president of the Korean petroleum dealers association (defunct in 1980) explained in 1978 that none of the association's 80 members bothered to pay the association's $10 annual dues because they were "too tight" to support the organization. The only successful Korean trade organization was organized by wig dealers with a monopoly in this field, but it was destroyed by an antitrust decree of the U.S. District Court in 1975. The case was exceptional because most Korean trade associations collapsed *without* government interference.

By contrast, several New York Korean trade associations have been very successful in regulating competition and protecting members' common interests: the Korean Green Grocers' Association, the Korean Fish Retailers' Association, and the Korean Drycleaners' Association (Min 1984). The situation among Surinamese retailers in Amsterdam is similar to that of the Koreans in Los Angeles. All recognized the importance of cooperation but were unable to resolve their jealousies.

The Gypsies have developed another formal means of regulating competition. Because there are more than a million Gypsies in the United States and all Gypsy clans are involved in fortune-telling, it is essential for them to regulate their industry. Internal regulation has produced a strict practice of territoriality by which Gypsy *kumpanias* (groups of extended families living and working together) are given exclusive rights to operate fortune-telling parlors in specific geographic locations. Within this territory they may conduct secondary business ventures such as used automobile and boat sales, but they have no right to seek business dealings beyond the boundaries of their territory. Adherence to territorial boundaries is enforced by the Gypsy court system called the *kris.* The *kris* is a mobile court that relies upon three to five prominent Gypsy men to hear cases and render decisions. Typically, these men are from nondisputing territories and are asked to serve as judges to ensure impartiality. Some professional groups such as medical doctors and dentists make use of similar territorial arrangements to limit competition, as do a notoriously successful group of immigrant entrepreneurs, the Sicilian American mafiosi (Demaris 1981).

The development of successful trading associations appears to be a function of the length of time an ethnic community has been established, the degree of acceptance of its leaders, and the pressure from competitors and from enemies from outside the ethnic group. The Dutch Italian Ice Cream Makers Association was established in the 1930s to combat pressure to control their numbers from the Dutch Ice Cream Vendors Association and government (Bovenkerk et al. 1983).

Although Koreans in Los Angeles were not able to establish successful trading organizations, the threatening experience of internal competition helped make manifest an anticompetitive normative consensus that had been latent in their cultural repertoire. Internal competition caused Koreans to remind one another that Korea's traditional culture denigrated competition. Under the banner of cultural tradition, Koreans rallied against the internal competition imposed on them by their market situation. Moreover, the rhetoric of ethnic cooperation caused Koreans to become aware of themselves as an ethnic minority competing with other ethnic minorities in America's pluralistic society. "We Koreans must stick together" simply meant in this context that Koreans recognized the destructive potential of internal competition and desired to build normative consensus and the ethnic institutions to support that consensus. "Ethnicity" was thus made more salient by the pressures of dealing with competition.

A fourth strategy that entrepreneurs used to eliminate competition among well-established competitors was *marriage,* as we observed among the Gypsies. While there is a high degree of compliance among Gypsies, each *kumpania* always seeks more and better territory, and marriage is a good way to acquire it. A marriage arranged between two *kumpanias* gives members of both *kumpanias* reciprocal trading rights in each other's territories. For this reason Gypsy marriages are based upon the estimated economic gain for each *kumpania* and are occasions for very large celebrations. In fact, we found that marriage was the only form of merger acceptable to ethnic entrepreneurs whose fierce independence and family loyalty precluded more conventional commercial mergers.

The various actions our entrepreneurs have taken to limit or contain the effects of competition also promote integration. Formal associations, territorial arrangements, horizontal and vertical extension, and marriage between important competitors contribute both to the integration of the ethnic community and to its members' ability to participate more successfully in the marketplace.

Protection

Ethnic entrepreneurs sometimes require protection from government regulators and inspectors because of their imperfect awareness of, and compliance with, the formal regulations and laws regulating their activities. Occasionally, they also need to defend themselves from the maneuvering of rival entrepreneurs from outside their ethnic communities.

The only case we encountered of a concerted attack by indigenous entrepreneurs was a campaign by black entrepreneurs in Los Angeles against Korean businessmen. Aggressive entrepreneurship had brought Koreans into conflict with local black groups. In this sense, as Bonacich (1973) predicted, the commercial activities of a middleman minority stirred up animosities in the host population. Opposition to Korean entrepreneurship stemmed from complex interconnections among the three principal groups: low-income customers, labor unions, and business competitors. The sharpest conflicts occurred in the black neighborhoods, where black nationalist political cadres claimed that Koreans were exploiting black consumers by taking their money in stores and then spending the funds in Korean neighborhoods, thus depriving black communities of the multiplier effect of consumer demand. With the influential support of black business owners, themselves in business competition with Koreans, the nationalists inflamed black opinion against Koreans, organizing boycotts and "buy black" campaigns to enforce their demands.

Although these campaigns obtained the active support of only a minority of the black population, the organized opposition intimidated the Koreans. Some Koreans reduced their commercial activities in black areas in response to this opposition. However, as a coherent and increasingly self-conscious ethnic minority, the Koreans also utilized methods of collective response that would have been unavailable had they represented a rabble of solo individualists. Under the leadership of the Korean Association of Southern California (itself in contact with equivalent Korean agencies in other American cities, where similar problems arose), the Koreans signed a "treaty" of friendship and mutual cooperation with the Watts Labor Community Action Committee, a leading black organization. At a festive banquet, Korean and black leaders discussed problems and sought accommodation. Korean churches also cultivated lines of communication with black churches, often hotbeds of anti-Korean sentiment, trying to improve relationships between blacks and Korean merchants in central Los Angeles. Their efforts were not completely successful, for incompatibilities of economic interests remained.

More common, however, are the ways in which ethnic entrepreneurs confronted the demands of established government. Their responses, though not notably differing from those of indigenous entrepreneurs faced with the same situation, are illuminating: bribing government controllers, paying fines, finding loopholes in existing laws, taking the government to court, and conforming to government regulations.

Gypsies have found perhaps the most striking accommodation, via bribery. Fortune-telling is illegal in all jurisdictions in the United States, with the exception of Virginia and Los Angeles County. The industry thrives, despite the laws, for one of two reasons. Either the laws are not enforced because the state does not feel that fortune-telling is harmful to the citizens or the laws are enforced intermittently to pressure the Gypsies into paying bribes to police chiefs and city attorneys in order to stay in business. One police chief derives $90,000 a year in graft from three fortune-tellers in an extremely wealthy West Coast beach town. Each fortune-telling parlor pays the chief $30,000 a year, which amounts to one-third of their annual income. The Gypsies seem to accept the fact that they will have to pay bribes and generally figure the amount into their overall operating costs. They also use their relationship with police chiefs and city attorneys to reinforce their own territorial control over an area. For example, any Gypsy operating "illegally" in another territory can be frightened into leaving the area by local authorities at the request of the Gypsies who pay them bribes.

Many Surinamese fail to conform to the maze of regulations that govern business activities in the Netherlands. The most frequent abuse is failing to obtain the necessary diplomas and licenses. If they are caught, they pay relatively modest fines, which they can deduct from taxes as business expenses. The various government control services inspect regularly, and thus nonconformity can become costly as well as time-consuming. One Turkish butcher, incensed at the frequent visits by the inspection service to his shop, which he regarded as harassment, became enraged, grabbed a meat cleaver, and started swinging it in manic fury while shouting at the inspector to leave him alone. His act of desperation helped, and for a while health inspectors avoided ethnic butchers.

Another way of coping with government laws is to manipulate them. Again the Surinamese in Amsterdam provided many examples. One successful manufacturer of leather clothing told us that he had registered his firm with the Chamber of Commerce under the art section: "For my leather business I needed a certificate for technical competence. But I did not have one. For an art business you need nothing. In this land of blossoms and barbed wire, you have to look after yourself, otherwise you get hurt!" Another informant provided further examples:

> To open a garage you must have a license and certificates of competence. On the other hand, you need none to sell new cars. Furthermore, you need no certificate to become a car mechanic. Thus you can open a garage as long as you make sure you have no formal roof over your head. You can also repair bicycles without license, but you cannot sell new parts—although you can get away with it [selling new parts] if your books "show" that you use these parts for your repairs. If you want to become a jeweler—which requires certificates—you register as a tinsmith. For that you don't need diplomas. If you repair one pan a year you meet the formal requirement!

Some businessmen rent the necessary diplomas or borrow them from acquaintances who ostensibly form part of the enterprise. To avoid tax assessment, which in the case of a newly established enterprise takes place only after the first five years, a number of entrepreneurs "terminate" their activities after four years. They drop out of the register and start up elsewhere under a new name. That is why, we were told by Amsterdam police controllers, small catering establishments change hands so frequently.

In West Berlin, during the early phase of immigration, small Turkish concerns were for the most part controlled by fictive German entrepreneurs who provided the required but missing trade license for the Turks (who were allowed to apply for this license only after five years' residence in Germany). These businesses were partly criminally organized, and a large part of the profits was taken by this criminal element. This was one of the reasons that small entrepreneurs were of limited importance during the early phase of the Turkish community in West Berlin.

Entrepreneurs sometimes find it necessary and advantageous to challenge government directly. In Los Angeles, the Korean-run garment industry violated a number of American laws, employing many illegal Mexican immigrants and paying wages below the statutory minimum under working conditions that also failed to satisfy the labor code, both common practices in the garment industry. In the late 1970s, the State of California initiated a series of garment industry "sweeps" in the interest of stricter enforcement of labor legislation. Government task forces raided factories, seeking evidence of labor law violations and subjecting factory owners to prosecution. The Koreans felt frightened and, in response, formed the Korean Sewing Contractors Association, a body whose principal function was to protect the membership against legal harassment. One coup was to hire the garment union's attorney, once a principal antagonist, who then, when securely on the payroll, became a valuable resource. Additionally, the Korean contractors compelled the state to translate the labor code into Korean, thus rendering its provisions accessible to their membership. Finally, the association represented Korean interests to the state, permitting the state to negotiate a solution rather than simply hound violator firms out of existence.

Sometimes a single entrepreneur can fight a case and score a point that benefits an entire community. The salt beef affair in Amsterdam was a case in point. Surinamese shopkeepers long ran the risk that, when they sold salt beef to their clients, they could be fined for cutting up the beef. Salt beef, a Surinamese staple, is imported in large chunks in vats of brine. The shopkeeper chops these chunks into smaller pieces according to the wishes of his customer. This operation is similar to the way grocers slice ham or sausage. The Meat Inspection Service classified salt beef as processed meat and saw nothing illegal in shopkeepers cutting it up, but the Economic Control Service disagreed.

One of our informants, Lo, who had been running a grocery shop for eight years, was inspected by the Economic Control Service. The inspector saw him preparing the salt beef. He regarded this as "the unauthorized exercise of the butcher's profession." The Economic Control Service ruled that because Lo was operating as a butcher, he had to have a special permit or an exemption to do so. He had neither. In 1981 Lo was fined a total of 750 guilders for acting as a butcher. Lo hired a lawyer, who pointed out to the magistrate (at our prompting) that the Meat Inspection Service had classified the salt beef as processed meat. The Economic Control Service finally accepted this point. It advised the police that the "suspect" in fact did not have to possess a butcher's permit or an exemption. Lo was acquitted by the judge, who ordered reimbursement of his fine. But he had to pay the lawyer's fee out of his own pocket. Lo fought this case as an isolated individual, without any support from the community that benefited from the court's ruling in his favor (Boissevain and Grotenbreg 1985). This miserable little bureaucratic episode illustrates the constricting effect excessive government regulations can have upon small businessmen. It also illustrates, as does the Korean example, that it is often worthwhile to fight a case through the courts.

CONCLUSION

We have examined the strategies that ethnic entrepreneurs employ to meet problems related to their enterprises. Our cases show how strategies emerge from the interaction of group characteristics and opportunity structures as entrepreneurs mobilize resources to meet market conditions, adapting to or creating solutions to problems. Our cases documented how very different and widely separated ethnic groups utilize rather similar *strategies* in their attempts to carve out economic niches in Western industrial societies.

The barriers all entrepreneurs must overcome if they are to succeed as entrepreneurs relate to their ability to contend with others competitively in securing low-cost labor, gaining access to skills, training, and capital, fighting prohibitive statutory regulations, and meeting price undercutting from competitors. Ethnic entrepreneurs need distinctive strategies for three reasons. First, distinctive strategies enable them to exploit distinctive sociocultural resources. For example, minority entrepreneurs utilize the cheap and loyal labor of coethnics available to them because of the discrimination and resulting underemployment imposed on those groups. Second, minority entrepreneurs must compensate for the typical background deficits of their groups in respect to wealth, valid educational credentials, political power, and influential contacts. Third, as social outsiders, they face political and economic obstacles that native-born or majority entrepreneurs escape. For example, because of difficulties in obtaining loans from commercial banks, minority entrepreneurs need to nurture kinship and friendship networks that provide alternative access to the savings of coethnics.

What emerges most remarkably from this account are not the differences among ethnic groups in their formation of small businesses, but the very similar strategies they adopt. Despite differences in their cultural and economic backgrounds, particular migration histories, and current circumstances, similar adaptations have occurred across different contexts. In stressing the similarities of resources and strategies that ethnic entrepreneurs recurrently utilize, we have not intended to reduce ethnic entrepreneurship to a lowest common denominator, thereby implying homogeneity among diverse groups. Ethnic groups do possess ethnic resources and deploy ethnic economic strategies, but the exact resources and strategies vary from group to group.

6

Business on the Ragged Edge:
Immigrant and Minority Business
in the Garment Industries
of Paris, London, and New York

Mirjana Morokvasic
Roger Waldinger
Annie Phizacklea

This chapter uses the framework developed in previous chapters — opportunities, group characteristics, and strategies — to analyze the immigrant garment industries of Paris, London, and New York. We focus on new immigrant garment entrepreneurs, the businesses they have founded, and the industrial environments in which they have grown up. The garment industry is the paradigmatic case of immigrant enterprise, as it is risk-laden, supportive of small concerns, and still dependent on traditional sewing skills.

Wherever they have settled, immigrant entrepreneurs have consistently gravitated to the clothing trade. In Holland, Turks have reintroduced garment manufacture to Amsterdam. In Britain, Cypriots and Asians have revived London's dying East End clothing trade, and Pakistanis and Indians have created a burgeoning clothing trade in the depressed West Midlands, where clothing production had never previously existed. Almost half of the Parisian garment trade is made up of immigrants, who are not only workers but also factory owners and even leading manufacturers. Virtually all new garment factories in New York are established by immigrant entrepreneurs. For example, in New York's Chinatown, the number of Chinese firms grew from 30 in 1965

to 480 in early 1985, with increasing spillover to newer Chinese neighborhoods. By 1985, 20,000 Chinese workers — more than one-sixth of
the city's entire apparel labor force — were employed in Chinese-owned
concerns.

Our inquiry focuses on a paradox: Why is it the small sector of the
garment industry that so persistently, and pervasively, survives? What
role do immigrant entrepreneurs play in the survival of this sector? As
with small business in general, the garment industry's small sector has
long been regarded as some archaic remnant, left over from industrialization's worst times. In the eyes of many observers, the industry's
future was leading to the same road that the rest of modern manufacturing industry had already followed: "concentration, automation, non-
entrepreneurial managements, and a strong marketing orientation"
(*Business Week* 1979). By contrast, the small clothing firms of the major
metropolitan centers, with their backward technologies and traditional
production structures, were slated for imminent demise. In his book
about homeworkers in the Parisian clothing industry, Klatzmann (1957:
132) argued that "the present situation is probably just a step [in the
development of the garment industry]. The trend seems to be towards
the industrialization of the production of clothing, the creation of
"conveyor belts' functioning with modern machines. Compared to that,
the present electric sewing machines are archaic."

Klatzmann's dire prognosis about technological and organizational
transformation has not come true, and perhaps one explanation involves
the immigrants themselves. Some have argued that the garment industry
survives only because of the newcomers. But not so long ago, the
industry's chief worry was a dwindling supply of available workers.
New York's clothing employers, for example, have suffered from a
persistent shortage of labor ever since the onset of postwar prosperity.
Writing in the 1950s, Helfgott (1959: 94) noted that the Italian and
Jewish workers, who had previously dominated work in New York's
needle trades, were "spurning the garment industry for occupations with
higher pay and prestige," and even recent entrants, like blacks and
Puerto Ricans, seemed likely to "forsake the garment industry for
alternative types of employment." In Paris, Klatzmann (1957: 132)
thought that modernization would be facilitated by the fact that the
industry's traditional sources of labor would not be renewed: "Among
the third generation (of Jews and immigrants) there will be very few
garment workers. Those of the present generation will probably have to
face a very difficult period."

Despite these bleak prognoses, the garment industry has gained a new infusion of immigrants in each of the three cities we studied. The maintenance of a sizable sector of small firms cannot be explained simply by the availability of a low-cost labor force willing to accept jobs that native workers spurn. Two additional explanatory factors must be considered: (1) the nature of the opportunity structure in the industry, especially limits to the techniques of mass production, and (2) the strategies that immigrants adapt in the struggle to make it in the very competitive economies of Western societies.

We will thus examine the paradox of small immigrant business in the garment industry in two stages. First, we will explore the conditions that give rise to a viable niche for small firms of the type set up by immigrants and minorities. Attributing the industry's survival to immigrants is at best a partial explanation, because it begs the logically prior question of why there are still ample opportunities for small firms and small entrepreneurs — predictions of modernization notwithstanding. We investigate the nature of the industry's opportunity structure in three cities, pursuing the hypothesis that small immigrant businesses will thrive where techniques of mass production do not apply.

Second, we look at the characteristics and strategies of the immigrants and the attributes that allow them to exploit opportunities created by broader market forces. Immigrants' expectations distinguish them from natives, to whom a garment shop has come in a poor second after a white-collar or service job. As one Dominican garment worker in New York put it, "I arrived hoping to find any job, it didn't matter . . . as long as it was a job." Exclusion from opportunities for good jobs is a potent source of entrepreneurial drive, especially among immigrants who have settled and no longer expect to return home. Immigrants are well positioned to exploit these opportunities, because their work situation connects them to others who can teach skills, and their social milieu provides attachments to a prospective source of labor.

THE OPPORTUNITY STRUCTURE

In markets dominated by the demand for standardized products, a number of barriers block the path of new immigrant firms' entry: scale economies, high absolute costs, and product differentiation. However, techniques of mass production and mass distribution are not applicable for products or services that are affected by uncertainty or differentiation or that are relatively small in size (Piore 1980). Immigrant firms are most likely to emerge in these markets.

In apparel, the critical structuring factors stem from the demand side: The demand for clothing falls into stable and unstable portions, each of which exerts different production demands. Consequently, the industry tends to be segmented into two branches: one that is dominated by larger firms that handle staple products and another that is composed of small-scale firms catering to the unpredictable and/or fluctuating portion of demand. Because the two branches thus involve noncompeting specializations, a sheltered niche exists for small firms of the type that immigrants might establish.

The apparel industry faces several sources of instability: fashion trends, the weather, and the state of the overall economy. The most important source of instability is fashion. Some clothing products fall into a staple category, and they can almost be worn year in and year out. At the other end of the spectrum are products whose existence is nearly ephemeral — for example, bridal gowns, which, even in today's world, are seldom worn more than once. Most items of clothing have greater longevity than do bridal gowns, but the nature of fashion is such that a dress or blouse is out of date fairly soon after its purchase. Weather is another factor making clothing purchases difficult to project; for example, if winter is delayed, consumers postpone buying coats until the next year. The overall state of the economy is another source of uncertainty; for example, spending on fashion rises when one's pocket is full and falls when there is barely enough for necessities.

Product-market conditions are correlated with particular types of production technology and organization: Staple products involve long production runs and can be handled and merchandised by large, bureaucratized firms. These same technological and organizational features are much less suited to product markets prone to instability and unpredictable changes, which are a more supportive environment for small firms (Waldinger 1986).

Fashion is an important influence in all three countries, but there is nonetheless substantial variation, with the United States falling at one end of the spectrum and France at the other. The French, always against uniformity and considering fashion to be a strong barrier against international competition, were historically slow to move away from an artisanal mode of production and toward standardization (Green 1986). Thus as late as 1951, only two-thirds of all garment production was made "ready-to-wear," as opposed to more than 90% in the United States (Guilbert and Isambert-Jamoti 1956).

The United States had completed the transition to factory-made production by World War II, but the life-style trends of the postwar years — suburbanization, the trend toward greater leisure, rising labor force participation among women — transformed American dress. As consumers opted for more standardized items of wear, the structure of the industry changed as well. Significant scale economies became possible, leading to larger establishment size, and production runs were lengthened, with the result that factory organization went from full-garment sewing to "section work," an assembly-line-type process in which each operator sews together a single part of the garment. Because standardization also meant a reduction in fashion uncertainty, internal economies of scale could be realized and hence a greater proportion of the work force was working for multiplant firms (Waldinger 1986).

In England and the United States, the shift toward standardized goods was further boosted by accompanying shifts in the related retail sector. Big business came to American retailing in the postwar era; as large retail chains grew, they sought to maximize transaction economies by shopping from the largest apparel makers. Increasingly, the success-ful firms were those with the capacity to supply large retailers' needs (Bluestone et al. 1981). In Britain, where the structure of retailing is even more centralized, the dominance of retail distribution by a small number of chains pushed a large section of the domestic clothing industry toward more standardized wear (Clairmonte and Cavanagh 1981). By contrast, French retailing remains small and the vast bulk of French-made clothes (about 70%) is distributed by boutique-type stores (Conseil Economique et Social 1982).

These disparities in standardization and in the structure of the retail-ing and apparel industries produced substantial differences in establish-ment size across the three countries. Factory size is largest in Britain, where the average establishment employs 76 workers (though this is surely an inflated figure, because the relevant data base excludes firms with fewer than 20 workers). In the United States the average establish-ment in the women's clothing industry employs 46 workers, whereas French firms employ an average of only 22 workers. Mean establish-ment size in the fashion markets of the three capital cities is smaller still: 29 in New York, 9.8 in Paris, and well over half the firms in London employ fewer than 10 people (Wilkins 1982). The most striking varia-tion is in the proportion of workers employed in very small shops: In

London and Paris, just over 50% of the low-skilled workers in the needle trades are in plants of 19 employees or fewer, whereas less than 20% of New York workers are found in such establishments.

The industry's changes in product-market and industrial structures brought about a new spatial division of labor. Concentration on standardized wear made garment producers increasingly sensitive to labor costs; hence the garment sector was one of the first to shift its production base to lower-wage countries abroad, primarily in the Orient. The greatest import market penetration has been in the United States: In 1959, imports were only 6.9% of domestic production of women's and men's apparel; by 1984, just as much clothing was imported to the United States as was made domestically (Waldinger 1986: 72-73). In Britain, the increase has been impressive, but not quite as substantial: Clothing and footwear imports, which averaged 12.2% of domestic consumption during the 1954-1964 period, captured an average of 33% of the market by the 1978-1981 years (Silberston 1984). In France, imports had risen to 21.6% in value of the home market by 1980, but accounted for 45% of the total number of units sold (Conseil Economique et Social 1982).

Though standardization has thus been a transforming force, it has not quite swept the field. The history of large apparel firms in the United States and, to a lesser extent, in the United Kingdom shows that the effects of style and fashion change pervade almost all apparel categories. Even the largest firms have found themselves imperiled when fashion shifts make product lines obsolete and plants and equipment are too specialized to be converted to other uses. Several large apparel firms have also found themselves shackled by cumbersome administrative structures that have kept them from adapting to the largest shifts.

The market for mass-produced clothing may have reached its limits at last. The prolonged crises of the Western economies have upset the stability needed for mass production and mass distribution. Manufacturers now need the ability to respond flexibly to fashion changes, and retailers are oriented toward a risk-averse strategy characterized by shorter buying cycles, smaller purchases, and an emphasis on keeping inventories down. Demographic changes have also altered consumption patterns: The aging of the baby boom cohort and the proliferation of two-earner families have shifted clothing expenditures to higher-priced, more fashion-sensitive goods (Piore and Sabel 1984; Kindel 1984). In Britain, the growing fragmentation and sophistication of the mass market have made it increasingly difficult to sell a single, rigidly planned "look" to broad categories of consumers. This development sparked the so-called High Street Fashion War, in which retailers began to target narrowly defined segments of the market on the basis of design innovation rather than price (Rosen 1984; Zeitlin 1985). U.S. retailers selling to the mass middle of the marketplace have also found themselves in the doldrums, with several major chains being chopped up or closed down, and the remaining giants seeking to move up-market into more fashion-sensitive lines (*Business Week* 1984a).

While importing has been greatest in the less fashion-sensitive lines, many other developments have also constrained the importing of higher-fashion items: the need for communication between designer and maker, the importance of short lead times, and the high costs of making small runs. Growing wage costs have also overtaken some of the chief clothing-exporting countries themselves. In the 1960s, rising wage costs forced Japan to cede its clothing industry to Hong Kong, and in the 1980s, rising wage costs were a damper on Hong Kong's competitive edge.

Increasing fashion consciousness is also taking a toll on the appeal of goods exported from distant, low-wage sources. In Britain, the main area of growth in clothing imports during the 1979-1983 period did not come from the Orient but from the higher-wage EEC countries, and in France other EEC countries furnished the greatest share of imports in value terms (Silberston 1984). The "big four" exporting countries of Hong Kong, South Korea, China, and Taiwan still dominate U.S. markets (Waldinger 1986), but the remarkable success of the Italian-based Benneton chain is evidence of the growing importance of design rather than price competition in the U.S. market (Belussi 1986; *Business Week* 1984b).

Finally, the web of protective rules drawn around the Western apparel-producing countries has made importing a source of rigidity. In most of the key exporting countries, goods must be ordered a year in advance of expected sale to ensure that they will enter before an exporting country's quota is exhausted. Retailers must, therefore, hold back some purchases to be furnished by nearby flexible domestic sources, once fashion and consuming patterns can be fully discerned (*Business Week* 1985; *Wall Street Journal* 1984).

Despite growing international competition and a shift toward larger units in the domestic industry, a space remains for a spot market that absorbs instability and specializes in fashion items and overruns on standardized goods. In this market, where rapid fashion changes and short runs predominate, the production process needs to remain very flexible. This is the niche that immigrant firms have filled.

Structural Characteristics of
the Garment Industry

Contracting arrangements between manufacturers and contractors appear wherever the garment industry is found. Though the vocabulary differs from one country to the next and the precise arrangements vary as well, the basic contours of the relationship are nonetheless the same. On one side are manufacturers or jobbers, responsible for designing and merchandising; on the other side are contractors, producing goods to the specifications set by the manufacturers. Typically, manufacturers employ several contractors; at the height of the season, the number may triple or quadruple. Contractors may do all the work in their own shops or may subcontract to still smaller entities. One recurrent possibility is the use of homeworkers or out-workers, a tendency more common in Paris and London than in New York, where the practice is virtually outlawed.

Contracting systems vary across the three cities, but in each case they originated in the 1880s with the influx of Russian Jews. In France, department stores took the lead in setting up the first garment factories. Because investment in stocks and machinery proved too risky, recourse was made to intermediaries — contractors (called *entrepreneurs* or *façonniers*) who organized small workshops or networks of homeworkers (Guilbert and Isambert-Jamoti 1956). Russian Jewish immigrants moved into this burgeoning contracting and homeworking sector as they filtered into Paris. Three factors accounted for this pattern of concentration: (1) Natives shifted into the factory sector; (2) the newcomers had a preference for family labor and found advantages in working at home and in easy access to other small shops; and (3) the immigrants were also skilled in the newer, highly seasonal women's clothing trades, where small-scale production was commonly found (Green 1985).

In London, a "sweating system," in which wholesale clothiers distributed cut cloth to the lowest-bidding "sweater," was fully developed by the 1860s (Hall 1962). This system, which recruited female and male hand-sewers, was transformed in subsequent decades by the advent of the sewing machine, used on a mass scale by 1870, and by the immigration of Russian Jews, who surged into London beginning in the 1880s.

With the arrival of the Jews came two developments: the subdivision of work and the subcontracting of labor. Some subcontracting existed prior to the influx of the Jews, originating in the bespoke (custom-made) end of the trade. Jewish entrepreneurs went even further in subcontracting, and pioneered in breaking up the work of artisan-tailors into as many as 25 different tasks and parceling those tasks out to a team of Jewish women and boy sewers. The ease with which newcomers could become small masters, and their tendency to recruit fellow townsmen (*landsmann*) to their shops, led to an explosion in subcontracting. By 1900, coat making, vest making, and trouser making had almost entirely fallen into the hands of Jewish entrepreneurs and workers (Hall 1962; Jones 1971; Schmiechen 1984).

In New York, most clothing was produced in larger workshops through the late 1880s, though a sizable number of homeworkers were to be found on the periphery. As the Russian Jews flocked into New York, they went to work for smaller contractors who often housed their factories in the same tenements where the immigrants lived. Contractors, usually also Russian-Jewish immigrants, were convenient intermediaries between manufacturers and workers. In contrast to the larger manufacturers, the contractors' connections to the newcomers were quite successful for recruiting a labor force and then holding on to it during periods of seasonal activity (Howe 1976; Rischin 1962).

Despite these variations in first causes, contracting arrangements persisted long after the original conditions disappeared. First, contracting allowed manufacturers to limit investment in fixed capital (factories, machines), and thereby considerably reduce risk, which is an important consideration in an industry as prone to instability as the garment industry. Second, contracting permitted both types of firms to become specialized—the manufacturers in designing and merchandising, the contractors in production. This specialization proved convenient because the small size and limited staff of most garment firms made it difficult for them to perform all the different activities efficiently.

Contracting Today

For today's prospective immigrant garment entrepreneurs, the survival of the contracting arrangement is decisive in influencing them to enter the garment business. Because manufacturers purchase the raw materials and engage in the required interactions with designers, merchandisers, and suppliers, prospective entrepreneurs need only two essentials to set up their own businesses: skills that one can pick up as a worker in a shop and connections to a reliable source of family or ethnic labor. Indeed, in Paris or London, where the scale of enterprise is smaller than in New York, a petty garment entrepreneur can start with as little as one sewing machine. Though shop sizes are larger in New York, a loft can be rented and machines obtained through a chattel mortgage at low risk to an entrepreneur. Even knowledge of the language is not always required — in some communities, there are intermediaries or brokers who connect immigrant contractors with native manufacturers — and, in any case, communication is usually stripped down to its essentials. As one manufacturer pointed out, "Language is not a major difficulty. If they don't understand, you simply sit down and show them."

Contracting has been the primary stepping-stone for immigrant entrepreneurs in the garment industry, but manufacturers have also provided inducements for new immigrants to set up on their own. Parisian garment producers, confronted with increasing international competition, have adopted the strategy of externalizing the labor-intensive parts of the production, leaving as little of the cutting, sewing, and pressing on their premises as possible, thus increasing the amount of work sent out to contractors. In New York, the hybrid system in which employment was divided among the workshops of manufacturers (who did designing and merchandising but also maintained facilities under their own roofs) and of contractors has largely collapsed as manufacturers have phased out their directly held operations. In Paris and London, some employers also have urged their salaried workers to become independent contractors as a way of avoiding contributions to national insurance funds and evading payments for sickness, holiday, redundancy, and maternity benefits that are mandated by law (Morokvasic et al. 1986).

In New York, larger firms' reluctance to expand and exploit an upturn in the demand for pleated dresses and firms had a similar impact on the business chances of Dominican immigrants. One organizer for the pleaters union offered this account, which was confirmed in interviews with owners of pleating firms:

When pleating took off, the larger firms had more business than they could handle. The owners preferred to concentrate on the fancy, specialized items on which they could make higher profits. So what would happen is that the owner would go up to one of his workers and say, "Hey, José, you want to be a boss? You set up your own pleating shop, and I'll keep you supplied with enough work to keep you busy." Of course, José jumped at the chance and started out as subcontractor to his old boss. But before long, José got to know his boss's customers; and it wasn't much longer that José was out in the market getting business for himself.

The ambiguity of the contractor's status forms one of the most important aspects of the subcontracting system. In some instances, the contractor may be literally employer and employee at the same time, shifting from one status to another, depending on the requirements of production. During the slow season, the contractor may be a simple worker or homeworker, and possibly even unemployed. But during months of intense activity, contractors become entrepreneurs, organizing both kin and ethnic workers when the pool of labor must extend beyond the orbit of the immediate family circle. In Paris, some immigrants regularly shift from one status to another several times a year, all the while maintaining their status of salaried worker ("what is sure is sure"), while others convert from *salarié* to *gérant* (manager) just once in their lives (Morokvasic 1987).

The ease of movement from worker to owner and the frequency of these transitions affects workers' occupational identities. In all three cities, the industry is filled with owners who started small and later made it big. Although the number of losers outweighs the number of winners, there are constantly new role models arising whose existence is reason to defy the odds. Moreover, the apparent facility of social promotion weakens the potential for class solidarity. Immigrants who become petty entrepreneurs also shift social class and no longer feel solidarity with those workers who, until yesterday, had been their counterparts.

What transpired in turn-of-the-century New York — when erstwhile Jewish revolutionaries went from proletarians to petty owners and ended up as "alrightniks" — occurs among today's immigrant populations as well. One example is the group of Turkish workers we interviewed who went on a hunger strike in Paris in 1980 to demand legal status and minimum, guaranteed wages from their employers. A few years later, we interviewed some of these former hunger strikers who in the interim had been legalized and had tried to settle as petty shop (*atelier*) owners.

IMMIGRANTS' STRATEGIES AND PREDISPOSITIONS

We have shown that the opportunity structure of the garment industry is very favorable for the entry and survival of small-scale businesses, and we turn now to the question: Why do immigrants provide the bulk of small garment owners? The answer involves group characteristics: the way in which skills and training are acquired for running a small garment business, the way in which resources are mobilized, and the predispositions of some immigrants toward this high-risk endeavor.

In some cases, immigrants apparently succeeded in the "rag trade" because they arrived with skills directly applicable to the business at hand. For example, many of the Jews who migrated to the three cities at various junctures over the past century had previously been tailors in their countries of origin. Though most were accustomed to working with needle and thread, they quickly adapted to operating a sewing machine. Later waves of Jewish immigrants (particularly in Paris) came with direct experience as either workers or petty owners in machine-run garment production.

Most of the modern-day immigrant garment entrepreneurs, however, arrive without prior exposure to the needle trades. Although lacking in specific skills, they make up for their deficits by readily adapting to a changing environment and acquiring the required proficiencies through kinship ties and patterns of ethnic reciprocity. As one Turkish owner in Paris commented in a discussion about sewing and sewing machines with other entrepreneurs: "What do I know about machines? I was a shepherd in Turkey, this one was a teacher, and that one there a football player."

Skills are obtained along two main paths: learning on the job or going into business with someone who knows the ropes. First, some immigrants learn how to sew through informal connections, as with Arif in Paris, who can ask the worker at the next machine, "Help me, brother, or do it for me so I get this job." In London, it is particularly common to find male entrepreneurs who have "learned the ropes" the hard way, that is, by learning all aspects of production themselves (Anthias 1983). Second, in the absence of direct connections, some immigrants go into business with someone who does have the specific skills, for example, their wives. In New York, the typical Chinese garment factory is owned by a former waiter who has saved enough money to open up a factory with his spouse, who knows how to run a sewing machine. These specific skills are also important for women who attempt to work on their own. Lacking access to the same resources as men, women's skills are practically the only resource they have.

Thus immigrants either come with business skills or else they acquire them through what we have called the "ethnic career ladder" (in Chapter 5). Having skills is not a sufficient reason to start a business, because immigrants want to know that their efforts are likely to be rewarded. In the garment industry, the likelihood of success is slim indeed, as new start-ups fail at an alarming rate. What drives the immigrants — and distinguishes them from natives — is that preferable alternatives to petty business ownership are few and far between.

Not having a job, so many studies have shown, often pushes un-employed persons into starting out on their own, and so it is with many small immigrant entrepreneurs in the garment industry. In London, the contraction of heavy industries employing immigrants has been severe (Newnham 1986). Having lost such a job, an immigrant with a small redundancy payment has enough to go into business as a clothing producer, especially if he or she has access to a skilled, cheap, and flexible labor force.

For example, Yosef had been made redundant from a plastics factory six months prior to the interview. Redundancy money was used to buy a secondhand cutter, textiles, and rent for very small premises. He and his brother marked up and cut out the cloth for women's and girls' dresses. These were put in his van and delivered to 12 homeworkers, all Asian women known personally to him and his wife. The sewn garments were picked up, brought back, and trimmed and finished by his wife. If there was no work, he had no employees to be retained.

For some immigrants, being one's own boss is attractive because it means an escape from the regimentation of factory work and its limited opportunities for economic advancement. Consider the case of Nikola, a Yugoslav garment entrepreneur who came to France in 1970 with a contract to work at Citroen, accompanied by his wife, who found work in a laundry:

> I started like all the mortals in this business: with one machine and go ahead. I have no idea about sewing, what for? But my wife does. Eleven

months at the assembly line at Citroen drove me crazy. My wife's work in the laundry was heavy too, her hands swollen. Then one day some compatriot asked me if my wife could sew. I said yes, but how much could she earn? If she worked well, 4-5,000 FF a month. A fortune, more than we both earned together at that time. I left my job, hired a machine, it was cheap. The first two pieces took the whole night, my wife thought she could never make it. But then the *patron* gave us eight pieces (dresses they were), then twenty. She already did them in one day. We earned 5,000 FF quickly. I saw that it worked and thought why should I be a bigger fool than the others. I rented three more machines, found three women, do more and more work, more and more machines. And we were doing well. Of course there were ups and downs; I closed [the shop for the] first [time] last year when my wife broke her leg.

Not every immigrant is driven by the desire for economic independence, however. Interviews with Chinese garment factory owners in New York and with Turkish and Yugoslav owners in Paris suggest that the small garment factory was a preferred way of making a living only because life provided few other chances. Thus, while most Chinese owners in New York agreed that "to really get ahead, the best thing is to get ahead in a big American corporation," they also acknowledged that "you have to be well educated if you want to work outside the community." Hence the limiting factor was that "for immigrants, it's either the restaurant business or the garment business." As several owners put it, "I had no choice; that's why I went into business" (Waldinger 1986).

Resource Mobilization

Immigrants are embedded in social structures that provide basic resources they can use to obtain an opening in the garment industry. Myriad ties connect them to other members of the immigrant community, and those ties are also imbued with special meanings within the community. Partnerships between husband and wife, between siblings, and between hometown friends are typically the ways in which immigrant firms start out. Family members provide labor if a firm suffers a labor shortage, if production problems crop up, or if additional work is needed to get an order out on time. "Relatives are a must," noted one recent immigrant from Hong Kong, operating a shop in New York. "You need people to take care of all the departments, and when you start out, you don't have enough money to hire as many people as you need."

Running a business with kin or coethnics for partners also provides the ingredients for resolving problems of trust and delegation. Commonly, one partner supervises internal operations, while another manages relations with outsiders: manufacturers who furnish work, truckers who haul goods back and forth to the manufacturers, and suppliers who provide needles and thread.

Ethnic entrepreneurs can also rely on informal networks to obtain a skilled, attached labor force. Word of mouth is the usual way of getting a job, or securing workers, in this industry. In recruiting, the immigrant owners who know a recruit have an advantage, perhaps because the recruit is a "friend of friends." An entrepreneur can bring workers from his place of origin, collect them from a common casual labor pool, or rely on informal networks of assistance and support to steer newcomers to him. When Yugoslavs were still immigrating in large numbers to Paris, an owner could simply arrive at the *Gare de Lyon* early one morning and pick up his labor supply as newcomers spilled off the train. In New York, new arrivals from the Dominican Republic seek work in shops owned by a compatriot, with the result that many shops are staffed by workers from the same hometown.

The terms of the labor exchange are altered under conditions where workers have some emotional tie to employers that often predates the employment relationship. Both worker and owner may have the impression that they have made a good bargain: The owner has gotten workers at a lower price, and workers perceive they are indebted to him for giving them jobs, giving them the opportunity to learn a skill, or having enabled them to immigrate in the first place.

As the more settled, more adept members of the immigrant community, owners also easily move into a paternalistic role, advancing funds to cover rent or emergencies, translating documents or writing letters, and even assisting workers in bringing relatives over from the home country. Moreover, both parties are often wary of the host society and its established procedures. Their mutual confidence often leads to a variety of practices—illegal transactions, cash payments, false bills, fake bankruptcies, off-the-books work—that ensure the survival of the ethnic business and partially compensate immigrant workers for their compatriots' unwillingness to pay the going rate.

For a long time, common ethnicity and paternalism can mask conflicts that would otherwise arise in a worker-employer relationship. Immigrant owners are usually quite limited in their ability to offer material inducements, but they can and do act as intermediaries and thereby develop a "good relationship with our workers," "make our workers happy," and "increase the rate of production." Moreover, ethnic commonalities also provide a repertoire of symbols and customs that can be invoked or manipulated to underline the cultural interests and similarities that owners share with their work forces. Chinese employers in New York, for example, celebrate ethnic holidays and shop anniversaries by holding banquets to which all workers are invited, pass out gifts on the Chinese New Year, and hold raffles whose proceeds go to the workers.

The ambiguity of the contractor's status is in some ways a further source of ethnic loyalty. Contractors are bosses of the shop, but in other respects they are merely elevated and frequently working foremen. "I work on the machines just like the workers do," pointed out one Dominican owner in New York. "We all earn our money here and we all share an interest in seeing that the work is done right." If there is often a rough functional equality within the shop, the contractor's subordination to the manufacturer—who is usually a member of a higher-status ethnic group—is visible to all. Thus the ambiguity in the contractor's status lends plausibility to claims of identification with the ethnic work force, as the following leaflet, distributed in 1982 by a group of Chinese employers during a labor dispute in New York, vividly suggests:

> No matter if we're bosses or workers, we are one, like fingers on a hand. We're in the same boat together in this garment industry, fighting for a decent living. Everyone in Chinatown can see the work of the bosses. Every cent is earned from sweat and blood. There's no difference at all with the workers, except go uptown to get the garments (from the manufacturers). When [the bosses] come back, they take off their coats and sit down and sew just as hard. (leaflet distributed by a "Group of Justice-Loving People" 1982)

Among Greek Cypriots in London, one even finds employers who are members of the Cypriot Communist party and yet maintain non-union shops. For these petty owners, Communist party membership is a symbol of identity as an oppressed member of the working class. But because these Cypriot entrepreneurs share the experience of racism and discrimination with their workers, unionization is seen as an act of ethnic disloyalty. The clothing workers' union has thus far gained few adherents among the Cypriot workers (Anthias 1983).

Because a new arrival or an undocumented immigrant often stops first in a coethnic's shop, ethnic owners have privileged access to the cheapest and most easily exploited members of the ethnic community. The newcomers provide a group of undemanding workers, either because they evaluate work in the host society relative to what they had known before migration, or because they see themselves as temporary immigrants for whom the expectation of upward mobility upon return is sufficient reward. A Yugoslav garment entrepreneur explained that

> the workers [in my shop] themselves insisted that they should not be insured, they knew that if I declared them they would earn much less. They wanted cash, as much as possible as quickly as possible. Some stayed a few months and returned to Yugoslavia, some were here for a longer time. Of course, in the long run, they were losers. No security, no pension, no health insurance. My wife and I were always declared as *salariés*; I wanted to have my future secured. I set up the company with that French guy; we were associates, but legally I was the *salarié* and he the manager (the *gérant*). We worked several years together, then he left the piano business, but remained my *gérant* for another year.

In Britain, in France, and, since June 1987, in the United States as well, undocumented workers are prohibited from taking jobs. In employing undocumented workers, ethnic entrepreneurs risk severe fines or possibly even the closing of their shops. But because undocumented workers have still more to lose, fear is a powerful incentive. As long as the labor force does not acquire security through legalization, bosses can drive them to work up to 70 hours a week, including Sundays, and under conditions that sometimes fit our idea of how the nineteenth-century sweatshop must have looked:

> Slavica, a skilled garment operator from Yugoslavia, joined her boyfriend in Paris and found work in an *atelier* as a machinist. She was expelled three times from the country until finally she married in order to get at least a resident's permit. Still without a labor permit, she found a Yugoslav entrepreneur who agreed to give her work to do at home. She was hardly paid. After a while she joined workers in her *atelier,* all women of different nationalities (so he could control them better). The boss gave her a year contract, a necessary condition for legalizing her situation. During that year, Slavica had to face sexual harassment and had to accept monthly wages corresponding to about one-fifth to one-sixth of the legal minimum. "When there was no work we were not paid, but he made us come and sit

at our machines, sometimes 60 hours a week. We had to because he threatened to break our contracts and we knew that he had in reserve other homeworkers waiting to replace us."

"Whoever says "entrepreneur' generally says exploiter," exclaimed one turn-of-the-century observer of the Parisian Jewish immigrant scene (Green 1985), and the same might be said today. The current pattern of exploitation, however, is ultimately a consequence of the structural changes that have transformed the clothing industries of the West. Large domestic makers have seen their profit margins dwindle as imports have taken an ever-larger share of the market; the profit squeeze is even greater as one moves down the contracting chain. The result is a highly competitive situation in an industry where entry barriers are so low that new firms continuously enter the business by undercutting already established firms. "People will take the work that you get," complained one Dominican contractor in New York, "and will make it at any price."

Competitive pressures on the contractors are then passed on to an already underrewarded work force whose real wages have diminished with each successive year. Labor costs can be still further reduced by insisting that all workers declare themselves "self-employed," by switching to homeworkers, or by keeping a large chunk of labor entirely hidden, "off the books."

WHO MOVES UP?
GENDER DIFFERENCES IN UPWARD MOBILITY

Entry into the garment industry is practically the same for men and women. Both start at the bottom of the job ladder as waged workers, often illegal. Over time, gender differences in employment emerge.

Women are more likely to remain in less visible jobs — as illegals, as homeworkers, or as "homeworkers' helpers." In some instances, they do not have access to the labor market (that is, no right to work); in other cases, they may have the legal status of a "dependent" and do not see any advantage in getting a properly declared job. In still other circumstances, all that they can obtain are undocumented jobs. Men are more likely to step out of the invisible jobs and become legally regis-tered workers (Morokvasic et al. 1986). The latest amnesty in France has, for instance, mainly benefited men — among the 10,000 legalized foreigners in this traditionally women's industry, only 22.5% were women (Morokvasic 1986, 1987).

Access of foreign women to entrepreneurship is also limited. The few immigrant women entrepreneurs whom we have encountered had to rely on men in their transactions with manufacturers, jobbers, retailers, or wholesalers. They said that they were often not taken seriously, could not enforce their rights, were often not paid back in timely fashion by the manufacturers for whom they worked, and were also subject to sexual harassment. Though these women entrepreneurs are usually highly skilled — in contrast to many of the men — skill is their only asset in the market. Unlike the men, they must rely exclusively on female workers. "We cannot command men," says one of them. Therefore, moving one step up in the system of subcontracting and becoming a contractor or small entrepreneur is virtually a male monopoly. While stepping out of someone else's *atelier* to work at home is a downward trend for women, for men this may be the beginning of a small business.

CONCLUSION

What is the future for immigrants and immigrant business in the garment industry? We can envision several scenarios. One scenario would have these small immigrant entrepreneurs moving up into the ranks of manufacturers — just as earlier immigrants did in the first part of the nineteenth century. Thus far, there is no movement into manufacturing to report, but in New York's Chinatown, at least, the nature of the immigrant garment business appears to be in flux. The current trend is a response to the industry's severely competitive environment. Owners who started out on easily made, low-skill items are trying to move into a higher-fashion niche where product margins are not razor thin. But carrying out this strategy means changing the conditions under which clothing is made — more capital is required and factories must be managed according to strict procedures, not just the rule of thumb.

Rationalization threatens unproductive workers and promises to harden work rules and increase supervision. Hence rationalization may undercut the compromise between ethnic labor and ethnic capital that has thus far kept the immigrant garment industry relatively free of strife. As one observer of the New York Chinatown scene pointed out to us: "Under the impact of modernization and concentration, Chinatown's former family-style management is disappearing. Under these circumstances, who will take care of the children, young people, and old people and immigrants who cannot be accommodated in the garment shops?"

Given the extent to which imports have penetrated Western markets, it may not be possible for immigrant garment makers to carve out a protected niche. Nonetheless, the domestic garment industries should not yet be written off. Problems with exporting goods before quotas are reached have already led Hong Kong producers to set up operations in England and New York (*Business Week* 1985). Cheapness of overseas labor is also offset by the importance of quick response. The immigrant garment businesses enjoy proximity to the centers of merchandising and design, and this should increase their lease on life.

Thus the most likely scenario involves more of the same, in which the only change is the succession of one group of immigrants for another. In Paris several years ago, Turkish workers struck to protest substandard conditions in small shops where they worked at the mercy of ethnic employers. The French government responded by issuing several reports that called for replacing the industry's outmoded technology and regrouping workers in large, modern factories. But the technological revolution has not yet arrived, and work in the industry continues just as it had before; the only new wrinkle is the arrival of Chinese refugees, whose garment shops are clustered in the *triangle du Choisy,* where this latest group of newcomers lives (Guillon and Taboada-Leonetti 1986; Hassoun and Tan 1986).

7

Conclusions and Policy Implications

Roger Waldinger
Howard Aldrich
William D. Bradford
Jeremy Boissevain
Gavin Chen
Hermann Korte
Robin Ward
Peter Wilson

Our explanation of immigrant enterprise has emphasized the interaction between the opportunity structure of the host society and the group characteristics and social structure of the immigrant community, and the strategies that emerge from the interaction of these forces.

Opportunity structures have been analyzed along two dimensions: the market — ethnic and nonethnic — for a business's products or services, and access to business vacancies produced either by expanding economic sectors or by the abandonment of sectors by previous owners. The demand for small business activities emanates from markets whose small size, heterogeneity, or susceptibility to flux and instability limit the potential for mass distribution and mass production. Because such conditions favor small-scale enterprise, they lower the entry barriers to immigrants with limited capital and technical resources. Opportunities for ownership result from the process of ethnic succession: Vacancies for new business owners arise as the older groups that have previously dominated small business activities move into higher social positions.

A group's position and success depend very much on the historical period during which it emigrates to a host society. Opportunities are continually opening (and closing) as the economies of Western nations mature. In our discussion of the United States, we pointed to the prevalence of petty entrepreneurship among the new immigrants as a reflection of the continuing, indeed enhanced, importance of small business in the national economy — the structural transformation of the American economy has expanded business opportunities, making small business an increasingly viable niche.

Economic restructuring is also occurring in western Europe, although the emergence of ethnic enterprise has mostly taken the form of a switch from marginal jobs to marginal businesses. However, sufficient signs of growth are evident to leave the long-term role of ethnic business in western Europe an open question.

The cases presented in Chapters 2 and 3 showed the complex interaction between the two dimensions of opportunity structures and group characteristics. Changing opportunity structures have presented immigrant groups with very different market conditions, depending upon when they arrived in the United States and western Europe. Opportunities have become available because groups previously dominating a market have left or been economically assimilated (such as the Japanese in the United States). A succession of immigrant groups, differing in predisposing factors and in their capacity for resource mobilization, have risen and fallen in visibility in the business sector. Our review indicated that any explanation of ethnic business participation must take account of the historically contingent nature of the process.

A group's position in a country's legal and political system, and the extent of restrictions imposed by the system on immigrants, has a major effect on its economic opportunities. Some immigrants are welcomed; others are merely tolerated. Some migrate to societies where business start-ups are simple and cheap, whereas in other societies, would-be business owners confront mountains of bureaucratic regulations. The United States is a business environment in which legal-political restrictions on immigrants are minimal, after the migrant is settled in the country. Immigrants in many western European nations, by contrast, must resort to a variety of strategies to evade legal constraints on their economic activities.

Some changes in opportunity structures are linked to changes in the residential distribution of groups, with some ethnic groups depending heavily upon residential concentrations of coethnics for their markets, and others diffusing to serve nonethnic markets in all areas. Business development is uneven, and businesses catering to a minority population coexist with those aiming for the majority market. The problems of immigrant adaptation give rise to "adjustment entrepreneurs" (ethnic real estate agents, ethnic professionals, and so on) early on in the replacement labor stage. In a later stage of settlement, an ethnic business enclave may develop in incipient form but provide neither the bulk of business services nor substantial local employment to a population mainly engaged in ethnic labor. Even in the most vibrant enclaves, business development will sooner, rather than later, reach its ceiling unless it can branch off into the broader market, given the limited size of the ethnic population.

As for *group characteristics,* our model emphasizes two factors that promote recruitment into entrepreneurial positions. First, the situational constraints that immigrants confront sometimes breed a predisposition toward small business and further encourage immigrants to engage in activities that are resource-conserving. Some ethnic groups have cultural norms that create a set of understandings about appropriate behavior and expectations within work settings. Second, resource mobilization is facilitated when immigrant firms draw on their connections with a supply of family and ethnic labor to resolve some of the organizational problems of small firms. While these factors lift the self-employment rate of the overall immigrant population, levels of business activity vary among specific immigrant groups. A group's success in attaining business ownership is determined by three characteristics — its premigration experiences, the circumstances of its migration and settlement, and its postmigration experiences — and how these characteristics interact with one another.

Among Afro-American and West Indian communities in the United States and the United Kingdom, there is no parallel to the growth of immigrant enclave economies — the self-employment rate among these groups remains far below the national average. New immigrants, rather than native-born blacks in the United States, or Caribbean immigrants in the United Kingdom, have emerged as the successors to whites as the suppliers of goods and services in black ghettos.

A group's position depends, in part, on the cultural, social, and economic resources it brings with it. However, lacking such resources, groups often enact *strategies* to compensate. Success with such strategies depends heavily on the nature of ties among coethnics and the shape of the social networks in which immigrants are embedded. The cases we reviewed showed how strategies emerge from the interaction of group characteristics and opportunity structures, as entrepreneurs mobilize resources to meet market conditions, adapting to or creating solutions to problems. We documented how very different and widely separated ethnic groups utilize rather similar strategies in their attempts to carve out economic niches in Western industrial societies.

We examined strategies involved in securing low-cost labor, gaining access to skills, training, and capital, fighting prohibitive statutory regulations, and meeting price undercutting from competitors. Distinctive strategies enable ethnic entrepreneurs to exploit distinctive sociocultural resources. Minority entrepreneurs develop strategies to compensate for the background deficits of their group in wealth, valid educational credentials, political power, and influential contacts. As social outsiders, ethnic entrepreneurs face political and economic obstacles that native-born or majority entrepreneurs escape, such as difficulties in obtaining loans from commercial banks.

Our account noted differences among ethnic groups in their formation of small businesses, but also pointed to the very similar strategies adopted by many groups. Despite differences in their cultural and economic backgrounds, particular migration history, and current circumstances, similar adaptations have occurred across different contexts. Ethnic groups do possess ethnic resources and deploy ethnic economic strategies, but the exact resources and strategies vary from group to group.

PUBLIC POLICY IMPLICATIONS

In virtually all of the countries discussed in this book, governments at differing levels have sought to promote the development of entrepreneurship among ethnic and immigrant groups. The appeal of business development strategies is not difficult to divine. Though many ethnic groups are afflicted by high levels of structural unemployment, governments are far more reluctant than in the past to undertake either macroeconomic or training and employment policies to alleviate this situation. In this context, a business development policy is an attractive option for governments trying to encourage job creation in ethnic and minority communities.

Immediate political necessity is not the only reason that governments pursue ethnic development policies. As we noted in the very beginning of this book, there are precedents, in the experience of earlier ethnic and immigrant groups, for the view that business development may be an effective engine of group social mobility. An ethnic business development policy is also consistent with the widespread view that economic growth depends on a society's ability to encourage and foster the birth of new, small firms, whether ethnic or not. Ethnic business development policies have an obvious political attraction to conservative or neoliberal governments, for whom the petite bourgeoisie is an important political constituency (Bechhofer and Elliot 1985). An emphasis on entrepreneurialism as a response to discrimination is also appealing insofar as it reinforces beliefs in the accessibility of rewards for those willing to take the risks of independent action.

In this chapter, we take a skeptical look at ethnic and minority business development policies in four countries: Germany, the Netherlands, the United Kingdom, and the United States. We argue that the rationale for business development policies is fundamentally inconsistent with the underlying social structural dynamics of ethnic business development, which we have explicated in this book. While we agree that governments should undertake policies aimed at promoting ethnic or minority business development, we argue that those policies can be thought of only as part of a much broader strategy aimed at tackling the multiple problems of unemployment, discrimination, and low earnings.

In this chapter, we also note that governments may promote the development of ethnic businesses while simultaneously maintaining policies that impede the attainment of that goal. Such policies may be directed at reducing competition in the small business sector; they may be directed at controlling the conditions under which labor is employed; or they may be directed at controlling the occupational or geographical mobility of immigrant workers. Regardless of intent, all of these policies heighten barriers to the formation of small ethnic firms.

Because the experience with ethnic business development policies is so uneven among the four countries under discussion, our principal focus is on the United States. In contrast to the European countries, minority business development has been a policy goal in the United States for almost a quarter century. During that time, the United States has compiled a record — of few successes and many failures — that provides a benchmark against which to evaluate the viability and appropriateness of a business development strategy.

The chapter is structured in the following way. We begin with descriptions of business development policy in each of the European countries. We then move on to an evaluation of business development policies in the United States. Next, we briefly review policies that *impede* the formation of ethnic firms, with particular interest in the variations among the four countries discussed in this chapter. Finally, we consider the overall objectives and problems of ethnic business development policy and suggest some general considerations for policymaking in this field.

ETHNIC BUSINESS DEVELOPMENT POLICIES IN EUROPE

Great Britain

From the end of World War II until the late 1960s, successive British governments sought to promote large businesses to take advantage of economies of scale and scope inherent in large businesses. Governments felt that larger firms were also more able to operate and compete in international markets and thus were important in developing international trade for British products.

Because of this policy and other economic-related factors, the number of small businesses in Great Britain declined between World War II and 1970. Starting in the late 1960s and continuing to the present, both Labour and Conservative national administrations have adopted specific programs to assist small businesses. Although a wide range of national government assistance programs for small businesses exist, there has been no statutory legislation that formalizes these programs or provides a legal justification for the support of small business.

Concern with business development among Great Britain's black minorities arose in the aftermath of widespread civil unrest in 1981, paralleling events in the United States. Reporting on the causes of unrest in predominantly black areas, the chairman of the Board of Inquiry pointed to the lack of black businesses in the area, implying a causal link between dissatisfaction with the social and economic conditions and the traditional developmental role of the entrepreneur in ethnic communities (Scarman 1981).

These conclusions converged with the findings of a report on the state of West Indian businesses, which was undertaken for the Home Office just one year before the outbreak of the civil disorders (Ward and Reeves 1980). This report contended that the conditions for development that had traditionally favored business growth among immigrant groups were not present in Britain's contemporary economic climate.

Racial discrimination was still pervasive and, in combination with the disadvantage of inner-city markets and the inherent problems of small-scale production, reduced the rate of business formation among blacks and limited their business survival prospects. This study was soon followed by a number of research projects that looked into the problems and needs of local black businesses. Many of these were funded by the public sector (Kazuka 1980; London Borough of Lambeth 1982; Wilson and Stanworth 1983).

Although official attitudes toward the underrepresentation of black minorities in business and their problems have changed perceptibly since the early 1980s, no formal statement of policy toward ethnic business, distinct from that toward small business in general, has been made. The principal reason is the prevailing view that the problems facing ethnic businesses are not essentially different from those confronting other firms.

Consequently, the implementation of public policy toward ethnic minority business in Great Britain derives from two principal sources. The first is policies toward small firms in general (ethnic minority businesses are typically small), and the second is policies toward the inner cities in particular (where most ethnic minorities live). Although laws and programs created by Great Britain to eliminate racial discrimination may affect minority business development, these impacts are indirect and will not be discussed here.

Small business policy has had no impact on either the formation or the growth rates of ethnic minority businesses. Despite the plethora of small business measures introduced by government since the late 1960s, none has been designed specifically for the needs of ethnic firms until very recently. Indeed, research has shown that government assistance programs have failed to reach black owner-managers, principally because they are oriented to the needs of certain industrial categories (manufacturing, for example, in which there is a relatively low black minority presence), geographical areas (in which there are relatively few black firms), and performance categories (such as rapidly growing high-technology firms, of which there are virtually none in the black minority community; Wilson and Stanworth 1983).

Public policy toward the inner city in general also embraces elements of ethnic minority business support. Public sector concern for inner-city communities has resulted in a range of special programs aimed at relieving poverty through employment and training opportunities, housing improvement, and providing resources to exploit business opportunities. A 1977 government statement on policy toward low-income inner-city areas made a brief reference to the role of ethnic minorities in retailing in deprived areas, but none of the resulting programs was designed specifically for the needs of minorities.

Statutory powers vested in certain local authorities have enabled them to support local firms with business counseling, rent grants, premises improvement grants, market research grants, loan guarantees, and loans at subsidized rates of interest. Areas of high unemployment and severe physical and social decay receive a greater allocation of inner-city funds, and the worst areas are accorded special status providing a commensurately higher level of assistance for business development. For example, in Manchester, the Local Authority established the Moss Side and Hulme Enterprise Scheme to promote business development in an economically depressed area. Although not specifically entitled to preferential treatment under this legislation, black-owned businesses have increasingly benefited from the various programs as a result of deliberately targeted marketing by local authorities with large concentrations of ethnic minority communities.

The efficacy of local policy in assisting minority businesses has never been evaluated, however, largely because these activities are so recent. In a preliminary evaluation, these programs have produced mixed results; possibly these mixed results reflect the inexperience of local policymakers.

The central government of Great Britain launched a more substantial initiative in 1986, aimed at providing advice and other business development services to black minorities in London, Birmingham, and Manchester. These activities included private sector contributions of counseling and other services. As of 1988, however, the largest volume of resources devoted to ethnic minority business development in Great Britain has come from local government.

The Netherlands

In the Netherlands, laws regulating the establishment of a business date from the economic crisis in the 1930s. The conditions for the establishment of a business were formulated for the first time in 1935. Entrepreneurs had to be creditworthy and technically competent. Moreover, they had to establish that there was a "need" among consumers for the new enterprise.

In 1937, the Small Business Establishment Act came into effect at the national level. Although the "need" element in the 1935 law was dropped under this 1937 legislation, entrepreneurs still had to demonstrate that they possessed the necessary trade expertise and knowledge for any particular line of business. Subsequently, the Beverage, Hotel and Catering Act of 1964, the Retail Establishment Act of 1971, and the Business Establishment Act of 1974 created a dense network of rules regulating the establishment of an enterprise. Regulations applicable to all entrepreneurs include the following:

(1) registration with the Chamber of Commerce and the Register of Commerce;

(2) compliance with regulations of the line of business, as established by the respective agency; and

(3) granting of licenses only to entrepreneurs possessing the required diplomas, although a license can be procured if an entrepreneur employs someone with a license.

Exemptions from the trade knowledge/expertise provisions can be requested at the Chamber of Commerce. Exemptions are granted on the basis of similar foreign training, pressing local consumer needs, and "special cases."

When the government established the criteria for opening businesses, foreign-trained immigrant craftsmen and businessmen were not very numerous and thus their needs were ignored. No attention was given to the specific skills and qualifications of many skilled craftsmen trained in other countries. During the passage of the 1971 Retail Establishment Act, observers noted that the law could create problems for entrepreneurs from EEC states who applied for Dutch business licenses. Subsequently, the Council for Small and Medium Sized Business of the Netherlands questioned whether the minimum level of profitability according to Dutch standards should be applied without adjustment to ethnic minority businesses. Entrepreneurial activity, the council argued, is sensitive to cultural background and depends upon the cultural norms and customs of people. This same statement was put to the Dutch Parliament in 1981. These pressures linked to EEC membership, combined with legal activism by ethnic minority entrepreneurs, have prompted modest revisions allowing ethnic minority entrepreneurs to be exempted from some regulations.

However, in practice it is extremely difficult for foreign-born entrepreneurs who possess the required diplomas to obtain licenses. Their "pressing needs" and "special cases" are rarely judged acute enough to warrant exemptions. One of the results of this web of regulations is that firms already in the field are protected against new entrants (Menger 1980).

Thus ethnic entrepreneurs in the Netherlands face a highly structured set of barriers to operation, including professional associations, semigovernmental inspection services, controllers, and a conservative national government. These bodies have a vested interest in maintaining the status quo that has not yet been overcome by the ethnic minority business sector. Finally, formal recognition of a minority business sector has not occurred in the Netherlands, in part because members of the ethnic minority business community will not or cannot organize themselves to apply pressure to government or mobilize public opinion.

West Germany

Government policy in West Germany regarding the ethnic minority business sector is subsumed under the general laws governing the admittance requirements for self-employment (Esser and Korte 1985; Korte 1987). All self-employed entrepreneurs are automatically registered with the appropriate authorities. Trade associations, such as the chambers of commerce and industry, and the artisans' chambers, are required to issue statements to the local authorities as to whether an applicant fulfills the prerequisites for self-employment, commenting on local needs in specific sectors.

The ability to open a business is also regulated according to the native land of the foreign applicant through EEC treaties, laws affecting foreigners, special bi- or multilateral agreements, and the guidelines for trading by foreigners. The trading laws, which must also be considered, contain the generally applicable regulations for individual lines of business—for example, a master qualification (*Meisterbrief*) is a prerequisite for operating an independent artisan business (Bender 1979; Haag 1982; Kanein 1966; Kissrow 1980).

Even though, as of 1988, no special programs had been developed for the ethnic minority business sector, the West German government takes account of the participation of ethnic minority entrepreneurs in planning its existing programs, and regulates their participation by special provisions. Current laws enable ethnic minorities to operate their own businesses and to participate in assistance and support programs in much the same way as do German entrepreneurs.

For a variety of reasons, there is no formal recognition of the significance of an ethnic business sector. Compared with the number of employed foreigners or of German entrepreneurs, this sector has become quantitatively significant only recently. Furthermore, government planners use outdated conceptions of migration, reflecting a refusal to recognize that Germany is a country that is attractive to immigrants. The concept of migration for employment instead of for self-employment has obscured the importance of foreign ethnic businesses. This ambiguity has also slowed the pace of government programs to assist minority businesses.

Consequently, the minority business sector in West Germany has not been comprehensively examined, nor has it been the object of directed state or organizational economic policy. Boards, agencies, or organizations exclusively responsible for this economic sector have not been established, and assistance or development programs to boost the economic growth of ethnic minority businesses have not been implemented. Special *informal* support of this sector is also nonexistent.

The federal government and several quasi-government organizations are currently conducting and supporting research that will document ethnic minority businesses in West Germany. Current policy is one of cautious inactivity until it is clear what strategies should be followed with respect to this sector.

ETHNIC AND MINORITY BUSINESS DEVELOPMENT POLICIES IN THE UNITED STATES

We first discuss the historical background of public policies toward minority businesses and then evaluate the results of such policies.

Background

Ever since the expansion of the federal government's role in the 1930s, small business assistance has been a public policy issue in the United States. During the New and Fair Deal eras, various federal departments undertook programs to assist small business or guarantee small business a share of government procurements and contracts. With the advent of a Republican administration in 1954, these programs were consolidated in the Small Business Administration (SBA), established within the Department of Commerce. Although the formation of the SBA appeared to symbolize the institutionalization of small business interests in Washington, the allocations made to SBA were considerably less than what was available when small business assistance efforts were scattered among numerous agencies (Zeigler 1961). Thus, from the beginning, government has championed small business for ideological reasons but has been much less willing to provide meaningful financial support.

Government policies to promote minority business arose as a response to the black protest movements of the 1960s. Prior to the mid-1960s, minority businesses were virtually excluded from the loan programs administered by the SBA. For example, a study of the first ten and half years of the Philadelphia SBA office found that only 7 of 432 loans were made to black businesses (Foley 1967: 574-575). The first programs were initiated under the Johnson administration as part of the War on Poverty. The Kerner Commission on the civil disorders of the late 1960s advocated expansion of government efforts to give special encouragement to black ownership of business in ghetto areas. Even prior to that, the SBA had accelerated its search for qualified black borrowers by instituting special outreach programs, lowering equity requirements, and guaranteeing up to 90% of bank loans (Tabb 1971). However, it was not until the election of Richard Nixon that minority economic development was articulated as a coherent policy. In 1969 President Nixon signed an executive order creating an Office of Minority Business Enterprise (later renamed the Minority Business Development Agency — MBDA) in the U.S. Department of Commerce, and he assigned it the task of coordinating the activities of other agencies to promote minority business enterprise and private sector involvement.

Nixon's minority business development policies were first broached during his campaign under the rubric of "black capitalism." But that label was soon discarded after criticism from the leaders of other groups — Hispanics, Asians, and Native Americans — who had been swept up into the civil rights revolution under the galvanizing effect of black mobilization. Under the executive order creating the Minority Business Enterprise Agency, blacks were joined by Hispanics, Asians, Native Americans, Aleuts, and Eskimos as "minorities" eligible for business assistance. Thus the evolution of minority business development policies is yet another instance of the extension of civil rights and affirmative action policies from the originally targeted group — blacks — to a much broader set of minority groups.

Specific Problems

Federal activities in the minority business development arena fall into several categories. The SBA licenses private capital agencies called small business investment corporations (SBICs) or minority enterprise small business investment companies (MESBICs). Using the private capital with which they were started, and funds provided at subsidized rates by SBA, these firms provide financing to minority entrepreneurs by investing in their debt and/or equity capital. The SBA also operates a direct loan program that lends small amounts (about $25,000) to minority businesses. Finally, the SBA has a major program of guaranteeing 80% of the total loan that a commercial bank makes to a minority business, thus enabling banks to finance minority firms more readily.

Assistance in obtaining market access is provided by the MBDA (as coordinator) and the SBA. At the federal level, each federal department designates a portion of the agency's purchases that will be held out of general procurements competition and allocated only for small and minority business competition. This activity, which creates sheltered market access, is coordinated by the MBDA and operated by the SBA. The MBDA also coordinates efforts to improve minority businesses' access to state and local government contracts and to private firm markets. Both the MBDA and the SBA furnish managerial and technical support to minority businesses: the SBA on a direct basis and the MBDA through hiring private consultants who provide counseling to minority businesses. A similar approach has been tried by some Local Authorities in Great Britain.

Comparable programs are provided at the state and municipal levels. As of the early 1980s, 30 of the nation's 33 largest cities operated major or significant programs for minority economic development (Bates 1985). New York City, for example, has established specific minority business offices within its larger economic development agencies; these offices are charged with assisting minority firms in obtaining loans or contracts with other city agencies. In addition, New York City operates a locally based enterprise (LBE) program, which reserves 10% of all city construction projects for the primarily minority firms that are certified as LBE eligible.

Evaluation

The record of minority business development in the United States is spotty at best. To begin with, a serious dollar commitment to small business, let alone minority business, has never been made. As Zeigler (1961: 111) concluded, the establishment of the SBA meant that "small businessmen finally were going to have representation in Washington, but the agency which was to represent them was to be less powerful than the organization it was to replace." Agencies in the minority business field have been no more potent. Blaustein and Faux (1972) were certainly correct in discerning a "star-spangled hustle" in Nixon's attempt to foster "black capitalism" as an alternative to public employment or job training programs. Indeed, OMBD was created without any new allocations, but rather given money already allocated to the Office for Economic Opportunity budget (Tabb 1971). Throughout the Nixon tenure, scandals enveloped the minority business effort, underlining the narrowly political character of the entire enterprise. While the subsequent Ford and Carter administrations can best be described as tepid in their support for minority business development, the Reagan administration was actively hostile toward it. Despite its putative pro-small business stance, the Reagan administration actively campaigned to abolish the entire SBA. Although these efforts were eventually blocked by Congress, the agency fell on hard times, suffering from low morale, high staff turnover, and recruitment difficulties.

An examination of specific programs provides further ground for criticism. Small Business Administration loans to minority businesses fall into two categories: the 7(a) Regular Business Loan Program (named after the section in the original SBA enabling legislation) and the Economic Opportunity Loan (EOL) Program. The EOL Program, which accounts for the bulk of loans to minority businesses, is targeted to socially or economically disadvantaged individuals, which in practice means that recipients have low incomes, little business experience, and minimal capital assets. EOL loans have also been low compared with general SBA loans. It is not surprising that recipients have experienced extraordinarily high business failure and loan repayment delinquency rates. Overall, SBA loans tended to be directed at business lines in which black firms, in particular, have historically been concentrated: Thus retail and service businesses accounted for more than 70% of all the 7(a) and EOL loans provided during the 1970s (Bates 1981: 329).

The high rates of failure and loan delinquency have had negative impacts both on the implementation and the political support for minority business policies. As a General Accounting Office report noted, high failure rates "necessarily have an adverse effect on the credibility of the Federal minority business enterprise" (quoted in Bates and Bradford 1979: 145) and weaken the congressional constituency as well. To reduce the risk of delinquency, the SBA has shifted from direct lending to guaranteeing the loans provided by private financial institutions. This transition, as Bates and Bradford (1979: 141) noted, leads to "socializing the risk of bank small business lending. In the process, the power to initiate and control the allocation of loan funds passed increasingly out of the hands of SBA bureaucrats and into those of private bankers." Consequently, black businesses have been made dependent on the willingness of private bankers to provide loans, which has diminished in the recent years of high interest rates and capital scarcity.

The experience of MESBICs is similarly discouraging. Because the MESBICs are undercapitalized and experience cash-flow problems, they tend to avoid equity investments and offer loans instead. In turn, the MESBICs' borrowers, which are undercapitalized to begin with, find that they cannot keep up with the constant demands for debt repayment, and consequently fall into default (Bates and Bradford 1979). A study conducted for the U.S. Congress by the GAO during the mid-1970s showed that MESBICs responded to this situation in risk-averse ways, with less than one-third of their funds invested in minority and disadvantaged businesses and over 60% in risk-free liquid assets, such as certificates of deposit (U.S. Office of Management and Budget 1976).

The experience of programs designed to set aside government contracts for minority businesses is also disappointing. By targeting deprived minority firms, the availability of federal set-aside contracts has fostered the development of a "dependent sector" of minority-owned businesses that cannot function in the open market. As of spring 1987, only 971 of the 6,500 firms that had participated in the SBA's set-aside program had graduated to "self-sufficiency" (Matlack 1987). Moreover, effective participation in federal set-aside programs exceeds the capacity of most minority firms. Those minority firms participating in federal programs are very distinct from the broader universe of minority businesses: The former are much larger and overrepresent lines in construction, manufacturing, and wholesaling — sectors in which minority businesses are generally underrepresented. Even this selected tier of minority-owned firms compares unfavorably with nonminority firms participating in set-aside programs, being less profitable and more highly in debt (Bates 1985).

In addition, the conditions under which firms are selected for participation in set-asides has fostered corrupt practices, both within industry and within government. Establishing a "minority-owned" business as a front for white interests is an example of such practices; in 1979, the SBA's inspector general found that 20% of the firms receiving set-asides were neither "minority-owned" nor "disadvantaged." Because decisions on set-aside contracts are made on a noncompetitive basis, the risk of payoffs and bribes to government officials making awards is high.

Although many states and municipalities run minority business development programs as well, there is virtually no research on their effectiveness. What is clear, however, is that programs have emerged in response to political mobilization. Browning, Marshall, and Tabb, who appear to be the only social scientists to have examined minority contracting patterns at the local level, conclude in their study of northern California cities that minority contracting was strongly correlated with minority incorporation in dominant local coalitions and minority protest (Browning et al. 1984). Clinical evidence suggests that demands for greater state and local assistance to minority businesses rank high on the minority political agenda, even when minorities are not part of the dominant coalition.

GENERIC EVALUATION

This review of policies in the United States provides the groundwork for a generic evaluation of policies aimed at fostering the development of ethnic business.

The first issue is specifying the problem that ethnic business development policies are meant to address. If the problem is that of large-scale structural unemployment among ethnic or minority populations, then business development policies are clearly not the appropriate response. In any society, the overall self-employment rate sets an upper bound on the number of minorities or immigrants who can be working on their own. Small groups will be relatively unaffected by this constraint, but large groups will have much greater difficulty fitting into the small business niche. Thus in the United States even the most effective minority business development policy would be of only limited value to Afro-Americans or to such Hispanic groups as Mexican Americans or Puerto Ricans in cities where they are particularly concentrated. Moreover, the unemployed are precisely those persons who lack the social structures most conducive to the acquisition of business contacts, information, and skill. Indeed, we have argued throughout this book that employment in small firms is the start of entrepreneurial careers, and this appears to hold for *all* workers, not just for members of ethnic groups (OECD 1986).

If the problem is that of developing an existing, but inadequate, resource base in ethnic communities, then business development policies may indeed be the appropriate course. But here one runs into another problem: How is one to target assistance to the right recipients? The tendency is to help those business owners who are most disadvantaged; the difficulty, however, is that these are the business owners most prone to failure. This conundrum has affected minority business development policy in the United States right from the beginning: No sooner did the SBA begin to increase its lending in black ghetto communities than its default rate rapidly moved up. Defaults not only are expensive, but they also weaken the political constituency for a minority business program. The safer alternative, which the SBA has pursued, is to assist larger, more established firms. But this option is open to the criticism often launched at business development policies of all sorts, namely, that the assisted firms are not in need of government's help and would survive and prosper whether they received assistance or not. To the extent that *minority* business development policies are aimed at reducing poverty, efforts directed at established firms or individuals may have limited community spinoffs. A similar criticism has been made of recent British governmental interventions.

Assuming that the objectives of policy *can* be properly specified, one should note the divergence between the model of business development outlined in this book and the implicit model underlying most government policies. In our model, the demand side for ethnic businesses (the opportunity structure) and the supply side (group characteristics) come into play and interact with each other. By contrast, the conventional policy model takes into account only the demand side. Put another way, policy takes the supply of potential entrepreneurs for granted and attempts to alter only the demand side. And in doing so, it cannot manipulate many of the variables — the vacancies for business ownerships, the competition for vacancies, the size of the small business niche—that impinge so powerfully on the business development process.

Not only is the policy model incomplete, it also abstracts from the historical contingencies out of which ethnic businesses emerge. As we have argued in this book, immigrants' predispositions toward entrepreneurship are not imported but situational. A crucial element in the immigrant situation, as Bailey (1987) pointed out, is the transitional nature of the immigrant experience. The standards of the home country affect immigrants' evaluation of the attractiveness of small business opportunities, and the constricted range of employment possibilities enhances the relative desirability of small business. These are also the characteristics that distinguish immigrants from second- or later-generation groups. Thus Afro-Americans in the United States or second-generation West Indians in Britain, for example, are unlikely to use an immigrant's standards in evaluating the desirability of opening a small shop.

Even if policy took into account the supply side, it is not clear that the array of instruments thus far developed by governments is compatible with the fundamental characteristics of the ethnic business development process. As we have argued throughout this book, ethnic businesses emerge as a consequence of the formation of ethnic communities, with their sheltered markets and networks of mutual support. These conditions not only allow business owners to start out small—often very small—they also foster informal arrangements of raising capital and business organization. Furthermore, the skills-acquisition process is so deeply embedded in networks that it does not correspond to the conventional human capital or occupational choice model. Employment in a coethnic's firm provides opportunities for costless and almost incidentally acquired business skills and information, the value of which the potential entrepreneur may not recognize until years later.

Not only is putting these social structures in place completely beyond the scope of policy, but policy is in conflict with the social structures themselves. The modus operandi of the ethnic firm, with its cash payments, hidden partners, thin line between family and business, and occasional employment of illegal immigrants, is simply not that of the bureaucratic model required to receive government loans or technical assistance. Moreover, participation in government programs forces ethnic firms to a threshold that they can neither attain nor sustain. As noted in our discussion of government set-aside policies in the United

States, minority participants are bigger, better capitalized, and in some sense deviant relative to the universe of minority firms. Moreover, participation in set-aside programs involves costs that are difficult to maintain. In the United States, for example, many of the set-aside contracts are for government construction projects, in which union labor is often mandatory. But this entails much higher labor costs than the minority firm can absorb on its nongovernment jobs. Hiring union construction workers, a group among whom blacks, Hispanics, and Asians are greatly underrepresented, not only dilutes the employment objectives of a minority business development policy but prevents the minority firm from benefiting from the advantages of employing co-ethnic labor.

Policies Impeding Ethnic Business Development

Though the principal focus in this chapter is on policies designed to promote ethnic business development, it is important to note that all four countries under examination maintain policies that *impede* the growth of ethnic firms. The impact of these policies is most severe in Germany and the Netherlands, where the small business sector continues to bear the imprint of its traditional artisanal, or guildlike, past. That this "traditional" small business sector persists is in large measure the product of government regulations designed to reduce competition and thereby protect established small businesses. However, these same strictures impede the emergence of ethnic or immigrant entrepreneurs who are unable to comply with training or operating standards, especially in the early stages of business development.

The situation in these countries contrasts sharply with the flexibility and openness of labor and commercial markets in the United States. Restraints on commercial competition were never as fully developed in the United States as in Europe and have been greatly scaled back in recent years. Furthermore, apprenticeship plays a minor role in the U.S. economy and is insignificant in commerce; even in those trades where apprenticeships are common, the majority of workers acquire skills without passing through organized apprenticeships.

Whether the small business sector is tightly regulated or not, ethnic entrepreneurs are likely to encounter legal obstacles to the formation and operation of small firms. Licenses are required for many of the business lines in which ethnic businesses are quick to emerge. The food and beverage trade is a good example of this characteristic, with concern over sanitary conditions one of the factors that makes licensing almost universal. Licensing is also one way to reduce competition among petty traders or skilled craftsworkers. Given the aversion of store owners to sidewalk competitors who do business without paying rent, authorities are under constant pressure to control peddling through licensing laws; similarly, building trade unions keep the supply of skilled labor tight by pressuring governments to monitor licensing requirements.

As noted in Chapters 5 and 6, labor standard laws also adversely affect ethnic entrepreneurs. Access to cheap coethnic or family labor is diminished by laws that set a floor on wages or hours, determine which workers are legally eligible for employment, and prohibit or regulate the use of homeworkers.

These various legal strictures provoke ethnic entrepreneurs to operate beyond or in spite of the law. Regulations that prevent immigrants from owning businesses lead immigrants to find natives who pose as "frontmen." Licensing requirements, as noted in Chapter 5, can be evaded by finding a related business line where certification is more easily obtained. Moreover, the tendency of ethnic entrepreneurs to fall back on ethnic networks reduces their exposure to state regulation. As we have argued, greater trust and confidentiality are among the advantages of a coethnic labor force, thus reducing the risks entailed in paying in cash, employing illegal immigrants, or violating overtime laws. Furthermore, the ethnic community itself offers a supportive and partially self-enclosed environment from which state monitors, as well as the interest groups that impel them, are effectively excluded.

To note that some regulations impede the formation of ethnic businesses is not to argue that small firms should be given a free hand. On the contrary, the objective of policy should be to locate the appropriate balance between ease of access to business opportunities and protections for workers and consumers.

Future Policies

Despite our harsh appraisal of many current policies, there is a future for minority and ethnic business development policy. That future, however, lies in a broader context, one in which business development policies are part of a broader strategy aimed at redressing the economic problems of ethnic and minority groups.

Effective policies might be developed along two lines: (1) building an infrastructure that fosters small business development in general and (2) enacting and enforcing systemic policies of equal economic opportunity for ethnic and racial minorities. We have argued that governments simply do not have the resources or the foresight to pick winners and losers from among competing small businesses, whether owned by majority or minority group members. Recognizing this constraint, some national, state, and local governments have turned their attention to creating conditions under which ambitious, resourceful (and perhaps lucky) entrepreneurs are tempted to start their own businesses. As a substantial literature exists on entrepreneurship and regional economic development, we simply note here that deregulation, enforcement of laws against monopolistic or predatory business practices, and investments in public education, highways and airports, public utilities, and so on create a climate within which business foundings increase. Governments have so far shown themselves unable to formulate policies with any long-run effect on business dissolutions, but if foundings are increased, the typically high level of business dissolutions is not problematic.

We have shown that ethnicity is often a powerful resource for minority group members, and we have argued that there is little governments can do to intervene in the social structures supporting ethnic businesses. However, majority groups should not be able to use ethnicity as a weapon *against* ethnic minorities. Legal and political strictures against discrimination are needed: At the very least, ethnic and minority groups should be able to play the game on an equal footing with dominant group members. Under the most optimistic scenario, these policies will significantly increase the level of business activity for *some* ethnic groups. As our model emphasizes, opportunity structures are only half of the equation, and the transitional nature of the immigrant experience means that many groups will not have the characteristics required to take advantage of favorable market conditions. Hence serious attempts to improve opportunities for all ethnic and minority groups will include business development policies, but only as part of a much larger effort to create jobs and provide relevant skills for the whole population.

References

Alain, L. 1980. *Le commerce indépendent, le phénomène maghrebin. Paris et la region parisienne.* Paris: Editions CIGMA.

Aldrich, Howard. 1973. "White-Owned Businesses in Black Ghettos." *American Journal of Sociology* 78 (6, May): 1403-1426.

Aldrich, Howard. 1975. "Ecological Succession in Racially Changing Neighborhoods: A Review of the Literature." *Urban Affairs Quarterly* 10 (3, March): 327-348.

Aldrich, Howard. 1977. "Testing the Middleman Minority Model of Asian Entrepreneurial Behavior: Preliminary Results from Wandsworth, England." Paper presented at the annual meetings of American Sociological Association, Chicago.

Aldrich, Howard, John Cater, Trevor Jones, and David McEvoy. 1983. "From Periphery to Peripheral: The South Asian Petite Bourgeoisie in England." Pp. 1-32 in Ida Harper Simpson and Richard Simpson (eds.), *Research in the Sociology of Work.* Vol. 2. Greenwich, CT: JAI.

Aldrich, Howard, John Cater, Trevor Jones, David McEvoy, and Paul Velleman. 1985. "Ethnic Residential Concentration and the Protected Market Hypothesis." *Social Forces* 63 (4, June): 996-1009.

Aldrich, Howard and Albert J. Reiss, Jr. 1970. "The Effect of Civil Disorders on Small Business in the Inner City." *Journal of Social Issues* 26 (1, Winter): 187-206.

Aldrich, Howard and Albert J. Reiss, Jr. 1976. "Continuities in the Study of Ecological Succession: Changes in the Race Composition of Neighborhoods and Their Businesses." *American Journal of Sociology* 81 (4, January): 846-866.

Aldrich, Howard, Robin Ward, and Roger Waldinger. 1985. "Minority Business Development in Industrial Society." *European Studies Newsletter* 14 (4, March): 4-8.

Aldrich, Howard and Catherine Zimmer. 1986. "Entrepreneurship Through Social Networks." Pp. 3-23 in Donald Sexton and Raymond Smilor (eds.), *The Art and Science of Entrepreneurship.* Cambridge, MA: Ballinger.

Aldrich, Howard, Catherine Zimmer, and David McEvoy. 1989. "Continuities in the Study of Ecological Succession: Asian Businesses in Three English Cities." *Social Forces* 67 (4, June): 920-943.

Anthias, Floya. 1983. "Sexual Divisions and Ethnic Adaptation." Pp. 73-94 in Annie Phizacklea (ed.), *One Way Ticket.* London: Routledge.

Armington, Catherine and Marjorie Odle. 1982. "Small Business — How Many Jobs?" *Brookings Review* 1 (2, Winter): 14-17.

Armstrong, John. 1976. "Mobilized and Proletarian Diasporas." *American Political Science Review* 70 (2, June): 393-408.

Auster, Ellen and Howard Aldrich. 1984. "Small Business Vulnerability, Ethnic Enclaves, and Ethnic Enterprises." Pp. 39-54 in Robin Ward and R. Jenkins (eds.), *Ethnic Communities in Business: Strategies for Economic Survival.* Cambridge: Cambridge University Press.

Bailey, Thomas R. 1987. *Immigrant and Native Workers: Contrasts and Competition.* Boulder, CO: Westview.

Bakker, J. and L. J. Tap. 1984. "Varianten in het etnishe ondernemerschap." *Kroniek van het ambacht/klein-en middenbedrijf* 38: 24-27.

Ballard, Roger and Cathleen Ballard. 1977. "The Sikhs: The Development of South Asian Settlement in Britain." Pp. 21-56 in James L. Watson (ed.), *Between Two Cultures.* Oxford: Basil Blackwell.

Barber, A. 1985. "Ethnic Origins and Economic Status." *Employment Gazette* (July): 467-477.

Baron, Salo W., et al. 1975. *Economic History of the Jews.* New York: Schocken.

Barth, Gunther. 1964. *Bitter Strength.* Cambridge, MA: Harvard University Press.

Barton, Josef. 1975. *Peasants and Strangers: Italians, Rumanians, and Slovaks in an American City.* Cambridge, MA: Harvard University Press.

Bates, Timothy. 1981. "Effectiveness of SBA in Financing Minority Business." *Review of Black Political Economy* 11 (3, Spring): 321-336.

Bates, Timothy. 1985. "Impact of Preferential Procurement Policies on Minority-Owned Businesses." *Review of Black Political Economy* 14 (1, Fall): 51-66.

Bates, Timothy and William Bradford. 1979. *Financing Black Economic Development.* New York: Academic Press.

Baumol, William J. 1968. "Entrepreneurship in Economic Theory." *American Economic Review* 58 (2, May): 64-71.

Bechhofer, Frank and Brian Elliot, eds. 1981. *The Petite Bourgeoisie: Comparative Studies of the Uneasy Stratum.* London: Macmillan.

Bechhofer, Frank and Brian Elliott. 1985. "The Petite Bourgeoisie in Late Capitalism." *Annual Review of Sociology* 11: 181-207.

Becker, Eugene. 1984. "Self-Employed Workers: An Update to 1983." *Monthly Labor Review* 107 (7, July): 14-18.

Belussi, Fiorenza. 1986. "New Technologies in a Traditional Sector." Working Paper. Berkeley, CA: Berkeley Roundtable on the International Economy.

Bender, K. 1979. "Erwebstätigleit durch Auslander." *Gemeinsame Broschure der Industrie-und Handelskammern North-Rhine-Westphalia.* Brochure (October).

Benedict, Burton. 1968. "Family Firms and Economic Development." *Southwestern Journal of Anthropology* 24 (1, Spring): 1-19.

Benedict, Burton. 1979. "Family Firms and Firm Families: A Comparison of Indian, Chinese and Creole Firms in Sechelles." Pp. 304-326 in Sidney M. Greenfield, Arnold Strickon, and Robert T. Aubey (eds.), *Entrepreneurs in Cultural Context.* Albuquerque: University of New Mexico.

Berger, Suzanne. 1981. "The Uses of the Traditional Sector in Italy: Why Declining Classes Survive." Pp. 71-89 in Frank Bechhofer and Brian Elliot (eds.), *The Petite Bourgeoisie: Comparative Studies of the Uneasy Stratum.* London: Macmillan.

Berlin, Ira. 1974. *Slaves Without Masters.* New York: Vintage.

Berroll, Selma C. 1987. "The Jewish West Side of New York City." *Journal of Ethnic Studies* 13 (4, Winter): 21-45.

Berteaux, Daniel and Isabelle Berteaux-Wiame. 1981. "Artisanal Bakery in France: How It Lives and Why It Survives." Pp. 155-181 in Frank Bechhofer and Brian Elliot (eds.), *The Petite Bourgeoisie: Comparative Studies of an Uneasy Stratum.* London: Macmillan.

Birch, David. 1981. "Who Creates Jobs?" *The Public Interest* 65 (Fall): 3-14.

Birch, David. 1987. *Job Creation in America: How Our Smallest Companies Put the Most People to Work.* New York: Free Press.

Black Enterprise. 1982. "The Black Enterprise 100: A Decade of Steady Progress." (June): 76-81.

Blaschke, Jochen. 1985. *Von der Kontraktarbeit zur Immigrantenkolonie.* Berlin: Arbeitsheft des BIVS.

Blaschke, Jochen and Ahmet Ersoz. 1986. "The Turkish Economy in West Berlin." *International Small Business Journal* 4 (3, Spring): 38-45.

Blaschke, Jochen and Ahmet Ersoz. 1987a. *Herkunft und Geschäftsaufnahme turkischer Kleingewerbetreibender in Berlin.* Berlin: Express Edition.

Blaschke, Jochen and Ahmet Ersoz. 1987b. *Legale Diskriminierungen von Auslandern bei der Gewerbeaufnahme.* Berlin: Unveroffentlichtes Gutachten.

Blaschke, Jochen, Ahmet Ersoz, and Thomas Schwarz. 1986-1987. *Formationseleme ethnischen kolonie am Beispiel der turkischen Community Berlin: Die Vervollstandigung ökonomischer, politischer und freizeitlicher Organisationen.* Hamburg: MS.

Blaustein, Arthur and Geoffrey Faux. 1972. *Star-Spangled Hustle.* Garden City, NY: Doubleday.

Bluestone, Barry, Patricia Hanna, Sarah Kuhn, and Laura Moore, eds. 1981. *The Retail Revolution.* Cambridge, MA: Auburn House.

Bodnar, John, Roger Simon, and Michael Weber. 1982. *Lives of Their Own: Blacks, Italians, and Poles in Pittsburgh, 1900-1960.* Urbana: University of Illinois Press.

Boissevain, Jeremy. 1981. *Small Entrepreneurs in Changing Europe: Toward a Research Agenda.* Maastrich: European Centre for Work and Society.

Boissevain, Jeremy and Hanneke Grotenbreg. 1985. "Survival in Spite of the Law: Surinamese Entrepreneurs in Amsterdam." Paper prepared for Wenner-Gren Symposium 7, "Ethnohistorical Models for the Evolution of Law in Specific Societies," Bellagio, Italy, August 10-18.

Boissevain, Jeremy and Hanneke Grotenbreg. 1986. "Culture, Structure and Ethnic Enterprise: The Surinamese of Amsterdam." *Ethnic and Racial Studies* 9 (1, January): 1-23.

Boissevain, Jeremy, Hanneke Grotenbreg, and August Choenni. 1984. *Een kleine baas is altijd beter dan een grote knecht. Surinaamse kleine zelfstandige ondernemers in Amsterdam.* Amsterdam: Antropologisch-Sociologisch Centrum & Ministerie van Economische Zaken.

Bonacich, Edna. 1973. "A Theory of Middleman Minorities." *American Sociological Review* 38 (5, October): 583-594.

Bonacich, Edna and John Modell. 1980. *The Economic Basis of Ethnic Solidarity in the Japanese American Community.* Berkeley: University of California Press.

Boswell, Terry E. 1986. "A Split Labor Market Analysis of Discrimination Against Chinese Immigrants, 1850-1882." *American Sociological Review* 51 (3, June): 352-371.

Boswell, Thomas and James Curtis. 1984. *The Cuban-American Experience: Culture, Images, and Perspectives.* Totowa, NJ: Rowman & Allanheld.

Boubakri, Hassan. 1984. "La restauration tunisienne à Paris." *Marchands ambulants et commerçants étrangers en France et en Allemagne.* Paris: Poitiers.

Boubakri, Hassan. 1985. "Mode de gestion et reinvestissements chez les commerçants tunisiens à Paris." *Revue Europeene des Migrations Internationales* 1 (1): 49-66.

Bovenkerk, F., A. Eyken, and W. Bovenkerk-Teerink. 1983. *Italiaans IJs. De opmerkelijke historie van Italiaanse ijsbereiders in Nederland.* Meppel: Boom.

Briggs, Vernon. 1984. *Immigration Policy and the American Labor Force.* Baltimore: Johns Hopkins University Press.

Brooks, A. 1983. "Black Business in Lambeth: Obstacles to Expansion." *New Community* 11 (1-2): 42-54.

Brown, C. 1984. *Black and White Britain.* London: Heinemann, PEP.

Browning, Rufus, Dale Marshall, and David Tabb. 1984. *Protest Is Not Enough.* Berkeley: University of California Press.

Budike, F. n.d. *Surinamers naar Nederland. De migratie van 1687 tot 1982.* Amsterdam: Inst. Voortgezet Agogisch Beroepsonderwijs.

Business Week. 1979. "Apparel's Last Stand." (May 14).

Business Week. 1984a. "K Mart: The No. 2 Retailer Starts to Make an Upscale Move — At Last." (June 4).

Business Week. 1984b. "Bennetton: Bringing European Chic to Middle America." (June 11).

Business Week. 1985. "Hong Kong's End Run Around U.S. Protectionism." (August 26).

Butler, John Sibley and Kenneth L. Wilson. 1988. "Entrepreneurial Enclaves: An Exposition into the Afro-American Experience." *National Journal of Sociology* 2 (2, Fall): 127-166.

Carey, S. and A. Shukur. 1985-1986. "A Profile of the Bangla Deshi Community in East London." *New Community* 12: 405-417.

Carter, Wilmoth. 1960. "Negro Main Street as a Symbol of Discrimination." *Phylon* 21 (3, Fall): 234-242.

Castles, Stephen, Heather Booth, and Tina Wallace. 1984. *Here for Good: Western Europe's New Ethnic Minorities.* London: Pluto.

The Chinatown Garment Industry Study. 1983. New York: Local 23-25, International Ladies' Garment Workers' Union and the Skirt and Sportswear Association.

Chiswick, Barry. 1974. *Income Inequality: Regional Analysis Within a Human Capital Framework.* New York: National Bureau of Economic Research (distributed by Columbia University Press).

Chiswick, Barry. 1978. *Human Resources and Income Distribution: Issues and Policies.* New York: Norton.

Clairmonte, Frederick and John Cavanagh. 1981. *The World in Their Web: The Dynamics of Textile Multinationals.* London: Zed.

Cobas, Jose. 1987. "On the Study of Ethnic Enterprise." *Sociological Perspectives* 30 (4, October): 467-472.

Cohen, Steven. 1983. *American Modernity and Jewish Identity.* New York: Tavistock.

Conseil Economique et Social. 1982. "Le devenir des industries du textile et de l'habillement." *Journal Officiel* 25 (Fevrier).

Creed, R. and Robin Ward. 1987. *Black Business Enterprise in Wales.* South Glamorgan: South Glamorgan Council for Racial Equality.

Curran, James and Roger Burrows. 1986. "The Sociology of Petit Capitalism: A Trend Report." *Sociology* 20 (2, May): 265-279.

Curry, Leonard. 1981. *The Free Black in Urban America.* Chicago: University of Chicago Press.

Dahya, B. 1974. "Pakistani Ethnicity in Industrial Cities in England." Pp. 77-113 in Abner Cohen (ed.), *Urban Ethnicity.* London: Tavistock.

Dei Ottati, Gabi. 1986. "Distretto industriale, problemi delle transazioni e mercato communitario: prime considerazioni." *Economia e Politica Industriale* 51: 93-121.

Demaris, Ovid. 1981. *The Last Mafioso: The Treacherous World of Jimmy "The Weasel" Fratiano.* London: Phantom.

Department of Employment. 1988. "Ethnic Origins and the Labour Market." *Employment Gazette* (March): 164-177.

Doeringer, Peter and Michael Piore. 1971. *Internal Labor Markets and Manpower Analysis.* Lexington, MA: D. C. Heath.

Drake, St. Clair and Horace Cayton. 1962. *Black Metropolis.* New York: Harper & Row.

DuBois, W.E.B. [1899] 1967. *The Philadelphia Negro.* New York: Schocken.

DuBois, W.E.B. 1907. *Economic Co-operation Among Negro Americans.* Atlanta, GA: Atlanta University Press.

Ebron, Betty Liu. 1985. "Chinese-American Developers Poised to Smash Old Barriers." *Crain's New York Business* (September 9).

Ehrlich, Paul. 1986. "Hong Kong Firm Eyes U.S. Production." *Women's Wear Daily* (March 19).

England, Keith. 1980. "The Persistence of the Private Retailer: A Sociological Enquiry into Community Problems." Unpublished M.A. thesis, University College, Swansea.

Esser, Hartmut and Hermann Korte. 1985. "Federal Republic of Germany." Pp. 165-205 in Tomas Hammar (ed.), *European Immigration Policy.* Cambridge: Cambridge University Press.

Eurostat. 1984. *Employment and Unemployment.* Luxembourg: Statistical Office of the Organization for Economic Cooperation and Development.

Eurostat. 1987. *Employment and Unemployment.* Luxembourg: Statistical Office of the Organization for Economic Cooperation and Development.

Fain, T. Scott. 1980. "Self-Employed Americans: Their Number Has Increased." *Monthly Labor Review* 103 (11, November): 3-8.

Fairchild, Henry Spratt. 1911. *Greek Immigration to the United States.* New Haven, CT: Yale University Press.

Foley, Eugene P. 1967. "Negro Businessmen in Search of a Tradition." Pp. 555-592 in Talcott Parsons and Kenneth B. Clark (eds.), *The Negro American.* Boston: Beacon.

Foner, Nancy. 1979. "West Indians in New York City and London: A Comparative Analysis." *International Migration Review* 13 (2, Summer): 284-297.

Fothergill, S. and G. Gudgin. 1982. *Unequal Growth.* London: Heinemann.

Fratoe, Frank. 1986. "A Sociological Analysis of Minority Business." *Review of Black Political Economy* 15 (2, Fall): 5-30.

Frazier, E. Franklin. 1937. "Negro Harlem: An Ecological Study." *American Journal of Sociology* 43 (1, July): 72-88.

Frazier, E. Franklin. 1949. *The Negro in America.* New York: Macmillan.

Fusfeld, Daniel and Timothy Bates. 1984. *The Political Economy of the Urban Ghetto.* Carbondale: Southern Illinois University Press.

Gallo, Carmenza. 1983. "The Construction Industry in New York: Black and Immigrant Entrepreneurs." Working Paper, Conservation of Human Resources. New York: Columbia University.

Gandoulou, Justin-Daniel. 1984. *Entre Paris et Bacongo.* Paris.

Gans, Herbert. 1962. *The Urban Villagers.* New York: Free Press.

Gans, Herbert J. 1979. "Symbolic Ethnicity: The Future of Ethnic Groups and Cultures in America." *Ethnic and Racial Studies* 2 (1, January): 1-20.

Gelder, P. Van. 1984. "Werken onder de boom, Dynamiek en informele sektor: de situatie in Groot-Paramaribo, Suriname." Ph.D. dissertation, Amsterdam.

Glazer, Nathan and Daniel P. Moynihan. 1963. *Still Beyond the Melting Pot.* Cambridge: MIT Press.

Gold, Steven J. 1985. "Refugee Communities: Soviet Jews and Vietnamese in the San Francisco Bay Area." Ph.D. dissertation, University of California, Berkeley.

Gold, Steven J. 1988. "The Employment Potential of Refugee Entrepreneurship: Soviet Jews and Vietnamese in Southern California." Washington, DC: U.S. Department of Labor, Division of Immigration Policy and Research, International Labor Affairs Bureau (September).

Goldscheider, Calvin. 1985. *Jewish Continuity and Change.* Bloomington: Indiana University Press.

Goldscheider, Calvin. 1986. *The American Jewish Community: Social Science Research and Policy Implications.* Atlanta, GA: Scholars.

Goldscheider, Calvin and Frances Kobrin. 1980. "Ethnic Continuity and the Process of Self-Employment." *Ethnicity* 7 (3, September): 256-278.

Granovetter, Mark. 1984. "Labor Markets and Establishment Size." *American Sociological Review* 49 (3, June): 323-334.

Granovetter, Mark. 1985. "Economic Action and Social Structure: The Problem of Embeddedness." *American Journal of Sociology* 91 (3, November): 481-510.

Granovetter, Mark and Charles Tilly. 1988. "Inequality and Labor Processes." Pp. 175-222 in Neil J. Smelser (ed.), *Handbook of Sociology.* Newbury Park, CA: Sage.

Green, Nancy. 1985. *Les travailleurs immigres juifs à la Belle Epoque.* Paris: Fayard.

Green, Nancy. 1986. "Immigrant Labor in the Garment Industries of New York and Paris: Variations on a Structure." *Comparative Social Research* 9: 231-243.

Greenberg, Jerome, Martin Topol, Elaine Sherman, and Kenneth Cooperman. 1980. "The Itinerant Street Vendor: A Form of Nonstore Retailing." *Journal of Retailing* 56 (2, Summer): 66-80.

Greenfield, Sidney M., Arnold Strickon, and Robert T. Aubey, eds. 1979. *Entrepreneurs in Cultural Context.* Albuquerque: University of New Mexico.

Greenfield, Sidney M., Arnold Strickon, Robert T. Aubey, and Morton Rothstein. 1979. "Studies in Entrepreneurial Behavior: A Review and Introduction." In Sidney M. Greenfield et al. (eds.), *Entrepreneurs in Cultural Context.* Albuquerque: University of New Mexico Press.

Guilbert, M. and V. Isambert-Jamoti. 1956. *Travail féminin et travail à domicile.* Paris: C.N.R.S.

Guillon, M. and I. Taboada-Leonetti. 1986. *Le Triangle de Choisy. Un Quartier Chinois à Paris.* Paris: Ciemi L'Harmatan.

Guillon, M., V. de Rudder, and I. Taboada-Leonetti. 1985. *Pratiques Urbaines et Transformations Sociales dans 3 Quartiers Pluri-ethniques.* Paris: Ministere de L'Urbanisme et du Logement.

Gurock, Jeffrey. 1979. *When Harlem Was Jewish.* New York: Columbia University Press.

Haag, C. 1982. "Die rechtliche Situation der Ausländer in der Bundesrepublik Deutschland." Pp. 161-194 in Martin Frey and Ulf Muller (eds.), *Ausländer bei uns-Fremde oder Mitburger?* Vol. 186. Bonn: Federal Centre for Political Education.

Haber, Sheldon, Enrique J. Lamas, and Jules H. Lichtenstein. 1987. "On Their Own: The Self-Employed and Others in Private Business." *Monthly Labor Review* 110 (5, May): 17-23.

Hall, Bruce F. 1983. "Neighborhood Differences in Retail Food Stores: Income Versus Race and Age of Population." *Economic Geography* 59 (3, July): 282-295.

Hall, Peter. 1962. *The Industries of London.* London: Hutchinson.

Harries, Keith D. 1971. "Ethnic Variations of Los Angeles Business Patterns." *Annals of the Association of American Geographers* 61 (4, December): 736-743.

Harris, Abram L. 1936. *The Negro as Capitalist: A Study of Banking and Business Among Negro Americans.* Philadelphia: American Academy of Political and Social Science.

Harrison, Bennett. 1974. "Ghetto Economic Development: A Survey." *Journal of Economic Literature* 12 (1): 1-37.

Hassoun, J. P. and Yinh Phong Tan. 1986. *Les refugiés de l'asie du sud-est de langue chinoise.* Paris: Mission du patrimoine ethnologique.

Heilbron, W. 1982. "Kleine boeren in de schaduw van de plantage. De politieke ekonomie van de na-slaverijperiode in Suriname." Ph.D. dissertation, Rotterdam.

Helfgott, Roy. 1959. "Women's and Children's Apparel." Pp. 19-134 in Max Hall (ed.), *Made in New York.* Cambridge, MA: Harvard University Press.

Henri, Florette. 1976. *Black Migration: Movement North, 1900-1920.* Garden City, NY: Anchor.

Herman, Harry Vjekoslav. 1979. "Dishwashers and Proprietors: Macedonians in Toronto's Restaurant Trade." Pp. 71-92 in Sandra Wallman (ed.), *Ethnicity at Work.* London: Macmillan.

Hershberg, Theodore. 1981. *Philadelphia: Work, Space, Family and Group Experience in the Nineteenth Century* (Essay Towards an Interdisciplinary History of the City). New York: Oxford University Press.

Higgs, David. 1976. *A Future to Inherit: Portuguese Communities in Canada.* Toronto: McClelland and Stewart.

Higgs, Robert. 1977. *Competition and Coercion: Blacks in the American Economy, 1865-1914.* Cambridge: Cambridge University Press.

Holzman, M. and R. Guidicelli. 1983. *L'Asie à Paris.* Paris: Editions Rochevignes.

Howe, Irving. 1976. *World of Our Fathers.* New York: Simon & Schuster.

Hurh, Won Moo and Kwang Chung Kim. 1984. "Adhesive Sociocultural Adaptation of Korean Immigrants in the U.S.: An Alternative Strategy of Minority Adaptation." *International Migration Review* 18 (2, Summer): 188-216.

Hurh, Won Moo and Kwang Chung Kim. 1985. "Korean Immigrants in America: A Structural Analysis of Ethnic Confinement and Adhesive Adaptation." *Contemporary Sociology* 14 (5, September): 599-600.

Immigration and Naturalization Service. 1985. *Statistical Annual.* Washington, DC: Government Printing Office.

INSEE (Institut national de la statistique et des études économiques). 1982. *Recensement de population des Etrangers.* Paris: Author.

INSEE. 1984. *Enquete sur l'emploi.* Paris: Author.

INSEE. 1985. *Recensement general de la population de 1982.* Paris: Author.

INSEE. 1986. *Countours et caractères. Les étrangers en France.* Paris: Author.

Instituut voor Toegepaste Sociologie. 1986. "Ethnisch ondernemerschap in Nederland." Unpublished manuscript, Amsterdam.

James, Estelle. 1975. "A Note on Uncertainty and Evaluation of Public Investment Decisions." *American Economic Review* 65 (1, March): 200-205.

Jenkins, Richard. 1986. *Racism and Recruitment.* Cambridge: Cambridge University Press.

Jenkins, Richard and J. Solomos, eds. 1987. *Racism and Equal Opportunity Policies in the 1980s.* Cambridge: Cambridge University Press.

Jones, Gareth Stedman. 1971. *Outcast London: A Study in the Relationship Between Classes in Victorian Society.* Oxford: Clarendon.

Jones, Trevor P. and David McEvoy. 1978. "Race and Space in Cloud-Cuckoo Land." *Area* 10 (3): 162-166.

Joseph, Isaac. 1984a. "Bronzeville 1984." *Terrain* 3: 20-32.

Joseph, Isaac. 1984b. "Situation Migratoire et Double Appartenance Culturelle." Pp. 95-110 in *Du bon usage de la ville. Utilisateurs et Decideurs.* Bruxelles: Facultés Universitaires Saint Louis.

Joseph, Isaac. 1985. "Urbanité et Ethnicité." Pp. 135-146 in *Sociétés Industrielles et Urbaines Contemporaines.* Paris: Ministere de la Culture — Maison des Sciences de l'Homme.

Joseph, Isaac. 1986. "Métaphores spaciales et Cultures urbaines: La question du local." In *Questions de la Sociologie urbaine.* Lausanne: Societe Suisse de Sociologie IREC, Cyclostyled.

Kalbert, Sylvia. 1986. "Probleme der Auswertung der Gewerbekartei." Unpublished manuscript, Bochum.

Kanein, W. 1966. *Das Ausländergesetz.* Munich: Beck'sche.

Katzman, David. 1973. *Before the Ghetto: Black Detroit in the Nineteenth Century.* Urbana: University of Illinois Press.

Kazuka, Martin. 1980. "Why So Few Black Businessmen?" Hackney: Hackney Borough Council (November).

Kessner, Thomas. 1977. *The Golden Door: Italian and Jewish Immigrant Mobility in New York City.* New York: Oxford University Press.

Kilby, Peter. 1971. "Hunting the Heffalump." Pp. 1-40 in Peter Kilby (ed.), *Entrepreneurship and Economic Development.* New York: Free Press.

Kim, Illsoo. 1981. *The New Urban Immigrants: The Korean Community in New York.* Princeton, NJ: Princeton University Press.

Kim, Illsoo. 1986. "Korean Immigrants' Enterprises in the New York Metropolitan Area." Paper presented at the annual meetings of the American Sociological Association, New York.

Kim, Illsoo. 1987. "The Koreans: Small Business in an Urban Frontier." Pp. 219-242 in Nancy Foner (ed.), *New Immigrants in New York City.* New York: Columbia University Press.

Kim, Kwang Chung. 1980. "Koreans." Pp. 601-606 in Stephan Thernstrom (ed.), *Harvard Encyclopedia of American Ethnic Groups.* Cambridge, MA: Harvard University Press.

Kindel, Stephen. 1984. "The Workshop Economy." *Forbes* 133 (10, April 30): 62-77.

Kissrow, W. 1980. *Ausländerrecht.* Neue Kommunale Schriften series no. 25. 6th ed., rev. Berlin: Kohlhammer.

Klatzmann, Joseph. 1957. *Le travail à domicile dans l'industrie parisienne du vêtement.* Paris: Armand Colin.

Kobrin, Frances E. and Calvin Goldscheider. 1978. *The Ethnic Factor in Family Structure and Mobility.* Cambridge, MA: Ballinger.

Korte, Hermann. 1987. "Guestworker Question or Immigration Issue? Social Sciences and Public Debate in the Federal Republic of Germany." Pp. 163-173 in Klaus J. Bade (ed.), *Population, Labour and Migration in 19th- and 20th-Century Germany.* New York: Berg and St. Martin's.

Korte, Hermann. n.d. "Case Study of Ethnic Entrepreneurs in Germany: Research Questions and Comparative Data." Unpublished manuscript, Bochum.

Krcmar, Karisa. 1984. "Immigrant Retail in Glasgow." M.B.A. thesis, Strathclyde University, Glasgow.

Kruijer, G. J. 1977. *Suriname. De problemen en hun opglossingen.* Utrecht/Antwerpen: Het Spectrum.

Kusmer, Kenneth. 1976. *A Ghetto Takes Shape: Black Cleveland, 1870-1930.* Urbana: University of Illinois Press.

Ladbury, Sarah. 1984. "Choice, Chance, or No Alternative? Turkish Cypriots in Business in London." Pp. 105-124 in Robin Ward and Richard Jenkins (eds.), *Ethnic Communities in Business.* Cambridge: Cambridge University Press.

Landry, Bart. 1987. *The New Black Middle Class.* Berkeley: University of California Press.

Leibenstein, Harvey. 1968. "Entrepreneurship and Development." *American Economic Review* 58 (2, May): 72-83.

Leonetti, Isabelle Taboada with Michelle Guillon. 1987. *Les immigrés des beaux quartiers: la communauté espagnole dans le XVIe.* Paris: CIEMI-L'Harmattan.

Lessinger, Johanna. 1985. "Painful Intimacy: The Establishment of Trust in Business Partnerships Among New York's Indian Immigrants." Paper presented at the conference, "The Anthropology of Experience, Feeling, and Emotion in South Asia," Houston, December.

Levine, Barry B. 1985. "The Capital of Latin America." *Wilson Quarterly* 9 (5, Winter): 47-69.

Lieberson, Stanley. 1958. "Ethnic Groups and the Practice of Medicine." *American Sociological Review* 23 (5, October): 542-549.

Lieberson, Stanley. 1980. *A Piece of the Pie.* Berkeley: University of California.

Lier, R. van. [1949, Dutch ed.] 1971. *Frontier Society: A Social Analysis of History of Surinam.* s.-Gravenhage: Martinus Nijhoff.

Light, Ivan. 1972. *Ethnic Enterprise in America.* Berkeley: University of California Press.

Light, Ivan. 1974. "From Vice District to Tourist Attraction: The Moral Career of American Chinatowns, 1880-1940." *Pacific Historical Review* 43 (3, August): 367-394.

Light, Ivan. 1977. "The Ethnic Vice District, 1880-1944." *American Sociological Review* 43 (3, June): 464-479.

Light, Ivan. 1979. "Disadvantaged Minorities in Self-Employment." In William Petersen (ed.), *The Background to Ethnic Conflict.* Leiden: E. J. Brill.

Light, Ivan. 1980. "Asian Enterprise in America." Pp. 33-57 in Scott Cummings (ed.), *Self-Help in America.* Pt. Washington, NY: Kennikat.

Light, Ivan. 1984. "Immigrant and Ethnic Enterprise in North America." *Ethnic and Racial Studies* 7 (2, April): 195-216.

Light, Ivan and Edna Bonacich. 1988. *Immigrant Entrepreneurs*. Berkeley: University of California Press.

Light, Ivan and Angel A. Sanchez. 1987. "Immigrant Entrepreneurs in 272 SMSAs." *Sociological Perspectives* 30 (4, October): 373-399.

London Borough of Lambeth. 1982. "Black Businesses in Lambeth." Report, Rm. 20 (March).

Long, Norman. 1977. "Commerce and Kinship in the Peruvian Highlands." Pp. 153-176 in Ralph Bolton and Enrique Mayer (eds.), *Andean Kinship and Marriage*. Washington, DC: American Anthropological Association.

Long, Norman. 1979. "Multiple Enterprise in the Central Highlands of Peru." Pp. 123-158 in Sidney M. Greenfield et al. (eds.), *Entrepreneurs in Cultural Context*. Albuquerque: University of New Mexico Press.

Lyman, Stanford. 1974. *Chinese-Americans*. New York: Random House.

Ma Mung, Emmanuel and Michel Guillon. 1986. "Les commerçants étrangers dans l'agglomération Parisienne." *Revue Europeene des Migrations Internationales* 2 (3): 105-134.

Marable, Manning. 1983. *How Capitalism Underdeveloped Black America*. Boston: South End Press.

Matlack, Carol. 1987. "Ripe for a Rip-Off." *National Journal* (June 6): 1462-1463.

McEvoy, David, Howard Aldrich, John Cater, and Trevor Jones. 1982. "Asian Immigrant Business in British Cities." British Association for the Advancement of Science (September 24).

Meier, August. 1962. "Negro Class Structure and Ideology in the Age of Booker T. Washington." *Phylon* 23 (3, Fall): 258-266.

Menger, P. J. 1980. *Vestigingswet Detailhandel*. Amsterdam: Zwolle Tjeenk Willink.

Mills, C. Wright. 1958. *The Causes of World War Three*. New York: Simon & Schuster.

Min, Pyong Gap. 1984. "A Structural Analysis of Korean Business in the United States." *Ethnic Groups* 6 (1, June): 1-25.

Min, Pyong Gap. 1986-1987. "Filipino and Korean Immigrants in Small Business: A Comparative Analysis." *Amerasia Journal* 13 (1): 53-71.

Min, Pyong Gap. 1988. *Ethnic Business Enterprise: Korean Small Business in Atlanta*. Staten Island: Center for Migration Studies.

Modell, John. 1977. *The Economics and Politics of Racial Accommodation: The Japanese of Los Angeles, 1900-1942*. Urbana: University of Illinois Press.

Mohl, Raymond. 1983. "Miami: The Ethnic Cauldron." In Richard M. Bernard and Bradley R. Rice (eds.), *Sunbelt Cities: Politics and Growth Since World War II*. Austin: University of Texas Press.

Moore, Joan W. 1985. *Urban Ethnicity in the United States: New Immigrants and Old Minorities*. Beverly Hills, CA: Sage.

Moore, Joan and Harry Pachon. 1985. *Hispanics in the United States*. Englewood Cliffs, NJ: Prentice-Hall.

Mormino, Gary Ross. 1986. *Immigrants on the Hill: Italian-Americans in St. Louis: 1882-1982*. Urbana: University of Illinois Press.

Morokvasic, Mirjana. 1986. "Recours aux immigrés dans la confection parisienne. Éléments de comparaison avec la ville de Berlin Quest." Pp. 199-242 in *La lutte contre les trafics de la main d'oeuvre en 1985-86*. Paris: la Documentation Francaise.

Morokvasic, Mirjana. 1987. "Immigrants in Parisian Garment Industry." *Work, Employment and Society* 1 (4, December): 441-462.

Morokvasic, Mirjana. 1988. *Minority and Immigrant Women in Self-Employment and Business in France, Great Britain, Italy, Portugal, and the Federal Republic of Germany* (V/1871/88-Engl.). Paris: EEC.

Morokvasic, Mirjana, Annie Phizacklea, and Hedwig Rudolph. 1986. "Small Firms and Minority Groups: Contradictory Trends in the French, German and British Clothing Industries." *International Sociology* 1 (4): 397-420.

Morokvasic-Muller, Mirjana. n.d. *De l'industrie de l'habillement aux retouches: les étrangers à Berlin-Quest.* Paris: MS.

Mullins, David. 1980. "Race and Retailing: The Asian-Owned Retailing Sectors in Croyden." Paper presented at the annual conference of the Institute of British Geographers, Lancaster.

Myrdal, Gunnar. 1944. *An American Dilemma: The Negro Problem and Modern Democracy.* New York: Harper & Row.

Nee, Victor and Brett de Bary Nee. 1973. *Longtime Californ': A Study of an American Chinatown.* New York: Pantheon.

Newnham, A. 1986. *Employment, Unemployment and Black People.* London: Runnymede Trust.

New York Chinese Business Guide & Directory. 1984. New York: Key Advertising.

OECD. 1985. "Self-Employment in OECD Countries." *Employment Outlook*, pp. 30-42.

OECD. 1986a. "Employment in Small and Large Firms: Where Have the Jobs Come From?" *Employment Outlook*, pp. 64-83.

OECD. 1986b. "Self-Employment in OECD Countries." *Employment Outlook*, pp. 40-66.

OKU (Onderzoeks Kollektief Utrecht). 1985. *Islamitische Slagerijen in Nederland.* s.-Gravenhage: Hoofbedrijfschap Ambachten.

Olzak, Susan. 1983. "Contemporary Ethnic Mobilization." *Annual Review of Sociology* 9: 355-374.

Ong, Paul. 1981. "An Ethnic Trade: The Chinese Laundries in Early California." *Journal of Ethnic Studies* 8 (4, Winter): 95-113.

Orlick, Anneliese. 1987. "The Soviet Jews: Life in Brighton Beach, Brooklyn." Pp. 273-304 in Nancy Foner (ed.), *New Immigrants in New York City.* New York: Columbia University Press.

Osofsky, Gilbert. 1966. *Harlem: The Making of a Ghetto: Negro New York, 1890-1930.* New York: Harper & Row.

Palmer, Robin. 1984. "The Rise of the Britalian Culture Entrepreneur." Pp. 89-104 in Robin Ward and Richard Jenkins (eds.), *Ethnic Communities in Business.* Cambridge: Cambridge University Press.

Pedraza-Bailey, Sylvia. 1985. *Political and Economic Migrants in the United States.* Austin: University of Texas Press.

Penninx, R. 1979. "Naar een algemeen ethnisch minderhedenbeleid?: schets van de sociale positie in Nederland van Molukkers, Surinaamse en Antilliaanse Nederlanders en Mediterrane werknemers en een inventarisatie van het Nederlandse overheidsbeleid." Pp. 3-174 in *Etnische minderheden Wetenschappelijke Raad voor het Regeringsbeleid (WRR).* s-Gravenhage: Staatsuitgeverij.

Petersen, William. 1980. "Concepts of Ethnicity." Pp. 234-242 in Stephen Thernstrom (ed.), *Harvard Encyclopedia of American Ethnic Groups.* Cambridge, MA: Harvard University Press.

Pieke, F. N. 1982. "De Chinese Gemeenschap van Nederland." Ph.D. dissertation, Department of Anthropology, University of Amsterdam.

Pierce, Joseph. 1947. *Negro Business and Business Education.* New York: Harper.

Piore, Michael J. 1979. *Birds of Passage: Migrant Labour and Industrial Societies.* London: Cambridge University Press.

Piore, Michael J. 1980. "The Technological Foundations of Dualism and Discontinuity." Pp. 55-81 in Suzanne Berger and Michael J. Piore (eds.), *Dualism and Discontinuity in Industrial Society.* Cambridge: Cambridge University Press.

Piore, Michael J. and Charles Sabel. 1984. *The New Industrial Divide.* New York: Basic Books.

"Policy for the Inner Cities" (White Paper). 1977. London: HMSO.

Pollins, Harold. 1982. *The Economic History of the Jews in England.* London: Associated University Presses.

Pollins, Harold. 1984. "The Development of Jewish Business in the United Kingdom." Pp. 73-88 in Robin Ward and Richard Jenkins (eds.), *Ethnic Communities in Business.* Cambridge: Cambridge University Press.

Portes, Alejandro. 1987. "The Social Origins of the Cuban Enclave Economy of Miami." *Sociological Perspectives* 30 (4, October): 340-372.

Portes, Alejandro and Robert Bach. 1985. *Latin Journey.* Berkeley: University of California Press.

Reeves, Frank and Robin Ward. 1984. "West Indian Businesses in Britain." Pp. 39-54 in Robin Ward and Richard Jenkins (eds.), *Ethnic Communities in Business: Strategies for Economic Survival.* Cambridge: Cambridge University Press.

Reid, Ira De A. 1940. "The Negro in the American Economic System." Unpublished manuscript (prepared for Gunnar Myrdal, 1944, *An American Dilemma: The Negro Problem and Modern Democracy,* New York: Harper & Row).

Reimers, David. 1985. *Still the Golden Door: The Third World Comes to America.* New York: Columbia University Press.

Reiss, Albert J., Jr., and Howard Aldrich. 1971. "Absentee Ownership and Management in the Black Ghetto: Social and Economic Consequences." *Social Problems* 18 (3, Winter): 319-339.

Reubsaet, T.J.M. and J. A. Kropman. 1985. *Beter opgeleide Antillianen op de Nederlandse arbeidsmarkt.* s-Gravenhage: Ministrie van Sociale Zaken en Werkgelegenheid.

Rieff, David. 1987. *Going to Miami: Exiles, Tourists, and Refugees in the New America.* New York: Penguin.

Rischin, Moses. 1962. *The Promised City.* Cambridge, MA: Harvard University Press.

Ritterband, Paul and Steven Cohen. 1984. "Social Characteristics of the New York Area Jewish Community." *American Jewish Yearbook* 84: 128-161.

Rose, H. M. 1970. "The Structure of Retail Trade in a Racially Changing Trade Area." *Geographical Analysis* 2 (2, April): 135-148.

Rosen, M. 1984. "A Study of Market Segmentation and Target Marketing." *Hollings Apparel Industry Review* (May).

Russell, Raymond. 1985. *Sharing Ownership in the Workplace.* Albany: State University of New York Press.

Saifullah Khan, Verity, ed. 1979. *Minority Families in Britain: Support and Stress.* London: Macmillan.

Salem, G. 1984. "Les marchands ambulants et le systeme commercial sénégalais en France." In *Marchands ambulants et commerçants étrangers en France et an Allemagne Federale.* Poitiers: University of Poitiers.

Saloutos, Theodore. 1964. *The Greeks in the United States.* Cambridge, MA: Harvard University Press.

Sanders, Jimmy M. and Victor Nee. 1987. "The Limits of Ethnic Solidarity in the Enclave Economy." *American Sociological Review* 52 (6, December): 745-767.

Sawyer, A. 1983. "Black Controlled Business in Britain." *New Community* 11 (1-2): 55-62.

Scarman [Lord]. 1981. "The Brixton Disorders, 10-12 April. Report of an Inquiry." London: HMSO (November).

Scase, Richard and Robert Goffee. 1982. *The Entrepreneurial Middle Class.* London: Croom Helm.

Scheiner, Seth. 1965. *Negro Mecca: A History of Negroes in New York City.* New York: New York University Press.

Schmiechen, James A. 1984. *Sweated Industries and Sweated Labor: The London Clothing Trades, 1860-1914.* Urbana: University of Illinois Press.

Schor, R. 1985. *L'opinion française et les étrangers en France 1919-1939.* Paris: Publications de la Sorbonne.

Sen, Faruk. 1986. *Kurzbericht: Studie zur selbständigen Erwebstatigkeit von Ausländern, insbesondere der Turken in der Bundesrepublik Deutschland.* Bonn: MS.

Silberston, Z. Aubrey 1984. *The Multi-Fibre Arrangement and the U.K. Economy.* London: HMSO.

Simon, G. 1979. "L'espace des travailleurs tunisiens en France." Ph.D. dissertation, Poitiers.

Simon, Gildas and Emmanuel Ma Mung. 1987. "La dynamique des commerces maghrebins et asiatiques et les perspectives du marché intérieur européen." Paper presented at the Atelier Cultures Urbaines, Universite Lyon 2, December 17-18.

Smith, Barbara. 1974. "Employment Opportunities in the Inner Area Study Part of Small Health, Birmingham in 1974." Research Memorandum no. 38. Birmingham: Birmingham University, Centre for Urban and Regional Studies.

Smith, Barbara. 1977. "The Inner City Economic Problem: A Framework for Analysis and Local Authority Policy." Research Memorandum no. 56. Birmingham: Birmingham University, Centre for Urban and Regional Studies.

Smith, David John. 1977. *Racial Disadvantage in Britain: The PEP Report.* Harmondsworth: Penguin.

Smith, Judith E. 1985. *Family Connections: A History of Italian and Jewish Immigrant Lives in Providence, R.I., 1900-1940.* Albany: State University of New York Press.

Smith, M. G. 1984. "The Nature and Variety of Plural Unity." Pp. 146-186 in David Maybury-Lewis (ed.), *The Prospects for Plural Societies: 1982 Proceedings of the American Ethnological Society.* Washington, DC: American Ethnological Society.

Soni, S., M. Triekor, and R. Ward. 1987. "Ethnic Minority Business in Leicestershire." Leicestershire: County Council; Leicester: City Council.

Spear, Allan H. 1967. *Black Chicago: The Making of a Negro Ghetto, 1890-1920.* Chicago: University of Chicago Press.

Spence, Michael. 1974. *Market Signalling.* Cambridge, MA: Harvard University Press.

Spilerman, Seymour. 1977. "Careers, Labor Market Structure, and Socioeconomic Achievement." *American Journal of Sociology* 83 (3, November): 551-593.

The State of Small Business: A Report of the President. 1987. Washington, DC: Government Printing Office.

Sullivan, Teresa A. and Stephen D. McCracken. 1988. "Black Entrepreneurs: Patterns and Rates of Return to Self-Employment." *National Journal of Sociology* 2 (2, Fall): 167-185.

Sway, Marlene B. 1981. "Simmel's Concept of the Stranger and the Gypsies." *Social Science Journal* 18 (1, January): 41-50.

Sway, Marlene. 1984. "Economic Adaptability. The Case of the Gypsies." *Urban Life* 13 (1, April): 83-98.

Tabb, William. 1971. *The Political Economy of the Ghetto.* New York: Norton.

Tap, L. J. 1983. *Het Turkse Bedrijfsleven in Amsterdam. Rapport naar aanleiding van een afstudeeronderzoek.* Groningen: Interfaculteit Bedrijfskunde.

Tenenbaum, Shelley. 1986. "Immigrants and Capital: Jewish Loan Societies in the United States, 1880-1945." *American Jewish History* 76 (1, September): 67-77.

Tillhaart, H., J. M. van den, H.C. van der Hoeven, F. W. van Uxem, and J. M. Westerlaak. 1981. *Zelfstandig Ondermen. Onderzoek naar de problemen en mogelijkheden van het zelfstandig ondernemerschap in het midden-/en kleinbedrijf.* Nijemgen: Instituut voor Toegepaste Sociologie/Economisch Instituut voor het Midden-en Kleinbedrijf.

Time. 1985. "Special Issue: Immigrants." (July 8).

Torres, David L. 1988. "Success and the Mexican American Businessperson." Pp. 313-334 in Samuel B. Bacharach (ed.), *Research in the Sociology of Organizations.* Vol. 6. Greenwich, CT: JAI.

U.S. Department of Commerce. 1987. *The State of Small Business, 1987.* Washington, DC: Government Printing Office.

U.S. Department of Commerce, Bureau of the Census. 1980. *Census of Population, General Population Characteristics, United States Summary. Washington, DC: Government Printing Office.*

U.S. Department of Commerce, Bureau of the Census. 1985a. *Survey of Minority-Owned Business Enterprises, 1982, Blacks.* Washington, DC: Government Printing Office.

U.S. Department of Commerce, Bureau of the Census. 1985b. *Survey of Minority-Owned Business Enterprises, 1982, Hispanics.* Washington, DC: Government Printing Office.

U.S. Department of Commerce, Bureau of the Census. 1986. *Survey of Minority-Owned Business Enterprises, 1982, Asians, American Indians, and Other Minorities.* Washington, DC: Government Printing Office.

U.S. National Advisory Commission on Civil Disorders. 1968. *Report.* New York: Bantam.

U.S. Office of Management and Budget. 1976. *Interagency Report on the Federal Minority Business Development Program.* Washington, DC: Government Printing Office.

Veeman, H. 1984. *De werkloosheid van Molukkers.* s-Granvenhage: Ministerie van Sociale Zaken en Werkgelegenheid.

Vermeulen, H. 1984. *Etnische groepen en grenzen. Surinamers, Chinezen en Turken.* Weesp: Het Wereldvenster.

Vermeulen, H. 1985. *De Grieken.* Muiderberg: D. Coutinho.

Vietorisz, Thomas and Bennett Harrison. 1970. *The Economic Development of Harlem.* New York: Praeger.

Wacquant, Lois J.D. and William J. Wilson. 1988. "Beyond Welfare Reform: Poverty, Joblessness and the Social Transformation of the Inner City." Paper presented at the Rockefeller Foundation Conference on Welfare Reform.

Waldinger, Roger. 1984. "Immigrant Enterprise in the New York Garment Industry." *Social Problems* 32 (1, October): 60-71.

Waldinger, Roger. 1986. *Through the Eye of the Needle: Immigrants and Enterprise in New York's Garment Trades*. New York: New York University Press.

Waldinger, Roger. 1987. "Immigrant Enterprise: A New Test of Competing Explanations." Paper presented at the Symposium on Hispanic Enterprise, Arizona State University, Tempe.

Waldinger, Roger and Michael Lapp. 1988. "Immigrants and Their Impact on the New York Garment Industry." Washington, DC: U.S. Department of Labor, International Labor Affairs Bureau, Division of Immigration Policy and Research.

Wall Street Journal. 1984. "Apparel Import Curbs." (August 8).

Ward, Robin. 1984. "Minority Settlement and the Local Economy." Pp. 198-212 in Bryan Roberts, Ruth Finnegan, and Duncan Gallie (eds.), *Approaches to Economic Life: Economic Restructuring, Employment, and the Social Division of Labor*. Manchester: ESRC and Manchester University Press.

Ward, Robin. 1986. "Evaluation of Shopping Centre Improvements Funded Under the Urban Programme in the West Midlands: The Ethnic Dimension." Working Paper no. 8. Birmingham: Aston University, Public Sector Management Research Unit.

Ward, Robin. 1987. "Small Retailers in Inner Urban Areas." Pp. 275-287 in Gerry Johnson (ed.), *Business Strategy and Retailing*. New York: John Wiley.

Ward, Robin and Richard Jenkins, eds. 1984. *Ethnic Communities in Business: Strategies for Economic Survival*. Cambridge: Cambridge University Press.

Ward, Robin, Richard Randall, and Karisa Krcmar. 1986. "Small Firms in the Clothing Industry: The Growth of Minority Enterprise." *International Small Business Journal* 4 (3): 46-56.

Ward, Robin and Frank Reeves. 1980. "West Indians in Business in Britain" (Home Affairs Committee). London: HMSO (December).

Watson, James. 1977. *Between Two Cultures: Migrants and Minorities in Britain*. London: Blackwell.

Werbner, Pnina. 1984. "Business on Trust: Pakistani Entrepreneurship in the Manchester Garment Industry." Pp. 166-88 in Robin Ward and Richard Jenkins (eds.), *Ethnic Communities in Business: Strategies for Economic Survival*. Cambridge: Cambridge University Press.

Werbner, Pnina. 1985a. "The Organization of Giving and Ethnic Elites: Voluntary Associations Amongst Manchester Pakistanis." *Ethnic and Racial Studies* 8 (3, July): 368-388.

Werbner, Pnina. 1985b. "Ethnic Enclave and Family Firms: A Dynamic Approach to the Study of Ethnic Business." Unpublished paper.

White, Paul D. 1984. *The West European City: A Social Geography*. New York: Longman.

White, Paul D., Hilary Winchester, and Michelle Guillon. 1987. "South-East Asian Refugees in Paris: The Evolution of a Minority Community." *Ethnic and Racial Studies* 10 (1, January): 48-61.

Wilken, Paul. 1979. *Entrepreneurship: A Comparative Historical Study*. Norwood, NJ: Ablex.

Wilkins, R. 1982. "The Problems of Training and Recruitment in Hackney's Clothing Industry." Unpublished paper.

Wilson, Franklin D. 1975. "The Ecology of a Black Business District." *Review of Black Political Economy* 5 (4, Summer): 353-375.

Wilson [The Rt. Hon. Sir, H.]. 1979. "The Financing of Small Firms" (March). London: HMSO.

Wilson, Kenneth and W. Allen Martin. 1982. "Ethnic Enclaves. A Comparison of Cuban and Black Economies in Miami." *American Journal of Sociology* 88 (1, July): 135-160.

Wilson, P.E.B. and J. Stanworth. 1983. *Black Business Enterprise in Britain: A Survey of Afro-Caribbean and Asian Small Business in Brent*. London: Runnymede Trust.

Wilson, William J. 1978. *The Declining Significance of Race: Blacks and Changing American Institutions*. Chicago: University of Chicago Press.

Wilson, William J. 1987. *The Truly Disadvantaged*. Chicago: University of Chicago Press.

Wirth, Louis. 1928. *The Ghetto*. Chicago: University of Chicago Press.

Wirth, Louis. 1938. "Urbanism as a Way of Life." *American Journal of Sociology* 44 (1, July): 1-24.

Wong, Bernard. 1987. "New Immigrants in New York's Chinatown." Pp. 243-272 in Nancy Foner (ed.), *New Immigrants in New York*. New York: Columbia University.

Young, Ken. 1983a. "An Agenda for Sir George: Local Authorities and the Promotion of Racial Equality." *Policy Studies* 3 (1, July): 54-70.

Young, Ken. 1983b. "Ethnic Pluralism and the Policy Agenda in Britain." In Nathan Glazer and Ken Young (eds.), *Ethnic Pluralism and Public Policy: Achieving Equality in the United States and Britain*. Lexington, MA: Lexington Books.

Young, Philip K.Y. 1983. "Family Labor, Sacrifice, and Competition: Korean Green-grocers in New York City." *Amerasia* 10: 53-71.

Zeigler, Harmon. 1961. *The Politics of Small Business*. Washington, DC: Public Affairs Press.

Zeitlin, Jonathan. 1985. "Markets, Technology and Collective Services: A Strategy for Local Government Intervention in the London Clothing Industry." London: Greater London Council, Industry and Employment Branch.

Zenner, Walter P. 1982. *Jewish Societies in the Middle East: Community, Culture and Authority*. Washington, DC: University Press of America.

Zimmer, Catherine and Howard Aldrich. 1987. "Resource Mobilization Through Ethnic Networks: Kinship and Friendship Ties of Shopkeepers in England." *Sociological Perspectives* 30 (4, October): 422-455.

Zukin, Sharon and Gilda Zwerman. 1984. "Housing for the Working Poor: A Historical View of Jews and Blacks in Brownsville." *New York Affairs* 9 (2): 3-18.

Zunz, Olivier. 1982. *The Changing Face of Inequality*. Chicago: University of Chicago Press.

Author Index

This name index was compiled by Deborah Tilley.

Subject Index

This subject index was compiled by Howard E. Aldrich.

About the Authors

Howard Aldrich, Professor of Sociology, Director of the Industrial Relations Curriculum, and Adjunct Professor of Business, University of North Carolina, Chapel Hill, North Carolina, USA, is the author of *Organizations and Environments* (Prentice-Hall, 1979) — one of the first comprehensive statements of a modern evolutionary perspective on organizational foundings, transformations, and dissolutions — and *Population Perspectives on Organizations* (Uppsala University, 1986). He has published more than 70 articles in the areas of organizational change, ethnic business, entrepreneurship, industrial relations, and business strategy.

Jochen Blaschke, Department of Political Science, the Free University of Berlin, Berlin, West Germany, is the author of *"Dritte Welt" in Europa* (Syndikat, 1980) and *Handbuch der Europäischen Regionalbewegungen* (Syndikat, 1980), and edits *Migration: A European Journal of International Migration and Ethnic Relations*. He is also editor of the annual *Jahrbuch zur Geshichte und Gesellschaft des Vorderen und Mittlerer Orients*.

Jeremy Boissevain, Centre for Anthropological and Sociological Studies, University of Amsterdam, Amsterdam, the Netherlands, is the author of *Friends of Friends: Networks, Manipulators, Coalitions* (Blackwell, 1974), and coeditor, with J. Clyde Mitchell, of *Network Analysis: Studies in Human Interaction* (Mouton, 1973).

William Bradford, Department of Finance, College of Business and Management, University of Maryland, College Park, Maryland, USA, is the author of *Financing Black Economic Development* (Academic Press, 1979).

223

Gavin Chen, Senior Economist, Minority Business Development Agency, Department of Commerce, Washington, D.C., USA, has written numerous articles on minority economic development, economic integration, trade, and development. His current research interests are in the international economic development of Latin America and the Caribbean.

Hanneke Grotenbreg is a member of the Centre for Anthropological and Sociological Studies, University of Amsterdam, Amsterdam, the Netherlands.

Isaac Joseph, Department of Anthropology and Sociology, University of Lyon 2, France, is the editor and translator of *L'école de Chicago* (Grenoble, 1979) and also of Ulf Hannerz's *Explorer la ville: Éléments d'anthropologie urbaine* (Minuit, 1983). He is currently doing research on space and territoriality on the Paris Metro.

Hermann Korte, Professor of Sociology, Ruhr-Universitat Bochum, Bochum, West Germany, and codirector of the Norbert Elias Foundation, is the author of numerous works on international migration, urban sociology, and social theory, including *Stadtsoziologie* (1986), *Eine Gesellschaft im Aufbruch. Die Bundesrepublik in den 60er Jahren* (1987), and *Über Norbert Elias, Das Werden eines Menschenwissenschaftlers* (1988).

Ivan Light, Professor of Sociology, University of California at Los Angeles, Los Angeles, California, USA, is the author of *Ethnic Enterprise in America: Business and Welfare Among Chinese, Japanese, and Blacks* (California, 1972), and coauthor, with Edna Bonacich, of *Immigrant Entrepreneurs: Koreans in Los Angeles, 1965-1982* (California, 1988).

David McEvoy, Deputy Director, School of Social Science, Liverpool Polytechnic, Liverpool, England, is the author of "Two Views of British Asian Retailing in a Time of Recession" in *The Spirit of Entrepreneurship*, edited by R. G. Wyekham et al. (Simon Fraser, 1987). He and Trevor P. Jones received grants from the Commission for Racial Equality, the Economic and Social Research Council, and the Canadian federal government in 1988-1989 to study ethnic minority small business.

Mirjana Morokvasic, Chargé de Recherche at the Centre National de la Recherche Scientifique, Paris, is the author of *Emigration und danach* (1987), and has edited special issues of *Current Sociology* (1984) and the *International Migration Review* (1984) on women and migration. She is currently doing research on the self-employment of immigrant women in five countries.

Annie Phizacklea, Lecturer in Sociology at Warwick University, Coventry, England, is the coauthor of *Labour and Racism* (Routledge, 1980) and *Unpacking the Fashion Industry: Gender, Racism, and Class in Production* (Routledge, 1989). She is currently researching women's employment, focusing on ethnic women involved in homeworking.

Marlene Sway, Research Associate, Department of Sociology, University of Alabama, Birmingham, Alabama, USA, is the author of *Familiar Strangers: Gypsy Life in America* (Illinois, 1988). Her main research interests are race and ethnic relations, social and economic organization, and gender.

Roger Waldinger, Associate Professor, Department of Sociology, the City College and Graduate School, City University of New York, New York, USA, is the author of *Through the Eye of the Needle: Immigrants and Enterprise in New York's Garment Trades* (New York: New York University Press, 1986) and numerous articles on immigration, labor markets, and urban change. In addition to continuing research on ethnic entrepreneurship, he is currently working on studies of ethnic change and persistence in New York City and of the impact of urban restructuring on immigrant and minority groups.

Robin Ward, Head of the European Business Centre and Professor of Corporate Strategy, Nottingham Business School, England, has done much to develop the study of ethnic business in Britain. His publications include *Ethnic Communities in Business* (Cambridge University Press, 1984) with Richard Jenkins.

Pnina Werbner, Research Associate, Department of Sociology, University of Manchester, U.K., has research interests focusing on economic networks among British Pakistanis. She is the author of *Capital Gifts, Offerings Among British Pakistanis* (Berg), *Black and Ethnic Leadership in Britain* (Routledge), and *The Migration Process* (Berg).

Peter Wilson, Partner in New Enterprise Development, London, England (a private sector organization engaged in small business development in the United Kingdom), has written several research reports on ethnic minority business in the United Kingdom and has recently contributed to an evaluation study of the British government's black business initiative.

NOTES

NOTES

NOTES

NOTES

NOTES

NOTES